AMERICA

Also in

REPRINTS OF ECONOMIC CLASSICS

By ALEXANDER H. EVERETT

NEW IDEAS ON POPULATION [1826]

AMERICA

OR

A GENERAL SURVEY

OF THE

POLITICAL SITUATION OF THE SEVERAL POWERS

OF THE

WESTERN CONTINENT

WITH CONJECTURES ON THEIR FUTURE PROSPECTS

BY

ALEXANDER H. EVERETT

[1827]

REPRINTS OF ECONOMIC CLASSICS

AUGUSTUS M. KELLEY · PUBLISHERS

NEW YORK 1970

First Edition 1827

(Philadelphia: H. C. Carey & I. Lee, *Chestnut Street*, 1827)

Reprinted 1970 by

AUGUSTUS M. KELLEY · PUBLISHERS

REPRINTS OF ECONOMIC CLASSICS

New York   New York   10001

.   .   .   .

I S B N   0 678 00651 2

L C N   70 117505

.   .   .   .

PRINTED IN THE UNITED STATES OF AMERICA
by SENTRY PRESS, NEW YORK, N. Y. 10019

AMERICA:

OR

A GENERAL SURVEY

OF THE

POLITICAL SITUATION OF THE SEVERAL POWERS

OF THE

WESTERN CONTINENT,

WITH CONJECTURES ON THEIR FUTURE PROSPECTS.

Matre pulchrâ filia pulchrior.

BY A CITIZEN OF THE UNITED STATES,

AUTHOR OF "EUROPE," &c.

PHILADELPHIA:

H. C. CAREY & I. LEA, CHESNUT STREET.

1827.

CONTENTS.

CHAPTER I.

AMERICA.

CHAPTER I.

Position of America and of the United States in the general Political System.

It has sometimes been suggested, that the United States ought to be considered as forming of themselves a political system, entirely distinct and separate from every other. The opinion expressed by Washington, in his farewell address, upon the subject of our foreign relations, has been thought to favour this idea; and it has also been apparently countenanced by other authorities of great and just consideration. But the general remarks of this kind, that have been occasionally thrown out, must be taken in connexion with the circumstances of the time when they were made, and with the character of the particular measures to which they had immediate reference. They must be understood to intimate, that we should avoid unnecessary interference in the public affairs of other countries; and that on account of our distance from Europe, the necessity of such interference would occur less frequently to us than to almost any other people. A complete separation of our political interests from those of all other countries could only be effected, by a complete abstinence from all intercourse with them; a plan which it would be extremely difficult to realise, which would be highly impolitic if practicable, and which has never been avowed nor defended by any one. All individual and personal intercourse between the members of different bodies politic carries with it political relations, to a certain extent; and no two nations which have any communication at all with each other, can be looked upon as completely independent and unconnected. Where community of origin, language, religion, laws and habits, produces continual and very intimate personal relations between the members of two or more communities, their national connexion becomes of necessity proportionably close, and they are said to constitute a political system. Each of the individual powers composing such a system, being independent of the rest in form, exercises a sovereign will in regulating its relations with them; but it is not in the power of any one to dissolve its connexion with the system, except as I have intimated above, by entirely prohibiting all individual intercourse with the other members; and even this would be only the establishment of one relation instead of another, and would leave the system as it stood before. The question, which of these relations would be more expedient, must be determined, in every case, by a just application of the principles of policy and duty to the particular circumstances of the time being, and not by any fixed ideas of a general kind: for prudence requires on the one hand that a nation should avoid entangling itself without necessity in the quarrels and concerns of its neighbours, and other considerations of interest and humanity make it proper to cultivate and encourage a good understanding and a friendly intercourse with all. A wise statesman will therefore regulate his conduct by a proper reference to both these rules, and by a careful notice of the signs of the times, in which he is called to act. As respects the United States in particular, their history sufficiently proves, if theory were wanting, that it is not in their power to separate themselves entirely from the great political system of Christendom, with which they are naturally connected by community of origin. It becomes therefore of high importance to ascertain precisely the nature of this connexion, and to form a clear idea of the position of this country and of America in general, in reference to the other Christian powers. This is the point which I propose to examine in the present chapter.

This immense political system, which now occupies so large a part of the earth's surface, which extends from Kamschatka on the one hand to Cape Horn on the other, comprehending the whole of Europe and America and a considerable portion of the two other continents and their neighbouring islands, dates from about fifteen hundred years ago, having grown out of the establishments formed upon the ruins of the Roman empire by its barbarous invaders. The several tribes, into which these rude sons of the north were divided, assumed in the first instance a complete sovereignty over the provinces which they respectively conquered.

The territory of the empire was thus parcelled out into a thousand petty states, engaged in perpetual wars with each other,—often unsettled in their turn by the inroads of new swarms from the old mother hive, and forming on the whole a real chaos rather than a system. In the course of two or three centuries, however, these originally independent settlements were gradually consolidated,—for the most part in conformity with certain great geographical lines of demarcation,—into a smaller number of considerable nations, separate in form, but closely connected by every other possible bond of union, and constituting what has often been called *the European commonwealth.* Of the larger states, that entered into the composition of this system, no one was sufficiently powerful to stand its ground permanently against a combination of the rest, or to acquire a decided superiority over the whole. The mutual jealousy of the great states afforded security to the smaller, and the *balance of power,* thus established, furnished a sort of rude substitute for a common government, and enforced upon all, to a certain extent, the observance of the rules of equity and justice. This state of things continued, without any very material or permanent alteration in the relative power of the several nations, until the middle of the last century. All, as they advanced in civilization, gradually increased in wealth and power, but preserved nearly the same comparative importance. France was on the whole the leading state, and threatened at times the independence of the others; but the predominance she acquired was never permanent, and was generally succeeded by a period of proportional weakness and exhaustion. Charlemagne united a great part of Europe under his government, but his empire fell to pieces upon his death, and France remained for two or three centuries after in a very feeble and distracted state. From that time, until the reformation, the power which really exercised the greatest influence was the see of Rome; and Europe may be said to have been, during this interval of four or five centuries, a sort of irregular theocracy. The reformation, which commenced by the preaching of a monk against the sale of indulgences, gradually assumed the form of a revolt of the military chiefs or kings, against the supreme ecclesiastical head, and finished by subverting the supremacy of the church in form over half of these chiefs, and in fact over all. Their relative power still remained in substance as before, and so continued, until the extension of the system beyond the limits of Europe effected a complete change in its character, or rather may be said to have substituted an entirely new one in place of the former. This revolution, as may well be supposed from the immense magnitude of the interests affected by it, was long in preparation, and very slow in its development. It is only, indeed, within a very few years, that its final results have become completely manifest.

The discovery and colonization of America and the East Indies, and the conquest of the whole north of Asia by Russia, which took place about the same time, prepared the way for the introduction into the European system of new elements, capable of becoming after a while much superior in weight and importance to the original mass. While the system was thus extended as it were over the whole face of the globe, and acquired as such a prodigious accession of positive power, it is evident that the relative influence of the several states must have been of necessity, as it was, completely altered. Had the new elements been distributed among these states, in exact proportion to their former weight, the old balance of power might indeed have been preserved; but this was hardly possible in the nature of things, and at any rate did not happen. France and Austria, on the whole the two leading powers in the former system, failed in securing any share of the distribution of this vast *treasure trove* of new continents; and consequently, although rapidly advancing in wealth and greatness, were doomed to suffer a gradual and constantly progressive decline of their comparative weight and general political influence. This decline was interrupted for a short time, as respects France, by the episode of the revolution, but has now resumed its course and will continue to proceed with accelerated rapidity. On the other hand, England, Holland, Spain, and Portugal, by dividing among themselves these *princely spoils*, rose at once,—the three first at least, from the rank of secondary to that of first rate powers. Spain for a time took the place of France and Austria as the leading European state; and being in other respects aided by circumstances, conquered Portugal, invaded France, threatened England, and made in short a very near approach to universal empire. With a better domestic system this preponderance might long have been maintained, but in consequence of gross misgovernment it soon passed away. After this, Holland, before a subject province, figured for a while as a leading power. England under the same circumstances assumed the same position, and of all the European powers is the one which has turned this revolution in the system to the best account. But in her case, as in that of the others, the accession of power acquired in this way was naturally transitory; because the colonies, separated as they were by immense distances and intervening oceans from the ruling state, had a natural tendency to fall off after a certain time and become independent. This consummation, of which our own revolution was the first great act, which is now proceeding in Spanish America, and will ultimately be completed by the emancipation of the remaining British colonies, exhibits the final development, in one of its great branches, of the revolution in the old European political system, or rather of the formation of a new one, to which I alluded above. In this way the European states, which had risen into temporary importance by the acquisition of colonies, were destined to return again to their former station. Spain, Portugal, and Holland, have already resumed their rank as inferior powers; and England, when she shall have lost entirely her colonial empire, must consent, however unwillingly, to do the same. Meanwhile the emancipation of America has added to the old family a cluster of new members, not inferior in number, nor (considering their immediate prospects) in importance, to the former ones; and this creation is the first remarkable point in the new political system.

Another important feature in this system was the result of the conquest of the north of Asia by Russia, and of circumstances occurring within the interior of that empire, which favoured in a very extraordinary manner, its progress in power and civilization. While the western and maritime states were appropriating to themselves the boundless regions of the new world, the Czars of Russia were stretching their jurisdiction over equally extensive territories, which being contiguous to their former possessions, were not liable to fall off, like the new acquisitions of the others, after a lapse of two or three centuries. Having succeeded about the same time, by favour of an almost miraculous concurrence of events, in forming a consolidated and vigorous body politic, out of the heterogeneous and before discordant materials of which this empire is composed; having finally, by a singular effort of genius, raised their subjects, in point of civilization, to a level with the rest of Europe, these princes, hitherto unknown and unheard of in the general system, now took their places, not so much in it as over it. Russia became at once not merely a leading, but in substance and effect the ruling state. I have dwelt, on a former occasion, upon the position and influence of this immense power, and need not therefore now enlarge upon the subject. A glance at the map of the world is sufficient to show, independently of any other argument, how completely the west of Europe is crushed, beneath the giant mass of this political Colossus. The whole course of history for a century past, beginning with the reign of Peter the Great, and ending with the recent invasion of Spain, demonstrates the same important truth. The continental states that figured as leading powers in the former system, such as France, Austria, and latterly Prussia, have lost, by the introduction of this new and overwhelming rival, not only their rank but virtually their independence. This feature of the new system has not yet assumed its perfect form; but the natural termination of the progress of events, which is now going on, will be the union of the whole continent into one military monarchy. Great Britain, while she preserves her colonial empire, will maintain her independence at home, and her rank as a first rate power; but when she loses her foreign possessions, and the sceptre of the ocean which will go with them, she must also lose her importance, and sink into a dependency of the neighbouring continent. Meanwhile the great political system, to which our country and continent belong, exhibits at present the three following principal elements:

1. The Continent of Europe with its dependencies in other parts of the world.

2. The British Empire.

3. America.

Each of these great divisions of the general system, comprehends one predominant power, and a number of others connected with it in a secondary order; and in every case on different principles. As respects the British empire, the multifarious and innumerable sections that compose it, scattered over every quarter of the globe, comprehending immense and unexplored regions in America, a hundred kingdoms in Asia and Africa, a whole continent in the south sea, and nearly all the islands in that and every other, (for Great Britain seems to claim a monopoly of islands,) are subject in form to the little ruling cluster on the northwest coast of Europe. In this division of the system, the subordination of the other members to the leading power, is therefore for the time complete; but as the connexion is not founded on any common principles of either right or policy, or even permanent and lasting power, it must be considered as in its nature accidental and transitory. On the other hand, the nations that occupy the continent of Europe, though in form independent, are subject to the influence of Russia, which, as I have just stated, exercises over them a decided predominance. This predominance being founded in a superiority of physical force likely to be durable, must also be expected to continue, and indeed to display itself more and more from year to year, until it brings about the consummation alluded to above. Finally, our own country enjoys the proud distinction of taking the lead in the great division composed of the various new nations that cover this continent—a lead not assumed in arrogance and maintained by force, but resulting in the course of nature from priority of national existence, and secured by continual good offices done, and to be done, to our sister republics. This connexion too being founded on the just and liberal principles of policy common to all the different parties, and which we may justly expect will long continue to be so, may be regarded as permanent, and, we may hope at least, perpetual. Russia, Great Britain, and the United States, are therefore now the three prominent and first rate powers of the civilized and christian world. All the rest stand at present, in an order secondary to one or the other of these. Some of the secondary powers of the two great European divisions, such as France, Austria, and even Turkey, are at present superior in population, and in disposable military and naval force, to the United States, and would doubtless consider it a signal piece of presumption in us, to claim in any respect a higher political importance. These celebrated empires, I mean the two first of the three just mentioned, in the pride of their antiquity, and of the brilliant part which they have constantly acted on the theatre of Europe, can hardly realize at once the effect of the new circumstances, which, without diminishing their actual power, have deprived them of a great part of their comparative weight among the nations; and they are rather disposed to underrate the pretensions of a new country, which emerged as it were only fifty years ago, from a continent that has been known to Europe but little more than three centuries. However natural such feelings may be with them, it is nevertheless certain, that it is not merely extent of population, and of organized military force, still less the date of its establishment, that determines the political importance of a country in the world. A favourable geographical position, and a good government, with the industry, wealth, and knowledge, the civilization, in a word, which naturally attend them, are matters of much more consequence. These are the causes which have given to the United States, at this early period of their national existence, the lofty position of a leading power among the nations; and, however the fact may now be doubted or disputed by some.

it will become in a very short time as evident to all, as it is at present to those who examine with unprejudiced minds, the situation of the world.

Such then is the position of America and of the United States, in the general political system, and such is now the aspect presented by that system, upon a large and comprehensive survey. It also happens, by a somewhat singular coincidence, that the great divisions which I have pointed out, exhibit at the same time a grand exemplification of each of the three principal forms of political institutions. No specimens of either of these forms have been held up to the world before, on any thing like so large a scale, in an equal degree of perfection. The United States are admitted by all to furnish the most finished model of a popular government that has yet been seen ; and they afford indeed the first instance, in which purely popular institutions have ever existed tranquilly for any length of time in a great community. The British constitution, on the other hand, is undoubtedly the most favourable specimen that has ever been exhibited of the mixed or intermediate system of government; while the Russian empire, although the aspect of its administration varies very much, like that of all despotic states, with the changes in the person of the despot, has displayed on the whole, since the time of Peter the Great, one of the best examples, as it certainly has the most imposing and remarkable one ever known, of the worst description of political institutions. Here then we have a vast and splendid panorama, in which those persons whose attention is directed by curiosity or habitual pursuits to the science of politics, may study the practical operation of the three great systems, developing themselves under every possible advantage and on the most extensive scale. Such a spectacle is surely well fitted to attract the observation of all those, who feel an interest in the fortunes of the human race, and have duly considered the permanent influence of political institutions upon their condition and happiness.

If the object were merely to settle, in the minds of the impartial inquirers, the question of the comparative advantages of liberal and arbitrary governments, it would perhaps be quite sufficient to survey, however superficially, the present situation of these different sections of the Christian world, especially of the continents of Europe and America, in which the two forms present themselves respectively in a pure and simple shape. Under the operation of the liberal system, we see throughout America an exhibition of prosperity, national and individual, such as probably the world never witnessed before upon the same scale; a substantial equality of property and of personal and political rights, a high degree of intellectual and moral activity pervading and animating the whole mass of society, a general diffusion of the material comforts of life, of knowledge and virtue, and, as a necessary consequence, of happiness; an increase of population and a progress of improvement, unheard of, unthought of, in any former age or region; gigantic enterprises in the way of internal development and foreign commerce, of which monarchs never dreamed, conceived and executed by states and individuals; tens of millions of busy, proud, and wealthy men, governed and defended almost without either armies or taxes; and finally, as if in mockery of the idle fears and vain pretences of the adversaries of this system, the whole movement going on in uninterrupted tranquillity, while at the same time the empires which are ruled upon the opposite principles, and whose professed object, and only supposed advantage, is tranquillity, are constantly convulsed with revolutions, and given up for ever to the standing curses of foreign and domestic war.

The despotic system, as exemplified on the continent of Europe, presents us with a picture in every respect precisely the reverse of this. We there see a few individuals in each separate state monopolizing all the property, and enjoying exclusively the material comforts of life, somewhat happier of course, but, from the vice of their position, not much wiser or better than their fellow citizens; the mass of the community poor, abject, and wretched; no intellectual or physical activity; no generous expansion of social feeling; no circulation of thought or diffusion of knowledge; no virtues but those of instinct, and all the vices which ignorance and misery constantly engender; wealth and population declining, or at best stationary; the useful and liberal arts at a stand; manifest improvement, familiar in more favoured regions, rejected and prohibited; loathsome and inveterate abuses in morals and politics retained and cherished, with a sort of affectation; we see, in short, in consequence of the very peculiar situation of these nations, the spectacle, altogether new I believe in the history of the world, of a number of cotemporary governments voluntarily shutting their eyes upon the lights of the age in which they live; spurning in practice, at truths which they cannot dispute in theory, and regulating their public conduct agreeably to known and acknowledged errors. Such is the singular condition of the vast communities professing the Greek and Catholic religions, which occupy so extensive a portion of the ancient continent, and whose policy, as I have already stated, is now preponderant through the whole of it, and unresisted except by the vain wishes and stifled complaints of a few individuals. It may be proper, however, to add that the Protestant countries, and also, to a certain extent, France and some parts of Catholic Germany, though moving in our order secondary to the great military power of the continent, are yet governed, as respects internal affairs, on a better system, commonly called the mixed or intermediate one, and which is also established in the British empire, or at least that part of it (not by any means the largest) which is subject to the British constitution.

This intermediate system exhibits the principle of liberty and that of despotism or arbitrary power, co-operating together, or rather contending for the mastery, within the compass of the same body politic. Institutions of this description have found, like those of despotism, their apologists and even their admirers; and have sometimes been extolled by men of high discernment, under the name of mixed governments, as the most finished products of political wisdom. In reality, however, although they argue a better state of society than that which exists of necessity in despotic governments, they may perhaps, when considered in the abstract, be fairly ranked as inferior to both the simple forms; or, to speak more properly, they should be described, not as a distinct class of governments, having a separate principle of their own, but as a sort of transition or passage from one of the simple forms of government to the other. This is the light, under which they are now viewed by some of the most intelligent European writers, as for example M. de Chateaubriand; and we find in fact, that, in all the countries in which we see them established, they have been the effect of accidental circumstances, which have planted the seeds of liberty and encouraged its growth, in a soil before appropriated to despotism. If this notion of the system be correct, it would seem that it can hardly be in any case a very durable one. When the new occupant becomes strong enough to display his character, a struggle must ensue between the two pretenders to the mastery, which, though it may endure for a considerable period of time, must apparently terminate in the complete triumph of one or the other. The intervening epoch of confusion and collision is the one, through which the constitutional monarchies of Europe appear to be now passing; and the incongruous forms of legislation and administration, naturally produced by this conflict of principles, constitute, at least on this view of it, the celebrated system of mixed governments.

We find accordingly, upon examining this system as exemplified in England, the only country where it ever grew up spontaneously, and where, if any where, it must be supposed to exhibit itself in its natural and proper shape, that it displays a combination of contraries, which no ingenuity can reconcile in theory and no art or skill unite in harmonious action. We find institutions existing together, which suppose the truth of directly opposite principles, and which, if they retain any real force, must lead of necessity to continual collision:—a king reigning by the grace of God, and a parliament claiming and exercising the right of deposing him at pleasure;—an established church, with universal liberty of conscience and worship;—equality of rights and hereditary privileges;—boundless prodigality in the public expenses, with a strict accountableness of all the agents;—with a thousand other incongruities of the same description. The administration of these countries presents in fact the appearance, which we should naturally expect from the view here taken of their political forms. We see in their proceedings and condition something of the favourable influence of liberty, and something of the ruinous effect of arbitrary government; but their most remarkable and distinctive feature is a continual collision between the two principles, and a ceaseless fluctuation in the public measures, as one or the other predominates in turn. When their power is pretty nearly balanced, the slightest accident is sometimes sufficient to determine which shall have the temporary prevalence. In the time of Queen Anne, the scale was turned in England in favour of passive obedience and non-resistance, by the duchess of Marlborough's gloves. In our own day, Lord Castlereagh's penknife (more potent than his pen) settled for a while the same great question in a different manner. And yet the discordance that takes place on these occasions in the public measures is not less strongly marked, because the accident that leads to it is a slight one. The ill humour of the duchess of Marlborough occasioned the recall of her husband, the greatest general that England ever possessed, from the head of his army, in the full career of victory, and when another campaign would have carried him to Paris,—rescued the monarchy of France from instant destruction, settled the succession of Spain, terminated a general war that had lasted ten years, and decided the politics of Europe for half a century. The second of the changes alluded to above, was not less complete. The British government had made war, for thirty years in succession, upon the principle of liberty exhibiting itself in the form of revolution. A ministerial movement occurs, produced by the little engine just mentioned ;—the scene immediately changes, another hand takes the helm, and the same government has now for several years been lending all its influence to the same principle, exhibiting itself in a different and even in the same quarter of the globe.—So it is in other nations, whose institutions are formed upon this model. France establishes a liberal constitution at home, and before the object is well accomplished despatches an army of a hundred thousand men, to put down a similar constitution in a neighbouring territory. The same fluctuation may be remarked in their economical systems. At one time the order of the day is prohibition, high duties, a continual intervention of the government in private concerns. Anon, without any perceptible change of circumstances, the favourite notions are liberty of commerce, low duties, and the *laissez faire* policy. Another natural effect of the conflict of principles, that forms the essence of this mixed government, is the existence of permanent and deep rooted party divisions. Such divisions naturally grow up even in free countries, and while kept within certain limits are not perhaps injurious; but in these mixed systems, where the nature of the constitution favours or rather creates them, they are apt to assume a dangerous and inveterate shape. They ruined the republic of Rome, and have always kept up in England, as Montesquieu, though a great admirer of the British constitution, remarks, a continual conflagration of discord and sedition.

It is not my object, however, to examine at present in detail, the respective merits of the different forms of government, but merely to present a hasty sketch of the internal situation of the three great divisions of the Christian world, for the purpose of completing the survey which I have taken of the whole, as a political system. Reverting, therefore, to the general conclusion at which I arrived before, it appears that the ancient commonwealth of Christendom, which was formed out of the broken fragments of the fallen Roman empire, and existed within the same limits for about a thousand years, has been gradually extending itself for two or three centuries, over the whole habitable globe, and has experienced, in consequence, a revolution hardly less violent, and certainly much more remarkable. than that which caused its foundation; that, in the course of this process, the old political landmarks have been broken up, as the physical divisions of the globe are subverted by a general inundation; that some great powers have disappeared entirely, others sprung into being as if by enchantment, and all assumed new shapes and combinations, according to principles that were not in operation before; that finally, within the last few years, the new system, which has thus risen from the wreck of the former, has arranged itself into three great divisions, each composed of various members, bound together by some common principle of union, and that one of these divisions is formed by the cluster of young and vigorous republics, occupying our western continent, and acting under the auspices and guidance of our own favoured country. A correct estimate of the nature and consequences of this position is indispensable in future, to all who desire to take part, with honour and advantage, in the conduct of the public affairs; and the proud satisfaction that we naturally feel, at seeing our country raised to this commanding height among the nations of the world, may well be tempered with a sentiment of awe, when we recollect the immense responsibility, the grave and sacred duties, involved in the exercise of so much power. To study these duties and their corresponding rights, is therefore a matter of high and pressing interest. It is the object of this imperfect essay to assist in this inquiry, and I shall deem the labour of it well bestowed, if I am able to throw any light, however feeble, on so vast and important a subject. On a former occasion, I attempted a rapid survey of the political situation of the ancient continent, including Great Britain, and I now propose to complete the work then commenced, by a similar review of our own western hemisphere. The indulgence with which the former sketch was received, by a few partial judges, affords me some encouragement in regard to the success of this; and with all the diffidence, which I nevertheless cannot but feel in undertaking it, I experience at the same time a high degree of satisfaction in reflecting, that I shall naturally be led, in treating this part of the subject, to dwell at considerable length upon the institutions, the policy, and the prospects of our own happy country, of whose present glory and splendid future destinies we are all so justly proud. In order to connect this part of the essay with the preceding one, I shall offer in the following chapter a rapid sketch of the principal political events of the last five years; and shall then take up in order the several subjects, that belong more immediately to the present occasion.

CHAPTER II.

*Brief Review of the principal Events of the last
five years.*

THE history of the last five years is replete with
events in themselves of imposing magnitude, and rendered still more remarkable by the vast influence
which they may hereafter exercise on the fortunes of
the human race. During this period the new political
system, of which a general outline was traced in the
preceding chapter, has put on, for the first time,
the form which it is likely to wear perhaps for centuries to come. Within this time, the patriots of
Spanish America have completed, by their perseverance and bravery, the great work of their emancipation; and the acknowledgment of their independence, by the United States and England, may be
considered as fixing the epoch when our western continent, under the auspices of our own country acting
as the leading American power, has assumed its proper
and permanent place in the political world. On the
other hand, this same acknowledgment of the independence of South America by England, afforded the
first decisive indication of the separation of the latter
power from the continental alliance, and therefore
marks the development of the new political system in
its second principal division. Finally, the overthrow·

of the Spanish constitution by the military power of France, acting under the influence, one might almost say the compulsion, of Russia, which has taken place within the same period, established the ascendancy of arbitrary principles among the western continental nations, and thus displayed for the first time in its full deformity the third prominent feature in the present aspect of Christendom. The great events that have taken place in America will form, in connexion with the present situation and prospects of the powers immediately affected by them, the principal subjects of the present work; and it will therefore not be necessary to discuss them particularly in this preliminary sketch. I shall confine myself in this chapter to a few remarks upon the two other leading occurrences in the history of the last five years, to which I have just alluded; viz. the counter-revolution in Spain, and the acknowledgment by Great Britain of the independence of Spanish America.

The former will probably be regarded hereafter as one of the most extraordinary as well as unfortunate events of modern times, and it is very difficult to give a reasonable account of it, upon any of the principles that commonly regulate the conduct of men. It is true that party spirit and fanaticism had some indirect share in bringing it about; and these motives are sufficient, as far as they go, to furnish an explanation of any act, however mad or foolish. But it does not appear after all that M. de Villèle and M. de Chateaubriand. the two leading statesmen under whose advice the measure must be supposed to have been adopted, were wholly or even mainly governed by either of these

principles. Though both are decided royalists, neither has ever been considered as attached to the blindly
fanatical section of the party, with which the invasion
of Spain was a favourite plan; and both had given,
and continued to give to the very last, repeated and
unequivocal proofs of their wish to avoid this extremity, while at the same time there was no apparent reason why they should resolve upon the measure, if they
did not like it. Their conduct, under these circumstances, displays a sort of unaccountable infatuation,
not unlike that of a fascinated bird, which is seen to
plunge suddenly, by a sort of desperate effort, into the
jaws of destruction, at the very moment when its wild
and anxious fluttering seems to show that it is fully
aware of the danger, and when an act of the will is
the only thing wanting to its safety. A brief recapitu-
lation of the facts immediately connected with the
adoption of this fatal policy, will prove sufficiently the
correctness of this statement.

The fall of M. de Cazes and the gradual elevation of
M. de Villèle, first to the ministry and then to the presidency of the council, indicated the ascendency of a
decidedly royalist party, in the cabinet of the Thuileries. But although the royalists, while contending with
the liberal, or, as they considered it, revolutionary party, had been pretty well united, they had no sooner
succeeded in completely discomfiting the common enemy, than they separated at once into two sections, sometimes called the *politicians* and the *fanatics*, which carried on the war against each other with nearly as much
violence as the royalists and the liberalists had done
before. The *politicians*, though not perhaps very fond

of representative government in the abstract, considered
it as expedient in the present state of France, and as
being at any rate an established institution, which it
would be highly imprudent and dangerous to attempt
to overturn or even to appear to dislike. Some of them,
as for example, M. de Chateaubriand, even go farther
than this, and have always professed a warm attachment
to the forms of constitutional monarchy. The *fanatics*,
on the other hand, make no secret of their utter contempt and detestation of all the modern political theories; and include in this number, with hardly a shadow
of reserve, the existing French charter. In their opinion, the only practicable and safe government is a virtual theocracy, in which the clergy are in fact the ruling
order, and superstition the principle of obedience in
the subject, and of authority in the government. Of these
two sections of the royalist party, the politicians were
decidedly predominant, and M. de Villèle, the minister,
was regarded as their leader. The fanatics were much
less numerous, and formed a small but very violent opposition corps in the house of deputies. Each party had
its daily papers, which served as regular organs of its
opinions, and from the opening of the Spanish revolution these journals had exhibited a strongly marked discordance of feeling in regard to it. The politicians,
though finding occasionally much to blame, viewed it as,
on the whole, a fortunate event, and treated the new
constitution as a plausible imitation of the French charter. The fanatics could hardly find words to express
their abhorrence for its forms and principles, and were
continually insisting on the necessity of a crusade for the

purpose of putting it down. When the northern powers
began to exhibit pretty strong symptoms of a disposition to
take such a step, these opposite opinions were expressed in France with still more decision. The *Journal
des Debats*, the ablest newspaper printed in Europe,
then a warm ministerial one, and supposed to be under
the immediate direction of M. de Chateaubriand, in-
sisted strenuously on the inexpediency and impolicy of
attempting to crush the Spanish revolution by force.—
Meanwhile the holy allies, having gradually and sufficiently matured their plan, determined upon holding a
congress at Verona, and invited France and England to
meet with them. The Duke de Montmorency was then
minister of foreign affairs, and was naturally one of the
persons appointed to represent the French government.
M. de Chateaubriand, then ambassador at London, was
united with him in the mission; and his sentiments in
regard to representative government were so perfectly
well known, that his appointment was considered as a
pretty decisive proof that nothing violent would be
attempted against Spain. The fanatics viewed it in
this light, and a certain Marquis de Jouffroy, a busy
officious scribbler, between agent and marplot in the
service of this party, addressed at this time a long letter
to Prince Metternich, which found its way afterwards
into the journals, in which he formally denounced Chateaubriand as a person, in whom the royalists had no
confidence, and as the *apostle of constitutions*. M. de
Montmorency, who is since dead, was a nobleman of
excellent feelings and intentions, but of no very great
intellectual power. He had been in his youth a decided
partisan of the revolution, but had since publicly abjured

his errors before the house of deputies, and had something of the excessive zeal of a new convert to the cause
of royalism. He therefore, if either, was the one of the
two French agents at Verona, who might fairly be considered as representing the fanatics, being in fact, himself, a real fanatic, in his own way.

Under these circumstances the congress met, performed its task, and separated. The session lasted for
two or three months, and during the whole time the
French ministerial papers preserved their usual moderate
tone, in regard to Spain, and the *Journal des Debats*
deprecated as strongly as ever an armed interference.
The public events that immediately followed the separation of the congress, are fresh in the memory of all.
England, it appeared, had refused to take any part in
the business; Russia, Austria, and Prussia, acting in
concert, withdrew their ministers from Spain, and addressed violent notes to the Spanish government, in
which they professed their intention to break off all
connexion with them, as long as the present system
lasted. France, on the contrary, took a different course,
kept her minister at Madrid, and addressed a note to
the Spanish government, which seemed to have little
or no actual object, except to show that her policy dif-
fered from that of the northern powers. At the same
time, the Duke de Montmorency resigned, and M. de
Chateaubriand was appointed minister of foreign affairs.
The natural, one may say, the necessary conclusion
from all this was, that France had come forward at the
congress as the advocate of constitutional monarchy, and
was determined not to attack Spain, or allow, if she
could help it, any one else to do so: and the change of

ministry at home was easily accounted for, by supposing that M. de Montmorency had been inclined to a different policy, and that M. de Chateaubriand, a known and declared friend of representative constitutions, would be a more suitable minister at the existing crisis. Such, I say, were the natural conclusions from the first events that followed the dissolution of the congress; but before the friends of liberal principles and of France, had time to realize their satisfaction at these results, within three or four weeks after the change of ministry, the chambers met, and the king addressed them in a speech, which amounted to a declaration of war. It was only a year before, that he had told them, in the same place and upon the same occasion, that the army of the Pyrenees was simply a *cordon sanitaire,* and that malignity alone *(malveillance)* could put any other construction upon the formation of it. The session opened, and M. de Chateaubriand himself, the apostle of constitutions, came forward in his new character of minister, and defended the policy of an armed interference in the affairs of Spain, for the purpose of destroying the established constitution. His journal followed his example, and, to use one of Lord Castlereagh's favourite phrases, also *turned its back upon itself,* and now stoutly defended the invasion, which it had so long deprecated, under pretext that it had become a government measure, which it was the duty of every loyal subject to support.

Of this singular *denouement* no satisfactory explanation has ever been given, nor is it yet known why the moderate section of the royalists, after apparently obtaining a complete victory over their adversaries, should

have adopted and carried into effect, at the very moment of success, the policy against which they had been
contendîng. They appear, therefore, as I said before,
to have acted under a sort of blind and unaccountable
infatuation. M. de Villèle, it is true, made no scruple
of affirming in the house of deputies, that *if they did
not make war at the south they should have it at the
north*, or, in other words, that the Emperor of Russia
had ordered him to invade Spain, and that he must
obey. But if this were the case, why remove M. de
Montmorency, and give his place to a known friend of
representative government, hitherto a declared and determined enemy of the invasion? What could have
induced M. de Chateaubriand to lend himself to such
a policy, and thus fix an indelible stain upon his high
and well deserved reputation? It has sometimes been
surmised indeed, that there was a secret understanding
between the French ministry and the military leaders
in Spain, by the effect of which the former were to be
put in possession of the country, and were then to establish a new constitution, somewhat different from the
existing one, and more resembling the French Chambers, but still substantially liberal, and in the representative form. These surmises are not, I believe, supported by any very strong positive authority, but they
appear to me to be extremely probable, because they
really furnish the only imaginable account, upon which
the conduct of the French ministry can be reconciled
with ordinary common rules, and a decent regard for
political consistency. If true, they illustrate very
strongly the danger of substituting a system of intrigue
and secret management, in place of a fair, open, and

generous policy. If it was really the object of the French ministry to establish in Spain a constitutional government, they found themselves completely disappointed and over-reached; and by their own impolitic proceedings lost the advantages of victory, at the very moment of obtaining it. Had they left the formal power in the hands of the Spanish constitutional party, and lent them a fair and honest support, they might, in concurrence with England, have finally prevailed upon them to modify their form of government. But by first invading the country and throwing the formal power again into the hands of the Spanish clergy, a body ten times more fanatical than even the French fanatics, they lost all their influence at once, and became the mere servile instruments of the very party whom they had just before beaten at home. The regency was no sooner established, than it became unmanageable, openly disputed the authority of the Duke of Angouleme, and, strange as it may seem, had influence enough at Paris, to prevent the latter from being sustained in his moderate measures by his own government which had prescribed them. The military leaders, Morillo, Ballesteros, Abisbal, and others, with whom the secret understanding, if any such existed, must have been concerted, and for whose proceedings it is indeed difficult to account upon any other supposition, were basely sacrificed. The French ministry, represented by a victorious general, a prince of the blood royal, at the head of a hundred thousand men, could not even gain a hearing from a troop of insolent and ignorant monks, whom they had just delivered from imprisonment and beggary; and the apostle of constitutions terminated his armed intervention in favour of representative government, by the establishment of a virtual theocracy, in the person of Victor Saez, the king's confessor.

Such may perhaps have been the secret history of this transaction, which, as it stands openly before the public, is, as I have observed, a wholly unfathomable mystery, and which, on this view of it, exhibits a singular instance of mismanagement and duplicity in a cabinet, which is willing enough to be considered as the most acute and skilful in the world, but which is too apt to lose sight of the first and most essential ingredient in all good policy. Whatever may have been the motives which led them to adopt this measure, its fatal operation, first upon Spain, and then upon the whole christian world, is but too perceptible. With the overthrow of the Spanish constitution, perished, probably for ever, all hopes of the revival of the industry, prosperity, and power of that ancient and once illustrious state. It is true, that, even under an arbitrary government, the great administrative measures required by the present situation of things, such as the acknowledgment of American independence, the establishment of public credit by the assumption of the debts of the Cortes, and a thorough reform of the whole system of internal administration, would, if adopted, accomplish a great deal of good. But this is only saying in other words, that if an arbitrary government were to act in the spirit of a liberal one, it would produce the same effects. The great advantage of reforming the constitution was, that such a reform naturally led to a reform in the administration, and with the present system of government no improvement in the administration can reasonably be expected. The complete ruin of Spain was therefore the first, but unfortunately not the only, nor perhaps even the worst of the evils produced by the French invasion. The overthrow of liberty in Spain completed the work which had been commenced in Italy, by securing at least against all present danger, the triumph of despotism throughout the continent. Considered under this point of view, it appears even more deplorable, than in its immediate effects on the welfare of the ill-fated kingdom in which it was accomplished.

It is difficult to read, without emotions of wonder and contempt, the pretences employed by the French ministers to justify the invasion, whatever we may suppose to have been their real views in undertaking it. The principal one was the danger resulting from the establishment of the Spanish constitution. Danger to France from Spain! danger to a kingdom that had just established a liberal constitution, from the establishment of a similar one in a neighbouring and weaker state! There was hardly reason enough in these notions, to give an appearance of method to the madness of the act they were intended to justify. In addition to this, M. de Chateaubriand alleged another consideration, in his speech in the house of deputies, which, for its very singularity, has acquired a sort of ridiculous notoriety. He said that it was necessary to make war, because the existing state of things injured the trade in mules between the border provinces of the two kingdoms. Does not charity itself require that we should suppose this eminent statesman to have been acting upon one set of motives, while he professed another, and these not the

most happily imagined? But the strength of the reasons against this measure was, if possible, still more conspicuous than the weakness of the pretences alleged in
its favour. I say nothing of the glaring and acknowledged injustice of interfering by force of arms, and
without necessity, in the internal government of a friendly power. I should expect to be charged with *niaiserie*,
now the fashionable bye-word with the enemies of liberty, if I were to pretend to suppose it possible, that
government should be deterred by a sense of right and
justice, from doing what they believed to be expedient.
I will even lay out of the case the obvious consideration, which, however, no enlightened French statesman
ought to have overlooked for a moment, that the development of the principle of liberty, in the west of Europe, is the great defence of France against the en-
croaching power of Russia. I admit that this is a truth,
which the party now predominant at the Thuileries
could hardly be expected to perceive. But looking at
the state of Europe, simply under the old diplomatic
point of view, and considering the several nations as
independent masses of power mutually dangerous to
each other in proportion to their greatness, the impolicy of the invasion appears so palpable, so enormous, that
it is almost inconceivable how it could have been undertaken. That France should look on quietly and see the
northern allies, or in one word, Russia cast her iron net
over the whole of Italy, after riveting it already over the
whole of Germany,—this of itself was passing strange.
This was policy that might have shaken in their cere-
ments the Sully's, the Richelieu's, and the Favier's, to

say nothing of Napoleon. But that France, not content with this silent acquiescence in her own degradation, should consent to become herself the instrument of carrying still further the influence of that portentous power, that now overshadows Europe,—that the Duke of Angouleme should be the person employed to plant upon the towers of Cadiz the fatal banner of despotism, which was waving before in triumph over every fortress, from Archangel to Naples; this was conduct to which epithets can do no justice, and of which the simplest description that can be given, is the strongest possible satire. Were the ministers then labouring under some delusion, that prevented them from seeing the precipice before they reached it? We know on the contrary, by their own public declarations, that they were fully aware of the nature of the course they were pursuing. M. de Villèle, as I have stated before, affirmed publicly in the house of deputies, that if he did not make war at the south he should have it at the north. It is true that M. de Chateaubriand affected to place great confidence in the moderation of the Emperor of Russia, and quoted in his speech, with much satisfaction, the assurance given him by that monarch at the congress of Verona, that providence had placed him at the head of an army of eight hundred thousand men, not to make war but to keep the peace of Europe. But were these grave and experienced statesmen persons to be cheated by a few fair words? More probably, as I have already observed, they were pursuing through a labyrinth of tortuous intrigues, some imaginary clue of policy which they thought would conduct them to a safe position; but which miserably failed them in the sequel. However this may be, their plans terminated in reducing France to a secondary rank in the great political sphere, and endangering even her independent national existence. Instead of being, as she had often been in former times, the arbitress of Europe, she now appears as a power of inferior order, sometimes led by England and sometimes by Russia, but never standing out firmly on the basis of a genuine French policy. Having thus carried their point in respect to foreign affairs, the fanatics have become more active and apparently more successful in their efforts to destroy the principle of internal improvement, and to bring back the exploded superstitions and abuses of the old *regime*. They meet with occasional rebuffs, but they seem on the whole to have their way, and at this very moment, with the ghastly spectre of Jesuitism at their head, are marching with rapid strides to the conquest of the country and the subversion of the charter. With this defection in the French councils, disappeared, however, every national hope of an early rescue of the civilized part of Europe from the influence of the barbarous empires of the north. The friends of liberty on the continent have now abandoned the expectation of any immediate improvement in its political condition, and derive their only comfort from the contemplation of the partial success of the cause to which they are devoted in England, and its rapid and brilliant triumphs in our western continent. In these more favoured regions, the prospect of the future is not less flattering and agreeable, than it is desolating and dreadful in the one we have now reviewed. To them, therefore, I turn with a feeling of relief and pleasure.

The next event of great and general interest that

occurred in Europe after the overthrow of the Spanish constitution, was the acknowledgment by England of the independence of the new governments of America. This was a measure of the highest importance, whether considered in its effects upon the nation which adopted it, or upon the whole political system. As it respects the latter, it completely established the alienation of Great Britain from the continental alliance, gave that power a distinct and independent position in the world, and confirmed for ever, beyond the possibility of doubt, the emancipation of Spanish America. This single stroke of policy, therefore, completed the development of the new political system, in all its three great divisions. As regards its operation upon the immediate interests of England, it favoured the progress of liberal principles at home, and exercised a very beneficial influence on the economical situation of the country. Several circumstances concurred to recommend and determine the adoption of this measure at the time when it took place; among which was the wish to secure, as far as possible, the American markets, jealousy of the advantage that the United States might obtain in this respect, in consequence of their prior recognition, disgust at the proceedings of the continental powers, and finally the accidental death of Lord Castlereagh, followed by the appointment of Mr. Canning as secretary of state for foreign affairs.

The alliance between England and Russia for the overthrow of Bonaparte, however cordial it may have been at the time, under the operation of a strong common interest, left them, when the object was effected, in their natural positions of rival and hostile powers.— This new relation was not very long in displaying itself.

and began to appear even at the congress of Vienna, which preceded the battle of Waterloo. The projects of aggrandizement manifested by Russia at that congress, were of course opposed by England, and their complete success afforded a pretty distinct indication of the actual weight of the two great rivals in the scale of Europe. The formation of the holy alliance, without the concurrence or participation of Great Britain, the violent intervention of the allies in the affairs of Naples and Sardinia, against her advice and wishes, and finally the repetition of the same action, on a still larger theatre, at the congress of Verona, fully established the fact of the preponderance of Russia, and the comparative nullity of England in reference to the continent. On all those occasions, the latter power had acted the part of a passive and unwilling spectator of measures, in which she could not co-operate, and which she avowedly disapproved, but which she could not venture to resist by force, and was even under a political necessity of sanctioning to a certain extent, by appearing at the assemblies at which they were adopted. Such was the not very brilliant position to which Great Britain found herself reduced, by a singular turn of the wheel of fortune, immediately after the close of a thirty-years' war, carried on at unheard of expense, for the express purpose of securing her influence in Europe, and crowned, as she supposed, with signal success. The worst of the case was that it did not admit of any effectual remedy. It was impossible for the nation, encumbered already with a debt of a thousand millions sterling, to engage in another interminable contest with the combined powers of the continent: and every thing short of a war had been tried without effect. It was therefore, to all appearance, a matter of necessity to acquiesce in this passive situation, and to sink quietly, and without a struggle, into the rank of the secondary powers. A minister of ordinary talent and resources would have probably done this, nor would any intellectual vigour have succeeded in preventing such a result, without the occurrence of some favourable accident. As it happened, a series of events of great importance was at the same time actually proceeding in South America, which afforded the British government the opportunity of taking a new stand in the political system of Europe and the world. In order to do this, however, with effect, it was necessary to make some little sacrifices on the score of consistency, and to brush away rather rudely some cobwebs of delicacy, which would probably have greatly embarrassed the wings of Lord Castlereagh. It may be doubted, whether that minister would have thought it consistent with the respect due to the supposed rights of the King of Spain over his colonies, to take precedence of him, in the acknowledgment of their independence. It required the action of a strong and independent mind in the cabinet, to remove these scruples, however idle they may now appear; and had it not been for the accidental death of Lord Castlereagh and the succession of Mr. Canning to the vacant place, at this very critical moment, this great measure might perhaps have been delayed for an indefinite length of time. Such delay would have exercised a material and probably very unfavourable influence upon the course of events in Europe and America. On this, therefore, as on other occasions, fortune as well as policy had effect in determining the movement of affairs.

It appears somewhat singular, that two statesmen, no-
minally attached to the same political party, bred in the
same school, professing an unbounded and sincere veneration for the same great master, and who in fact had
acted together for years, not very harmoniously it must
be owned, as members of the same cabinet, should entertain views so essentially different upon the foreign politics of the country. But the personal characters of Lord
Castlereagh and Mr. Canning were as opposite, as their
political course had been in some respects similar. Lord
Castlereagh was a statesman of mere routine, and possessed in no eminent degree the qualities that belong to that
character. He administered the government as it had
been arranged by Mr. Pitt, in the same way in which a
chief clerk carries on the affairs of a department in the
absence of his principal; but to do him justice he was a
chief clerk of a high order. Though incapable of original conceptions, he was indefatigably active and industrious in the work of his office. Though he wanted
power and eloquence, he was fluent, cool, and above all,
copious, as an orator. He never irritated, and could
often tire out his opponents, when he could not persuade
or convince them. As a writer, he had no pretensions to
purity or precision, and even made no great account of
grammar; but he was a safe diplomatist, because he never committed himself by expressing his ideas in a distinct and forcible way, so that his despatches would bear
any construction which he might find it convenient at
any time to put upon them. He was very imperfectly
acquainted with politics as a science, and he could therefore hardly be considered as a partizan or disciple of

either despotism or liberty. Although he told his continental friends that the mixture of the latter element, which exists in the British constitution, was not the best part of it, this was probably rather because he felt it at times as a present inconvenience, than because he approved of the theory or practice of pure despotism. Qualities like these made him a successful, if not a very distinguished minister, as long as affairs could proceed without detriment to the public interest, in the same course which they were pursuing when he took the direction of them. But when a crisis occurred, which required the adoption of new and original measures, he was found, and would have continued to be found unequal to it. The embarrassment and anxiety which he felt at seeing himself blown off shore in this way, out of sight of all the old sea marks, and without chart or compass to direct him, probably contributed to produce the state of mind that occasioned his death.

Mr. Canning's character was in almost every respect the reverse of this. He possessed most of the high intellectual and moral qualities that Lord Castlereagh wanted, but he united with them some of the quiet and practical merits that belonged to his predecessor. A finished scholar, a powerful and elegant writer in prose and verse, an eloquent orator, capable of deep thought, though not so much addicted to this as to some other intellectual exercises, he united almost all the endowments that constituted a mind of the highest order; but in the pride of these advantages he has some times forgotten the cool and steady prudence, which is at once the instinctive resource of conscious inferiority, and the

invariable policy of true practical talent. Fond of exhibiting his skill in the graceful sports of wit and humour, he has not only often indulged in this way to
excess, in his parliamentary speeches, but has even
pointed his gravest diplomatic despatches with irony
and sarcasm. He assured the Russian chancellor, Count
Romanzoff, in answer to a conventional and common-
place remark upon the inconveniences of the war, which
that minister had introduced into an overture for peace
addressed to Mr. Canning from Erfurth, that it was not
the king's fault, if the continental nations were distress-
ed by their own system. In like manner, he informed
our government, in reply to some similar expression,
that although his majesty regretted very much the inconvenience which the United States suffered from the
embargo, they could not reasonably expect him to relieve
them from it, by sacrificing his own rights and interests.
In this style there was as little good sense and good taste
as there was good feeling. On some other occasions he
has exhibited his natural independence and fearlessness
of character, in a way which did him much more honour, as in the affair of the queen. Though apparently
partial to freedom in the abstract, he was led by a just
and natural abhorrence of the excesses of the French
revolution and its adherents in England, to attach himself to the ministerial party; and in the theory of the
government he seems to have adopted the opinion, which
in its application to Great Britain is probably correct,
that the constitution is in that country a thing entirely
of practice and not of theory, that it was not founded
and cannot safely be reformed according to any known

political rule, but must be left without touching, to follow its own course, at least until desperate evils shall require desperate remedies. But with all his great and brilliant qualities, his political course was, on the whole, unsuccessful, and somewhat inglorious, until his second entrance into the cabinet of foreign affairs. His position in the ministry, after his first retirement from that department, was not honourable and did not appear to be easy. The ascendency of an inferior but more fortunate rival, was evidently unpalatable to him, and we saw him moving about like a restless spirit, in different parts of Europe, and finally preparing to embark for the east, when the death of Lord Castlereagh restored him at once to his proper post, at the very moment when it stood most in need of his energetic genius. Since that time, his career has been sufficiently brilliant, to atone for any preceding failure or defect. The crisis was eminently favourable to the exercise of superior talent, and Mr. Canning has proved himself to be fully equal to it. He saw the fearful and growing power of despotism in his neighbourhood, and felt that the only way in which England could avoid becoming a victim to it, was to attach her fate at once to the rising empire of freedom in America. Satisfied of this, and conscious of his ability to strike out a new course for himself and the country, he broke off abruptly his connexion with the continent, and, like another Columbus, turned his hopes and views to the world embosomed in our western ocean. His second entrance into the cabinet of foreign affairs marks, therefore, the opening of a new era in the policy, foreign and domestic, of Great Britain.

The powerful considerations of an economical character, which also conduced to recommend this great measure, and the favourable effect that it will have upon the
industry and commerce of England, are sufficiently obvious, and need not here be developed at length. The
opening of the immense market of Spanish America to
the manufacturers of England was sufficient, if the thing
be in any way within the compass of possibility, to relieve
that country from the immense burdens with which it
has been charged, by the unexampled efforts of the government during the late war. At any rate it will afford
a great temporary relief, and will delay, if it does not
ultimately prevent the coming on of the evil hour. A
natural fear that the United States, by means of a first
recognition, would pre-occupy, and in some degree appropriate this glorious field, was probably one of the
motives which operated most powerfully in inducing
Great Britain to accelerate her movements. But on this
head we have no ground for complaint, nor in fact for
jealousy. In thus consulting the economical interest of
their subjects, the British government only did what
was perfectly within their competence; and as for us,
experience shows that we need not desire a larger share
of the commerce of the world than we can obtain, by the
effect of the enterprise and talent of our citizens, entering into fair competition with those of all other nations.
Our nearness to Spanish America will always give us a
considerable advantage in this trade over England; and
it is understood that in some important branches of industry we are already, notwithstanding the infancy of our
manufacturing establishments, the successful rivals of

the mother country. This amicable contest for the palm of excellence in the fine and useful arts of life, is injurious to no one, and indeed promotes directly the advantage of all. Humanity rejoices over it, as much as she deplores the infernal scenes which so often result from the rival claims of nations to power and territorial dominion.

The political results of the recognition of Spanish America by England are, however, those which fall more immediately under our present consideration, and, as I have already remarked, are of such importance, that it would be difficult to exaggerate them by any statement, however highly coloured. To the new governments themselves, this event is only second in interest to the prior recognition by the United States, upon which I shall have occasion to enlarge hereafter, and which first gave them full assurance, that their struggle for emancipation would be successful. But if our recognition was of higher value, as well by its direct operation as by its effect in determining that of England, the latter was nevertheless of the most serious consequence, because it satisfied the continental powers that they could not with safety interfere, and must leave Spain to her own unassisted strength. To the United States it was also an event of signal interest, inasmuch as it confirmed and established the new condition of the American continent, and with it the pre-eminence of our country, as the leading American power, among the nations of the world. If therefore this measure did in any way affect us injuriously in an economical point of view, which there is very little reason to suppose, we are more than compensated by its favourable influence upon our political importance and security. To England herself the adoption of this policy was a thing of such moment, that it was almost equivalent in its consequences to a geographical removal from one quarter of the globe to the other. Distrusted by the continental powers, as a false friend and deserter of the common cause, banished from their markets, excluded from their councils, and an alien from their principles, Great Britain seems to have lost her hold on the other world in which she is situated, and to have become an American rather than a European state. We find accordingly that Mr. Canning, in his complimentary speech addressed to our countryman Mr. Hughes, at a public dinner at Liverpool, declared without scruple, that the mother and daughter, meaning Great Britain and the United States, were now to stand together and make head against the rest of the Christian world. The form which this alliance is likely to assume (and of which the United States will have no reason to be ashamed) I shall have occasion to examine, in the course of the present volume. As to its effects on the continental powers, the recognition of Spanish America by England struck them with a feeling of consternation and disappointment, which they have hardly thought it worth while to dissemble. It defeated their secret projects of ultimately aiding Spain in the war, and inspired them with sad forebodings, that the principle of liberty, being thus firmly and for ever established in the new world, would at some future period exercise a fatal reaction upon their own unnatural system. Finally this event, in its influence upon the whole brotherhood of christian nations, considered as forming one vast commonwealth, and in reference to the principles respectively prevailing among them, strengthened the cause of freedom, which was before perhaps the weaker in comparison with that of despotism, in such a way as to give it a decided and constantly increasing preponderance, secured the progress of improvement from the danger of future interruption, refreshed the hearts of the friends of humanity, and brightened the prospects of the world. For these great results, we are no doubt chiefly indebted to the ascendency in the British cabinet of the powerful and generous mind of Mr. Canning. In the gratitude we feel for these signal benefits conferred upon the whole human race, and especially upon our own country and continent, we may venture to forget our old quarrel with him, for his ill timed jest upon the embargo, more particularly as we have had a pretty serious revenge upon him for it at Platsburgh, Erie, and New Orleans.

Such have been the principal events of the last five years, in the two political divisions of Europe; on the continent, the overthrow of the Spanish Constitution, in England the acknowledgment of American Independence. Both of these appeared to be, at the moment of their occurrence, the results of tendencies, that were likely to operate for a length of time to come, and to determine, perhaps, for centuries, the aspect of the regions where they happened. Such, however, is the instability of human affairs, that before these events are fairly consummated, while the French troops are still occupying Spain, and while the English ministers are still making their first arrangements with the new American governments, an accident happens to an individual on the shore of a solitary sea, in a remote corner of Europe, which threatened, for a moment at least, to unsettle every thing, and give an entirely new form to the political affairs of the world. The short period of confusion, that immediately succeeded the first intelligence of the death of the Emperor Alexander, has, however, passed off, without any very important results ; nor does it now appear that any such will hereafter follow from it. It is nevertheless in itself an occurrence of a character so highly interesting, that it seems to call for a passing notice in a general review of political events.

The mass of men, who are fond of discovering in all extraordinary accidents the signs of a special interposition of Providence, and who considered the Emperor Alexander as responsible in part for the singular severity with which Napoleon was treated by the allies after his final fall, have been disposed to regard the untimely death of the former, in the peculiar way in which it took place, as a sort of judgment upon him, for his share in the banishment of his ancient friend and ally to St. Helena. There is, in fact, something singular, in the resemblance of the circumstances, under which these two individuals ultimately perished. Each, after wielding in turn for about ten years, the sceptre of continental Europe, leaves his strong castles and splendid palaces—his court and his army—all the pride, pomp, and circumstance of his rank, and retires to die in a lonely dwelling, situated in a distant corner of the globe, with no attendants but a few domestic servants and private friends. Alexander was at least in this respect more fortunate than Napoleon, that his last moments were soothed by the presence and affectionate endearments of his wife. It must be owned, however, that this supposed similarity of the circumstances attending their deaths was, on the whole, rather superficial than real. But, however much alike their positions may have been, at certain moments of their lives and at leaving of them, it would be difficult to mention two individuals, who have exhibited a stronger contrast of personal character. The Emperor Alexander was undoubtedly by no means free from faults. His earlier life was marked by doubtful passages of a very serious complexion. In his later years, he adopted erroneous theories on government and religion, which greatly affected the rectitude of his public conduct; and throughout his whole career his domestic habits, on some very delicate points, if we would not censure him too severely, must be judged by comparison with those of other princes, rather than by the rules of strict morality. He also made no pretensions to high intellectual powers of any description, nor was the want of brilliant endowments supplied in him by the presence of the plainer and more solid qualities, that serve quite as well for the practical objects of life. He was, on the contrary, rather remarkable for his deficiency in sound judgment and ordinary good sense. He exhibited, at times, but little discernment in the choice of his associates; and, as he advanced in life, fell into a kind of feverish and mystical enthusiasm, that did him but very little honour. But although he was thus destitute in greater or less degrees of many of the qualities, that go to form an elevated character, he possessed, nevertheless, virtues of a high order, that served in some measure to redeem his defects, and to give him, on the whole, a very favourable position in the eye of the world. He had talent enough to make him remarkable among his brother sovereigns, and to confer upon his actions an air of independence; and by great activity and industry, he made the most of the talent he had. But the only truly brilliant quality about him, was the nobleness and generosity of his spirit, virtues so graceful and yet so rare in hereditary princes. He was not like most of his brother monarchs, who, like the arcadian youth in Juvenal, feel no throbs under the left breast,—læva sub parte mamillæ nil salit;—nor yet like Napoleon, whose heart, according to his mother's remark, was as hard as one of his own cannon balls. The Emperor Alexander possessed a real heart of flesh and blood. He had a fund of unaffected goodness, which remained uncorrupted to the last, which formed the charm and beauty of his character, and made him at one time the Titus of the age and the delight of the human race. We saw it in most of his domestic relations, where real charity does and ought to begin. What a contrast there was between the beautiful harmony that prevailed in the imperial family of Russia, and the wretched wrangling which at the same time constantly disturbed the interior of the Thuileries. While Napoleon would not allow *Madame Mere*, as he called her, to sit in his presence, the empress mother was worshipped at St. Petersburgh as a sort of divinity, by all her sons, the emperor among the first. Neither was faultless in his nearest family connexion; but what a difference between the temporary neglect of Alexander, while the ardour of youth led him into excesses, venial if ever in a rank like his, and the cold-blooded calculating unkindness of Napoleon, who, for reasons of state, could put away for ever, and bring down in fact to an untimely grave, the companion of his life and the affectionate partner of his humbler fortunes! The quarrels of the latter with his brothers, were the scandal of Europe, while the world in regard to the others was ready to exclaim, in the language of Scripture, " Behold how good and how pleasant a thing it is, for brethren to live together in unity." But the generous spirit of the Emperor Alexander extended its influence beyond the walls of his palace, and gave an amiable and elevated cast to his whole deportment, public and private. He felt a real sympathy in the fortunes and concerns of other men, and was fond of mingling with them on equal terms. I have seen him repeatedly in the streets of St. Petersburgh, walking unattended, by the hour together, and conversing familiarly with persons of all classes, whom he happened to meet. His habits were the same in foreign countries, where the effect of them was heightened by the contrast with the cold and stiff manner of the sovereigns, by whom he was generally accompanied. When he appeared among the good people of Paris, winning their hearts with his charming and easy popularity, at the same time that he was bringing them the substantial blessing of deliverance from military despotism, they forgot for the moment the humiliation of receiving their liberty as a gift from a foreigner, and almost looked upon his presence as a supernatural intervention of providence. The free and genial warmth of his spirit made his intellect appear to greater advantage, or, to speak more correctly, actually increased his mental powers; for what we call understanding, is as much the result of moral as of intellectual qualities. The political nothingness of most sovereigns, and the pitiful emptiness of their conversation, do not perhaps arise so much from the want of understanding as from habitual subjection to form and etiquette. The Emperor Alexander had a spirit above this. He did not think it necessary to confine his conversation with distinguished foreigners to a few paltry remarks upon the weather and the walk, the last ball, or the next bull-fight. He entered boldly into the general field of observation, and with naturally respectable powers and an excellent education, in addition to the *prestiges* of his rank and title to heighten the effect of what he said, he acquitted himself in such a way, that he had no reason to repent of his temerity.

It belongs, perhaps, to the citizens of the United States of America to do full justice to the character of this prince, since whatever he may have been to other nations, he was to us a true friend in more than mere profession. He proved himself a most important and useful ally, at the critical epoch of the late war, and in consideration of this, we ought not to think too hardly of him, for employing a cypher or two more than was necessary, in stating the extent of his jurisdiction over

the Pacific ocean. It would be useless, however, to attempt to conceal his errors, which arose in part from the
same qualities that formed the principle of his best virtues. The freedom and activity of his spirit, while they
greatly increased his influence and reputation, were
also the immediate causes of some very dangerous mistakes. Great activity generally implies on occasions,
inconsistency and fickleness of purpose; and the emperor appears accordingly to have had no principle sufficiently stable, to resist the current of adverse circumstances, or the seduction of immediate interest. He
commenced his reign with the most liberal feelings and
intentions, and ended it by establishing the military colonies—the most illiberal and at the same time economi-
cally impolitic and impracticable institution, that was
ever deliberately adopted in any age or nation. At one
time, he favoured the introduction of representative
constitutions in foreign countries, founded one, at least
in form, in his own kingdom of Poland, and gave out
that he intended to do the same in Russia. A few years
after, we see him crushing these constitutions by force of
arms in several parts of Europe, out of complaisance to
the empty theories of a few interested declaimers; and
lending his influence, fortunately without the same success, to perpetuate the reign of superstition and military despotism over the vast and wealthy regions of the
new world. While, therefore, we acknowledge and do
full justice to his amiable qualities, while we admit that
he possessed the charity, that covers a multitude of sins,
we have little cause, as friends of liberty, to regret his
death. His opinions and feelings had taken a false direc-

tion, from which there is no probability that they would ever have returned; and under these circumstances it may almost be said, that his very virtues and graces were dangerous to the cause of humanity. But not to dwell too long either on his frailties or his merits, and leaving them both to the award of that great power to whom alone he would own himself to be accountable for his actions, let us follow his remains from the remote and solitary shore where his spirit took its flight, to the splendid abode of his living greatness, and consider for a moment the political effects of his sudden and unexpected death.

This event is still so recent, and was followed immediately by consequences of so singular a character, that it is rather early to attempt to anticipate its remote results. It displayed to the world the uncommon spectacle of two brothers, contending with each other for the privilege, not of possessing, but of resigning the empire of a quarter of the globe. There was possibly at bottom something less of disinterestedness on both sides, than appeared in mere outward show; but there is, nevertheless, a charm and beauty in the external forms of generosity, which make them in the highest degree valuable, even where the substance is wanting. That it was in this case altogether wanting, is, however, far from being evident. The Grand Duke Constantine may have originally waved his pretensions to the crown, from other motives than those which are assigned in his public letters; but there was nothing in fact or in right to prevent him from asserting them, had he thought proper to do so after his brother's death; and although prudence as well as fraternal affection would have dictated the conduct of Nicholas, it is still impossible not to see something better in it, than in the greedy eagerness with which sceptres have been generally grasped, by all who had any pretext for laying hands upon them. It is impossible not to consider the uncommon self command and mutual respect and kindness of these rival brothers, as in part effects and proofs of the unprecedented harmony, that has for some time past prevailed among the members of the imperial family of Russia, and which is generally attributed, in a great degree, to the ascendency over her children of the commanding and amiable character of the empress mother. The result of this forbearance, whatever may have been its cause, was undoubtedly the prevention of a civil war, which, under the complicated circumstances of the case, could hardly have been avoided, had the rival candidates for the crown displayed the spirit that generally belongs to that position.

This new form of fraternal competition, somewhat different from the famous example of the Theban brothers, was not the only interesting accident that attended the change in the person of the emperor. While these edifying scenes were in progress, others of an opposite character were opening upon the same theatre. It appears that a vast conspiracy against the life of the emperor, and the present form of government, had been lurking in the heart of the empire, had spread very extensively through the army, and included many distinguished and wealthy individuals. Such are the statements of the government itself, which has certainly no

interest in exaggerating the mischief. It is rather a
strange coincidence, and one that would almost lead to
some dark surmises respecting the mode of the late emperor's death, that it appears to have been a part of the
plot to assassinate him, while on his journey to the south,
and in the section of the country where he actually
died. Whatever may be the truth in regard to this
point, it is evident beyond dispute, from the fearful
revelations which have been made upon this occasion,
that the machinery of despotism, however effectually it
may operate in checking the publicity of thought and
feeling, cannot prevent their action; and that discontent, though hidden from the eye of the world by the
impenetrable covering of the police and the *censure*,
assumes at least as dangerous a form, as when it evapo-
rates in newspaper essays and popular harangues. The
results of this plot are far from being yet entirely dis-
closed. It evidently struck the government, as well it
might, with the deepest consternation; and there was
for some time a singular vacillation, probably occasioned
by it, in regard to some very important matters. No
less than three different resolutions appear to have been
taken upon the subject of the military colonies, within
the same number of weeks after the accession of Nico-
las. One of the very first official papers printed after
the event, was a report from Count Arakchief, the superintendant of these colonies, in which he declared openly against them, as having completely failed in their
objects, and as being in every way useless and injurious.
This report must be presumed not to have been disagreeable to the government at the moment when they

ordered its publication. But about a week after, there appeared in the official gazette a letter signed by the emperor, and addressed to this same Count Arakchief, highly commending the institution of the military colonies and the manner in which they had been managed, and ordering the count to proceed in the same course which he had pursued under the late sovereign. A few days elapsed, and it was officially announced that the superintendance of the military colonies was intrusted to Count Diebitch, and that Count Arakchief had obtained permission to travel for his health. The secret of these enigmatical proceedings is not yet known; but they have probably some connexion, more or less remote. with the conspiracy. Whether other consequences of still greater moment may not yet grow out of it, is still uncertain. Will it be completely stifled and crushed without producing any serious commotion in the empire? Will the emperor think it expedient to employ his discontented troops abroad, in order to keep them out of mischief at home, and determine to assist the Greeks, when all better motives have failed, from mere self-interest? The British cabinet, which under the influence of some strange fatality has been so long counteracting the cause of liberty in Greece, appears to be alarmed at the favourable prospect held out by the present state of Russia, and has despatched the Duke of Wellington to St. Petersburgh, at once to compliment the emperor upon his accession and to frighten him into keeping the peace with Turkey.

It would lead me too far, however, from my immediate subject, to examine the probability of a war between Russia and Turkey, or its influence, if it should occur, upon the politics of Europe and the world; nor is the subject in fact sufficiently mature to be treated yet in detail. It belongs more properly to some future chapter in political history. Laying this question entirely out of view, it does not appear that the change in the person of the Emperor of Russia, considered under any of its other aspects, is likely to affect materially the nature of the influence exercised by that country. This will probably still be exerted as before, in favour of what has been called by courtesy, *legitimacy,* and against the cause of liberty and good government throughout the world. Even should a civil war grow out of the controversy respecting the succession or the conspiracy, it does not appear that such an event would in any degree diminish the power of the empire, or make it less formidable to the independence or welfare of the rest of Europe. A military monarchy is in fact never more formidable, because its principle is never more active, than when it is distracted by internal convulsions. These are constantly developing by exercise the highest talents, which are first sharpened by contention with each other, and then, as soon as a moment's breathing time occurs at home, are turned with a sort of fury against every thing that comes within their reach abroad. A civil war in Russia would very probably give to that empire the only element which it wants, I mean an ambitious, ardent, and successful military chieftain, in order to effect the conquest of the whole of Europe. We should probably see, in that case, some Muscovite Cæsar subjugating Gaul, in order to reign with more security at home, or carrying his armies in pursuit of some new Sertorius beyond the Pyrenees. The sphere of Russia is now so vast that it comprehends the entire continent; and her battles are as likely to be fought on the banks of the Rhine or the Danube, as of the Volga. If, however, nothing of all this should take place at present, and the internal tranquillity of the empire should remain undisturbed, the new administration will be only a continuation of the last, and the same general course of opposition to liberal principles and of the extension of the ascendancy of Russia over the rest of Europe will be pursued in a more quiet, and of course, perhaps, in the end, a more effectual way, than it could be in the tumult and fury of civil and foreign war.

Such are the principal events that have occurred in Europe within the last five years. It will have been seen that they are by no means of an ordinary character. But important and interesting as they are, they dwindle into nothing, by the side of the mighty revolutions, of which, during the same period of time, our own continent has been the theatre; and which, whether we consider their immense present magnitude or their still more imposing future results, have no parallel in the history of the world. During this interval, the boundless regions of Spanish America have completed their emancipation from the government of the parent country; and our own United States have taken the stand which they are henceforth and for ever to occupy, in the political system of Christendom. What volumes of detail are comprehended in these few lines! How insignificant do the events of former times appear, by the side of those which this new epoch must bring to light! How confined the sphere on which the most distinguished actors in those events performed their parts, compared with the present political theatre, which has no limits but those of the globe! Is it too much to anticipate that the minds, which are to figure upon this more extended field of action, before this enlarged circle of observers, will be moved by purer and nobler views, and rise to loftier heights of patriotism and virtue, than those which preceded them? May we not hope at least that the new world will continue to produce Washingtons, instead of Cromwells and Bonapartes; and Adamses, Franklins, and Jeffersons, instead of Machiavels and Mirabeaus? Certainly the present appearances tend to encourage very strongly these ideas, and to cheer the hearts of the lovers of our race with delightful visions of the future.

To comment, however imperfectly, upon the great events to which I have just alluded, in connexion with the present state of the regions in which they have occurred, will be the principal object of the present volume; and the branch of this inquiry, which naturally first claims our attention, is the situation of our own country, which I shall accordingly proceed to examine in the following chapter.

CHAPTER III.

United States of America.—Form and Spirit of their Political Institutions.

THE extraordinary success which has thus far attended the political career of the United States, has naturally excited throughout the world a strong interest respecting the forms of their social institutions, accompanied with a general prepossession in their favour, in the minds of reflecting and unprejudiced inquirers. It is known and admitted by all such persons, that the welfare of nations depends almost wholly upon the nature of their governments. When, therefore, a nation prospers for a length of time, in a very remarkable way, the conclusion is, that the government is uncommonly good. If it be in form entirely new, the friends of humanity and the students of political science are led to examine it with great curiosity and attention, in order to ascertain its principles and peculiar virtues, for the purpose of applying them to the advancement of knowledge and the profit of other countries. We find, accordingly, that, since the close of the late convulsions afforded the observers of Europe an opportunity of directing their attention to objects of remote and general interest, they have been very much occupied in examining the situation and political institutions of the

United States; and the opinions which are expressed upon the subject, by the most distinguished authorities among them, are for the most part highly favourable and satisfactory. We have found, it is true, but little favour in the eyes of sundry respectable mechanics and tradesmen, who came out from the mother country to sell their wares, and made, on their return, but a meagre report of the state of our religion, government, morals, and manners, perhaps because they found our markets somewhat better stocked than they expected. But with all the regret that we naturally feel at not having given satisfaction to these honest people, it is some consolation that even in Great Britain such minds as those of Burke, Fox, Mackintosh, Canning, Brougham, Jeffrey, and others of the same class, have seen something to admire, as well as something at times to condemn, in our institutions and history; and have honoured us with their friendly dispositions and occasional discerning approbation. On the continent of Europe, there is also a general impression in favour of our country; not resulting from accidental sympathies, but common to various parties, and shared by almost all impartial and reflecting men. The Germans, in particular, have given much attention to the United States, and have always regarded them with peculiar good will. It was predicted by the celebrated Herder, that the eighteenth century would be known hereafter in history, as the age of Washington and Franklin. Schmidt-Phiseldeck, no bigotted republican, since he has written a work expressly to defend and vindicate the principles of the holy alliance, opens one of his books, by remarking that the fourth of July, 1776, was the commencement of a new era in the history of the world. In France, the other great intellectual section of the continent, the judgments are equally favourable. The opinions of the Constants, the Guizots, the De Staels, the Lafayettes, are too well known to require being stated in detail; but it may be worth remarking, that the Vicomte de Chateaubriand, not less decided as a constitutional royalist, than distinguished as a writer and philosopher, declared in his late *Note on Greece*, that the *representative republic*, of which the United States have given the world the first example, is the most splendid discovery of modern times. The great political economist Say, as competent a judge as perhaps any living individual, extends to the administration of the government the approbation, which the others have bestowed upon its principles; and exclaims, in his well known work, in allusion to the United States—"What a comfort it is to find at least one nation acting uniformly in obedience to the dictates of humanity and justice!"—I quote these favourable opinions of distinguished foreigners, not for the purpose of fostering an overweening national vanity, but in order to show that the strong predilection we feel at home for our political institutions, is not the effect of prejudice or ignorance, and that similar ideas are also entertained by the best judges and most eminent men in other quarters of the globe. Time has in fact already stamped our government with the seal of tried and approved excellence. It has now existed half a century,—the age of the British constitution, dating it from 1688, when it received the splendid eulogium

which Montesquieu passed upon it in his Spirit of Laws.
Ours has carried us triumphantly through dangerous
periods of intestine divisions and foreign war. Under
its benign influence we have doubled our territory,
quadrupled our population, centupled, if I may use
such a word, our wealth and influence; and at the close
of this first jubilee of our political existence, we have
the proud satisfaction of being able to look backwards
on a course of more brilliant success, and forward on a
fairer prospect of future greatness and glory, than ever
fell to the lot of any nation upon earth before. A government that affords such results may well be expected
to excite attention at home and abroad.

The constitutions of the United States, like that of
England, which furnished in part the model of them,
have been more admired and praised, than studied in
the abstract or examined in a scientific way. It is true
that the subject very frequently comes up in debate, as
well in congress as in the legislatures of the different
states, and that libraries have been written and published, upon the construction of the constitution, in the
shape of speeches and newspaper essays. These dis-
sertations, however, with some exceptions, have in general but little permanent value; not merely because
they are for the most part tinctured with personal and
party prejudices, but because, independently of this
objection, they are almost always formed upon a partial
and imperfect view of the system. Of the more deli-
berate treatises that have appeared upon this great
subject, two have attained a high degree of reputation,
and are justly entitled to it, as well by the authority of

their writers, as by their own intrinsic value; I mean
the Defence of the Constitution, by President Adams,
and the Federalist. Both these works may now be regarded as classical; and are equal perhaps, as scientific
essays on the subjects of which they treat, to any productions of the kind in the language. They are in some
measure complements to each other, and form together
a full commentary on our political system. The work
of President Adams, which was written before the
adoption of the federal constitution, is devoted to an
examination of those of the states, and of the general
principles of our government, while the Federalist is
merely a commentary on the instrument of union. After
a complete survey of the subject by these illustrious
authors, *summi auctores*, it may be thought, perhaps,
that little remains to be said; and it may even appear
presumptuous to undertake to add any thing to their
weighty and mature suggestions. I trust, however,
that the few hasty observations which I shall now offer,
limited as well by the character of the present essay, as
by other more imperious motives, will not expose me to
such a charge. The works to which I have now alluded
were both published about forty years ago, and the
eventful period which has since elapsed may have varied
a little the point of view, under which we consider certain subjects, or may have made familiar some notions
which were formerly less obvious. If there be any value
in the following remarks, it will be owing entirely to the
effect of this circumstance. In the present chapter, I
shall first sketch out, in a very general way, the theory
of the constitution as I conceive it, and then inquire into

the securities we have for the continuance of its present state of purity.

The *constitution* of a country is a thing upon which many persons write and reason with great freedom, without sufficiently considering the full extent of the term. By the constitution of the United States, for example, we generally mean the written instrument to which this title is affixed; and this is, no doubt, taken separately and distinctly from every thing else, a very important subject for consideration. But if the object be to acquire a distinct notion of the form and spirit of the government under which we live, we must take into view the whole mass of our political institutions; and in this case, the federal constitution, though the first and highest in value of the written acts and monuments that compose this mass, is far from being the only thing that calls for attention. Besides this charter, there are four and twenty others, each of which, though less important to the nation at large, is even of more direct and daily value to the state on which it operates, than the common covenant of union. But this is not all. Besides the five and twenty constitutions, we must take into view the statutes of congress and of the several state governments, and add to these the common law of the land, which forms in every state the basis of the local jurisprudence, and which comprehends, with the modifications under which they have been applied in this country, the whole law of England in its various branches of common, statute, feudal, chancery, admiralty, and so forth; the civil and canon law, the law of nature and nations, and, as a sanction to the whole, the truths of natural and revealed religion. The constitution of this country, therefore, taken in its broad and proper signification, is a very extensive code, including a variety of titles, of which the covenant of union is only one. I say not this for the purpose of depreciating the importance of the federal constitution, upon which, as will appear from the sequel of these remarks, I set as high a value as any one can. It is in fact the key-stone of our social arch, which crowns and consolidates the whole multifarious mass of materials, and infuses a principle of strength and order into what would otherwise be a mere chaos.

All important as this instrument is, as the necessary condition of our liberty and national existence, it is still, however, not the only thing we have of value; and there are several subjects of essential moment, that are not even touched upon in this our great charter. The principles, for example, that regulate the tenure and transfer of property, particularly land, exercise beyond a doubt more influence upon the character and happiness of nations, than any other part of their political institutions. They are not mentioned in the federal constitution. The punishment of crimes is left, with some exceptions, to the states; and the direct protection of our personal rights is still committed, almost wholly, to the common law of the land. These momentous subjects must nevertheless be studied, if we wish to obtain a complete and exact idea of our political institutions; for how could a correct opinion be formed upon the nature of the government of a country, without a knowledge of the state of property and the securities of personal rights? If the practical truths and rules that belong to each of these various titles, were any where stated with the same beautiful precision and simplicity that distinguish the federal constitution, the task of the student would be comparatively light; but this is far from being the case. Truth, the law, the constitution, must be discovered under most of these heads, by long and laborious research; must be pursued through mazes of controversy, wilds of speculation, mines of literature. Consider, for example, what masses of materials must be employed in order to ascertain the common law of England, which is yet only one of the titles or component parts of the common law of each of our states. Lord Coke assures us, that even the obscurity of the common law, great as it is, is broad daylight compared with the Cimmerian darkness that envelopes the British statutes; and yet these, with our own five and twenty collections at the end of them, not to speak of territorial and district enactments, are among the lighter labours of our political student. What patience is necessary, what libraries must be explored, in pursuing the progress and development of the Roman jurisprudence, from its rude elements in the twelve tables of the Decemvirs, down to its last and most perfect form in the code Napoleon! How comprehensive is the law of nature and nations, including as it does the great sciences of politics, morals, and political economy, together with the whole compass of history as evidence of usage! These must all be mastered. Finally, religion, natural and revealed, the most extensive and difficult subject upon which the human mind can be employed, has been declared by the competent authorities to be parcel of the common law; and is of course, from its nature, a most important parcel of every composition into which it enters. Such being the compass and variety of the elements that make up our political institutions, it is evidently not so easy and simple a task as is sometimes supposed, to become acquainted with their form and spirit; and it certainly requires much more than the half-hour's labour necessary for the perusal of the constitution of the United States.

In this, however, as in other cases, the machinery works in detail, under the operation of a few powerful springs, which create and determine the movement of all the parts. It may be possible, perhaps, to have some general conception of the nature of these, without possessing a thorough knowledge of all or any of the various divisions of our constitutional law; and it is to this part of the subject only, that the limits of the present essay will allow me to devote any attention.

The fundamental principle, or, to keep up the metaphor, the mainspring of our political machine to which all others are subordinate and secondary, is the sovereignty of the people. In most other nations, the right of administering the common concerns, or in other words, of making and enacting laws, is said to reside either in some family, possessing it by inheritance, as in absolute monarchies; or in a class of families holding it in the same way, as in aristocracies; or to be shared unequally among the different individuals or families composing the community, as in mixed governments, in which a single family is said to enjoy by inheritance, a large share of this right, a class of other families another large share, while the body of the people possess the remainder. The superiority of our system, considered as a theory, is sufficiently obvious, or at least does not require to be defended by argument before the American public. In fact the burden of proof lies in this case on the other side. That the affairs of every association, political, economical, literary, or religious, should be managed under the joint direction of all the members, and not by any other person or by any one or more members to the exclusion of the rest, is a proposition so plainly consonant with common sense and common right, that it would be thought madness, rather than mistake, to deny it in the abstract. If then it be affirmed, that this principle, though true in every other case, is false in its application to government; and that, in every political association, there is to be found some one family or families endowed by nature with a right to manage the concerns of the rest, it belongs to the person making this assertion to prove it, and to show us in every nation this ruling race, which come into the world with crowns on their heads and sceptres in their hands. Until this can be done, as long as men are born politically free and equal, we shall continue to regard the leading axiom of our government above alluded to, not only as true, but as it is said to be in the declaration of independence, self evident. The same principle is sometimes expressed in other forms, as when we say that the will of the people is the legitimate source of power, and that the voice of the people is the voice of God. It is not meant by these assertions, as some affect to suppose, that the opinion of the members of any one political society fixes the natural distinction of right and wrong. This has been done once for all and for ever, by the great sovereign of the universe. The office of human sovereignties is to declare these distinctions, for the use of the community, and enforce, as far as possible, the conduct corresponding with them; and the right of doing this, as of managing all other matters of common concern, belongs, in the last resort, to the members of each community, that is, to the body of the people. To say that the people may sometimes be mistaken, and declare as a rule of conduct some principle, which a better understanding of natural law would reprove, is only saying in other words, that men are not angels. This we know. But as the body of the people, though subject to error, intellectual and moral, possess, notwithstanding, in every political society, to the exclusion of any other human power, the right of proclaiming and enforcing the principles of natural law, that is, the decrees of the Divine Being, as by them understood, the voice of the people may be said with propriety and literal truth, to be the voice of God; because it is the only authoritative earthly expression that can rightfully be given, to the eternal decrees, which the Creator has stamped upon the face of his work, and engraved in the hearts of his rational creatures.

Indeed the sovereignty of the people is so far from being a doubtful principle, that it is supposed and admitted, in all the plausible theories that can be advanced of all forms of government. It may be said for example, by the advocates of monarchy, that it appears from experience that the general good is best promoted by investing one particular family with the hereditary office of declaring and enforcing the laws. This is no doubt the most plausible account that can be given of the matter. But what does it suppose? First, that the people naturally possess the right of self-government; secondly, that they have exercised this right, and finding by experience that such exercise was attended with inconvenience, have, thirdly, invested a particular family with the office of acting for them in this capacity. Monarchy, therefore, according to the only rational theory that can be given of it, is a form, in which the people exercise their inherent right of self-government; and the same remark may be applied to aristocracy, theocracy, mixed governments, and in general to all forms as far as they pretend to rest upon the basis of natural justice.*

---

* Another theory now much in fashion among the European *philosophers of anti-philosophy*, (as they were called by Madame de Stael,) founds the defence of monarchy upon some supposed analogy between communities and families. As the father of a family naturally possesses a controlling power over his wife, children, and servants, so there ought to be, and naturally is as they say, in every community, some chief or sovereign who exercises a similar control over the members. It is needless, however, to take the trouble of refuting a theory, which supposes, in opposition to all known facts and to the whole course of history, that hereditary sovereigns possess the same intellectual and physical advantages over their subjects, and the same instinctive and unconquerable love for them, which constitute the source of the paternal authority. It is enough to wait, as before, until they show us, in each community, an individual

As the sovereignty of the people is thus consonant to natural justice, and is even supposed in all rational theories of all forms of government, it would seem to follow that pure *democracy,* or a government in which the people actually exercise in person the sovereignty which they rightfully possess, would be the form of political association most expedient in practice, and most generally adopted. But a little reflection shows very clearly that this is not and cannot be the case. A community governed on a purely democratic system is necessarily limited to the number of families, whose heads can assemble conveniently in one place for deliberation on the common affairs, that is, to four or five hundred, or at the most as many thousand. Now communities of this size do not afford the necessary security, either against internal convulsion or foreign violence; and this form of government is, therefore, impracticable on a scale sufficiently large to ensure the objects of all social institutions. The great problem in politics is, therefore, to discover the form of government which best combines the security that can only be enjoyed in large states, with the acknowledgment and exercise of the right of self-government inherent in the people. Monarchy. aristocracy, theocracy, mixed governments, and whatever other forms may have been at times devised and

---

endowed by nature with the visible signs of this high pre-eminence. While these fathers of the nations continue as heretofore to acquire and maintain their paternal authority at the point of the bayonet, we shall consider the bayonet as the best argument they can urge in support of it, as well as the last.

essayed, must be considered, as far as they are in any way defensible and justifiable, as so many different modes of solving this problem. It remained for the people of the United States to furnish, in addition to these, an entirely new solution, which, as I have just remarked, has been pronounced by a very competent judge, to be the most splendid discovery of modern times. The object of this solution is not, as some affirm, *democracy rejected*, but *democracy made easy*. The secret of it lies in the application to government of two principles, neither of which had ever before been distinctly perceived or successfully practised, and which constitute the two next in order of the powerful springs in our political machine, to which I have alluded above. Every reader will perceive at once that the principles in question are the *representative* and the *federative*. They are not so much substitutes for democracy, as modes of reducing it to practice. The people exercise by responsible deputies the power which they cannot conveniently exercise in person; and obtain by a federal union the security, which they could not have enjoyed as independent states. It is wholly impossible to form a correct idea of the spirit of our political institutions, without attentively considering the nature and operation of these two great elementary principles. Pressed as I am for space, by the necessity of treating this large subject in a single chapter, I must confine myself to a few of the most obvious remarks upon each.

1. The principle of representation, to us who have become familiar with it, appears extremely simple as well as highly important. But this is the case with all

great improvements; and it is nevertheless true, that the application of this principle, in any thing like a pure and perfect state, (and it is only when applied in such a form that its real advantages are perceived,) was attempted for the first time, by the people of the United States. The hint was taken from the imperfect essays made in some countries of modern Europe, to employ this principle in accomplishing certain partial objects of a political character; but the merit of bringing the machine to perfection, and applying it to the great purpose of carrying on the whole affairs of the government, belongs to our own country. In ancient history, notwithstanding the frequent examples of popular institutions, and the constant experience of the insecurity of small states of this description, we find no traces of any effort to enlarge them, by the application of the representative principle to the business of ordinary legislation and administration. The democracies of ancient and of modern times have all been cities, in which every citizen possessed and exercised in person a share of the sovereign power. If the city made conquests, they were held as subject provinces, and enjoyed no political rights, unless the freedom of the conquering city was extended to them by special favour; and the rights thus conferred could only be exercised by appearing in person in the city. Even in Rome, where the restless spirit of the people led them to try successively almost every imaginable form of government, where the rapid extension of the territory of the republic would have made the representative system so extremely convenient, and where the practice of electing the executive magistrates might naturally have suggested it, it was never resorted to for the general purposes of legislation. Of the two legislative bodies that carried on the government, independently of each other, and with the sort of harmony that might have been expected under such an arrangement, one consisted of the citizens *en masse*, and the other of the executive officers whose term of service had expired, and who then took their seats for life in the senate, by virtue of the offices they had held. The rights of citizenship, though largely conferred in the later times of the republic on the inhabitants of the provinces, were never exercised by deputy. The council of the Amphictyons and others of the same description, which managed the concerns of the confederacies of independent states, so common in ancient times, exhibit something like the representation principle as practised with us; but this resemblance is little more than formal. These councils approached more nearly to the congresses of ambassadors, that occasionally sit in Europe, than to our legislative assemblies. They accomplished many important purposes, but they never brought into action the principle of representation, as applied to the general object of government. The first germ of this great improvement was the introduction of the deputies of cities into the states general of modern Europe. Although they acted quite a subaltern part in these assemblies, and although the assemblies themselves exercised a very limited portion of the legislative power, it is nevertheless true, that we discover in the popular portion of these bodies the first rude elements of the modern doctrine of representation. These elements have been more or less developed in the various parts of Europe, and especially in England, where the principle was applied for a short time, during the period of the commonwealth, in something like a pure and perfect form; but the government was then in a state of revolution, and can hardly be said to have possessed, even for a moment, a real and established existence. At other times in England, and generally in all the European governments, the principle has been applied in combination with others of an opposite character, which in a great measure neutralized its power. The same causes, which occasioned the temporary appearance in England of a pure form of representation, introduced it under better auspices into the British colonies that now constitute the United States. In this country there existed no political elements of an opposite tendency, except the imaginary rights of the crown; and when these were set aside, there was nothing left to prevent the representative principle from exhibiting itself in its natural simplicity, and putting forth all its force and virtue. In this way the discovery of its real value was finally made. Obvious as the idea may now appear, it was not, as we have seen, deduced from general reasoning, nor struck out at once by a single happy inspiration. No one age or nation can claim the exclusive merit of the invention, still less any one individual, although it was reserved for this country to exhibit for the first time its glorious results. It grew out of rude elements, which were intended originally to effect other objects, but were gradually modified by the course of years and events into their present shape. It was silently maturing for centuries in Europe, and would after all never have been brought to perfection, had not a new world been discovered, on which it could spring up, shoot forth, and spread itself without interruption, until it finally assumed its natural form. Even now, and in this nation, where we daily see its beauty and feel its virtue, where it gives refreshment to the air we breathe and fruitfulness to the soil we tread upon, we are yet hardly conscious of its real character and value. We accept the blessings it bestows upon us as a common bounty of providence, without distinctly perceiving and appreciating the immediate cause, to which we are indebted for them. When we have studied it more and understand it better, we shall perhaps be able to turn it to even better account than we do at present.

By means of this discovery, however, the system of popular government or democracy, which had been before generally regarded as a beautiful dream of a state of things too perfect to be realized on this terrestrial sphere, was at once rendered practicable without any material alteration of its essential principles. *Qui facit per alium, facit per se.* Where the people act by real and responsible deputies, the effect is the same, as if they acted in person; and so it has been found to be in practice. This system, being once ascertained to be practicable, naturally supersedes all others, when there is nothing to oppose its introduction, because the only motive (in theory) for resorting to any other, was the supposed impracticability of this. We find accordingly, that since the example of pure representative government was exhibited for the first time, by the United States, it has been eagerly imitated by every community in the old and new world, without I believe a single exception, which has undertaken to establish political institutions. Unfavourable circumstances have occasioned the failure of most of these attempts, and those which have succeeded, in our own continent, are so recent, that the system has hardly yet had a fair trial. There is, however, no reason to doubt, that in these and in all cases where it shall be fairly established and go into tranquil operation, it will produce the same results that it has with us.

The representative principle is therefore the vital spirit, the real life and soul of our body politic. It is this and this only, that makes our popular form of government practicable and durable. It is this which gives us peace and union at home, and security from abroad; which, taken in connection with the other great and leading principle of federalism, raises us from the precarious and tumultuary condition of a thousand independent petty sovereignties, wasting each other with perpetual wars, (the situation of Europe,) into one great, free, united, rich, glorious, and happy republic. As long as this principle, which pervades and animates alike the general and state governments, shall be preserved in its purity; as long as the people of the United States shall be really and truly represented in the legislative councils of both, there can be no fear of decay or abuse in either; no fear of oppression or anarchy, of military usurpation, civil commotion, or foreign conquest. We have amongst us, like all the rest of the world, and in continual activity, all the elements of political evil; but this divine principle is a perpetual and never failing fountain of good, that constantly neutralizes or purges off every thing noxious, and pours an unceasing flood of health and vigour through all the members of the state. Well, therefore, has it been called by the distinguished statesman, philosopher, and writer to whom I have before alluded, the most brilliant discovery of modern times; and strange enough it is, that such a genius as Mr. Ames, with such a principle as this in constant operation before his eyes, should have said that nothing new had been found out in politics, since the invention of the art of printing.

But is there no danger that this guardian spirit, whose presence ensures us all the blessings we enjoy, will desert his post? *Quis custodiat ipsos custodes?* What certainty have we, that the people of the United States will be always fairly and truly represented, as they are now, in the legislative councils of the states and of the union? These questions I shall endeavour briefly to resolve, after first devoting some attention to that other not less important and curious principle, in our social system, by which the sovereign power is held as it were in joint tenancy, by the people of the union and of the several states composing it, and is exercised by each in severalty in appropriate portions, according to the tenor of our great charters, and the laws and usages of the country.

2. The principle of representation prevails alike, as I have already observed, in the general and state governments, and is a necessary condition of the existence of the former as well as of the latter. Without representation there could be no free government of a larger size

than a society of a few hundred or a few thousand families. To what extent the system of simple representative democracy might be carried, without the intervention of the federal principle, is a question which is not yet settled and which we need not here investigate. In the late example of the republic of Colombia, this system is applied to a territory, twice as large as the principal kingdoms of Europe; but that republic is still under military government, and the civil constitution has therefore not yet been fairly brought to the test of experiment. Without pretending to anticipate whether it will or will not succeed, or to foresee the result of the movements now making in that quarter, it is sufficient for our present purpose to remark, that the circumstances under which our institutions were formed, naturally led to the introduction of the federal in connexion with the representative principle. In our situation both were necessary, and neither could have existed or produced its full effect without the other. Without the representative principle, we could not have possessed either free state governments or a union among them; and the country having been settled originally by distinct and independent colonies, the people would not have coalesced quietly (had it even been desirable that they should) in any other body politic, excepting a federal republic. The success of our political experiment depended therefore on the ability with which the problem of forming a federal republic out of the existing materials should be solved. The first trial proved ineffectual; the second produced the fortunate and beautiful system under which we live.

The plan first attempted, commonly called the *old confederation,* resembled very nearly the leagues of free states, which have existed in other ages and countries; and the scheme, however inferior it may have been to the one finally adopted, does no discredit to the learning or the discernment of our revolutionary statesmen. It was in fact highly honourable to their discretion, that, before they launched out into new experiments, they made trial of the most improved system then known to the world. The confederacies of free states, which have flourished in ancient and modern times, are illustrious in history, and had met the approbation of the most acute and judicious political writers. Montesquieu devotes a chapter to this form of government, and represents it as nothing less than *perfect.* " A republic of this character," he observes, " is in no danger from either foreign violence or domestic corruption; and is thus *clear of all defects.* It unites the strength and security of a great monarchy with all the internal advantages of a free state." In following the footsteps of the genius of ancient Greece, in imitating the examples of Etruria, the mother and nurse of Rome, of Switzerland, and Holland, favourite seats of learning, liberty, and virtue, in yielding to the authority of Montesquieu, our fathers did what all wise and good men would have done in their places. They were not ignorant of the misfortunes and fall of the ancient states that were organized in this form; but they also knew that we were placed under circumstances, in every respect more favourable, and might reasonably look for a better fate. Switzerland and Holland were still flourishing in all their glory, and were generally regarded by the friends of liberty, as among the best models of free government. Independently of these circumstances, which might have determined our fathers to give a preference, in the abstract, to a confederacy of independent states over any closer connexion, they had not in fact (morally speaking) the liberty of choice. The states were supposed as colonies to be wholly independent of each other; and had no political bond of union, excepting the imaginary rights of the crown. When this was dissolved, they remained entirely separate; and having certain common concerns to arrange, it was a matter of course, if not of necessity, that they should go to the management of them, as independent communities. The first act of confederation did not make them independent but found them so. It was a simple expression of their existing situation, and of the mode of administration to which it naturally led. Before they introduced any essential change in their political condition, it was right, not only to wait for tranquil times, but to wait until they found by experience, that any such change was necessary. They took things as they found them, like men of sound practical sense as they were; and the old confederation, defective as it afterwards proved to be, nevertheless justified their discretion, and carried us nobly through the revolutionary war. It was discovered in the sequel to be tainted with one fatal vice, which made a reform indispensable, and which naturally indicated as a remedy the adoption of the federal principle in its present shape. The radical defect of the old confederation, and it was one inseparable from the nature of the system, was, that the authority of the general government proceeded from and acted upon the state authorities and not the individual citizens; while it is the leading principle of our present federal union as such, that the authority of the general government proceeds from and acts upon the individual citizen, and has nothing to do with the states.

By virtue of this arrangement each state surrendered to the union a portion of its sovereignty, and received in turn, as an equivalent, a portion of the sovereignty of each of the others. No single state can, therefore, now be considered as completely sovereign or as independent of the union; nor is the union as such, and by virtue of the powers granted to it by the states, completely sovereign. Each state is sovereign for certain purposes, and possesses its appropriate share of the complete sovereignty belonging to the people of the United States: The union, by virtue of the powers granted to it, is also sovereign for certain purposes: And finally, the people of the United States, considered as comprehending in itself the people of all the states, and possessing as an aggregate mass the rights and powers belonging in severalty to each of its component parts, is the rightful owner of all the powers temporarily entrusted to the state and general governments; and being also the rightful owner of all the powers that are not granted to either, enjoys the only entire and complete sovereignty existing in the country. The sovereign power, thus belonging to the people of the United States, is exercised for many purposes immediately and in person, on the principle of pure democracy; as in all matters of a merely local character,

and in the designation of the persons who are to be invested with such powers as are exercised by deputy.
The persons thus designated have no pretensions to the
character of sovereignty, but are merely agents of the
people of the union or of the states, for the several purposes for which they are appointed. Such appears to
be in general the theory of our government, considered
as a federal republic.

The revolution thus accomplished in our government,
for it was in fact and in its consequences another revolution, not less important, although achieved without bloodshed, than the one which gave us independence—this
revolution removed at once with the principle of them,
the inconveniences that had been experienced under the
former system, and which belong to the essence of all
confederacies of sovereign states. In all such confederacies, the common concerns are managed in the way of
diplomatic negociation. The members of the union
engage to execute the decisions of the common council;
but if they fail to do so, there is no regular mode of putting them in force, and the only compulsory process is
war. In other words, there is really no common government; whereas in a federal republic like ours, the common concerns are managed in the ordinary methods of
legislation and administration, and the laws of the union
are enforced upon the individual citizen, in the usual
forms of legal process. The improvement, introduced
by the adoption of the present constitution, was therefore nothing less than the substitution of order for anarchy, and of the best of all governments for no government at all. It may appear indeed at first view, and is

very generally believed by persons not familiarly acquainted with the nature of our system, that as the sovereignty of the states is not entirely merged in that of the union, but is still retained for certain purposes, the dangers incident to all bodies politic composed of a union of sovereignties must still exist to a certain extent, and that they are only mitigated, but not completely removed. But this opinion will be found on examination to be erroneous; and it will be seen that the danger incident to all confederacies of completely sovereign states, is not incident in any degree, either in theory or practice, to such a system as ours. As the states with us retain no control whatever over the portion of sovereignty which they have surrendered to the union, and the union on the other hand has no control whatever over the portion of sovereignty retained by the states, there is no possibility of collision between them, as to the exercise of any power which they mutually acknowledge to belong to either. It is only as to powers of which the rightful possession is disputed between the persons composing the general and state governments, that there can be any appearance of difficulty. But the difficulty, that presents itself in such a case is essentially different from that which is incident to a confederacy of independent states. The disputes of this kind, which have occurred or which may occur hereafter, all turn upon questions of construction, which are in their nature legal and not political. The constitution provides a regular method of deciding all such questions in the usual forms of law, and enforcing the decision by the ordinary legal process; so that no agent of the general government or of a state government can usurp any portion of authority not rightfully belonging to him, nor refuse to comply with the lawful requisition of any other agent, without performing an illegal act and subjecting himself to the corresponding punishment. Where this is the case, the system is complete; and the vice of all confederacies, which consists in the absence of any legal jurisdiction of the union over its members, is fully remedied. In this system, the relation between the general and state governments, is that of two classes of public agents independent of each other, but executing the orders and subject to the control of a common superior. As long as the authority of the latter is maintained, as long as, in this case, the representation principle is preserved in its purity, it is evident that there is not only no danger, but that there is even no real delicacy in a relation of this kind. The two classes of agents alluded to are situated like generals of division, placed under the orders of a common commander in chief. Their fields of action are for the most part distinct. They rarely come in contact, and when they do, it is rarely on occasions that admit of collision. If some accidental circumstance gives rise to a difference of opinion or a burst of ill humour, the disturbance is appeased at once by a recurrence to head quarters; and as long as the rightful authority of the commander in chief is maintained, the worst that can happen, in such a case, is a court martial with its appropriate results. This is a faithful image and illustration of the respective relations between the general and state governments, and between them both and the sovereign people of the union. This part of the body politic, therefore, instead of being, as has sometimes been supposed, morbid and delicate, is in fact as healthy and vigorous as any other. The theory of the government on this head as on every other, is plain, intelligible, and perfectly consistent with natural justice. Such a system will bear examination, and will be more admired in proportion as it is more examined and better understood; while as respects some others, constructed on different principles, it is but too true, as was observed by a celebrated French politician, that the only way to avoid disputes upon the relative pretensions of rulers and subjects, is to say nothing about the matter.

Such was the nature of the reform made in the old confederacy, by the adoption of the federal principle in its present shape. On the other hand, the preservation of the state sovereignties as they are now defined and limited, while it was, as I have observed, a necessary result of our precarious situation, is also attended with great positive benefits.

It has the favourable effect of opening new springs of activity and improvement, in every quarter of the country, and of giving to the administration of justice a promptitude and efficiency unknown in other systems. The necessity of recurring upon every trifling question to some remote central authority, for a decision in the last resort, is an inconvenience serious in itself and still more serious from the opening it affords for abuse and corruption. It has been long and deeply felt in the great monarchies of Europe, especially in France, where the suffering parties, tormented with perpetual delays

and unceasing demands for new bribes, have invented,
in the anguish of their spirits, the hard name of *bureau-
cracy*, to express the whole system; and it is generally
admitted among them, that, of all the *ocracies* that have
yet been tried, this is decidedly the worst. With us, on
the contrary, the administration of justice and the business of government in general, being carried on for
the most part by the state authorities, is brought home
to the door of every citizen, and transacted with all the
despatch that its nature will admit. Add to this the
immense advantage of having dispersed about the country these masses of delegated power, inefficient for evil
but every way competent to do much good, and emulating each other in promoting the greatness and glory of
the section of the union peculiarly subject to their care.
See the New York canal, a work that would do honour
to the mightiest empires, a work not inferior to the splendid monuments of Egyptian, Chinese, or European enterprise, planned and executed by a single state, with its
own funds, in eight years. Look at Ohio putting forth,
in her fresh and youthful beauty, the vigour of maturity, and rivalling already the example of New York.
Behold the genius of improvement awaking in the other
states, Pennsylvania, New Jersey, Delaware, Virginia,
the Carolinas, and Georgia, intersecting their territories
with these precious conduits of wealth, and preparing
even now to apply the summit level to the tops of the
Alleghany Ridge, and thus realize the fable (already
antiquated in the age of Horace) of a time when the sea
gods drove their herds to pasture on the mountains—

> Omne cum Proteus pecus egit altos
> Visere montes.

Observe the venerable universities of Harvard and Yale, founded, endowed, nursed, patronized, and protected by their respective states; the recent and highly promising institutions of the same kind in Virginia and Kentucky; the literary fund of Connecticut and New York; and the various other establishments less conspicuous, but in some cases not less valuable, for which we are indebted either wholly or in part to the enlightened protection of the state governments. When we look at these things, it is impossible not to be convinced, that we can hardly appreciate too highly the direct advantages, resulting from the preservation of these governments as parts of our political system. When we see these things, and contemplate, at the same time, the general government, harmoniously co-operating with the states when necessary, in all their enterprises, while, in the exercise of its own immediate functions, it is spreading abroad among the nations the fear and the love of our country, until the very name of the United States has become with the wise and good throughout the world the symbol, as it were, of political justice, and a word of good omen, auspicious of something noble and fortunate, wherever it is pronounced, it is difficult not to be carried away beyond the line of cool and sober approbation, which belongs, perhaps, more properly to the nature of the subject, into something like enthusiasm. If the thought were not too bold, we might almost be tempted to believe that providence had specially interfered in our favour, and recompensed by these more than ordinary blessings, bestowed upon their offspring, the toils, the sufferings,

the manly virtues, the sincere though sometimes mistaken piety of our pilgrim fathers.

Upon the view of such a system as this, we may well
exclaim, and with more than equal propriety, in the
language of the great commentator on the laws of England, *may it be perpetual!* and it is with a sort of fearful anxiety that we inquire for the first time, is it likely
to be so? What security have we that this fair fabric
will be lasting? Is it not too bright to be durable; a
splendid castle in the air, which the first commotion of
the elements will sweep into nothing? I feel that this
branch of the subject is fast out-growing the limits of a
chapter; but I cannot refuse myself the pleasure of
stating the grounds we have for the belief, that our constitution, and with it the greatness and glory of our
country, if it should not be *perpetual,* (this would hardly come within the bounds of a reasonable hope,) will
enjoy, at least, in all probability, a long term of healthy
and vigorous existence. " All human things have their
date," says Montesquieu with a sort of stern conviction,
at the close of his chapter on the British constitution—
" all human things have their date, and England like
other nations must lose her liberty and perish. Rome,
Carthage, and Sparta have perished before her." Our
country too, the fairer daughter of this fair mother,
matre pulchra filia pulchrior, may be doomed to obey
the universal law. But however this may be, we may
venture, while yet as a nation in the freshness of early
youth, to withdraw our thoughts from such mournful
contemplations, and to indulge rather in a review of our
great political advantages and of the reasons we have
to expect their continuance.

The only security for the duration of any political institutions, good or bad, lies in their conformity to the condition of the society in which they are established. If, in a community consisting of a thousand families, the head of every family have, by law, the right of voting in the election of the chief and other magistrates, each possesses in form a portion of the sovereignty equal to a thousandth part of the whole, and the shares of each being equal, the government is purely democratic. If then it be asked, whether this constitution be likely to endure, the question can only be resolved by ascertaining in what manner the elements of real power are distributed among the members of this community, and whether each possesses a portion of them corresponding with the share which his vote represents. These elements are essentially wealth and knowledge, the political influence of mere physical force being in civilized society comparatively null; and as knowledge in general follows wealth, (not indeed in the individual case but in the final aggregate,) the question respecting the distribution of the elements of real power resolves itself into that of the distribution of property. If then, in the community supposed, each individual possesses with his right of suffrage a thousandth part of the property, and with it a proportional share of the means of acquiring knowledge or cultivating his intellectual capacity, his vote, in that case, represents a corresponding portion of real power. The government thus constituted is secure and durable, because no individual has the means of persuading or compelling the others to surrender their rights. If, on the other hand, while the right of suffrage is universal, the property of the country (with the means of education and improvement attached to it) belongs exclusively to ten or twenty individuals, it is evident that the form of the government is nugatory. The proprietors as such exercise the power of life and death, (the ne plus ultra of sovereignty) over the rest of the community; and as it is of no consequence to the latter under what names this tremendous prerogative is held, they are ready to confer by vote any official titles and characters upon the proprietor, which they may prefer. They will be elected at their discretion, representatives, consuls, kings, or priests; but as they, on the other hand, have no real motive for wishing in such a case to go through the farce of a popular election, the natural effect of such a distribution of property is to determine the form of the government in a manner corresponding with it, and to introduce, instead of an equal distribution of political power, a permanent aristocracy, composed of the ten or twenty families who hold the property. I have stated the example of a small community, in order to present the principle with more distinctness; but the conclusion increases in certainty, in proportion to the scale upon which the experiment is tried. In small communities much depends upon accident, and in a society of a thousand families the influence of property might be balanced or annulled, under certain circumstances, by that of mere physical force: but in larger states, where the slow progress of the action, and the immense theatre on which it is performed, preclude, in a great degree, the influence of accident, and leave every thing to be determined by the operation of general

causes, the correspondence between the form and substance of the government may be regarded as certain.
The history of the world confirms these principles.
Wherever property is very unequally distributed, we
uniformly find an arbitrary government under some of
its various shapes, which differ only in name, but are
the same thing in substance. On the other hand,
wherever property is pretty equally distributed, we
find in greater or less degrees an approach to free government; and we regularly find the form of government changing with the changes in the state of property. The equal distribution of property, which was
introduced at the first foundation of the city of Rome,
subverted the power that established it and changed the
government from a monarchy to a republic. The inequality of property occasioned by the extension of the
territory of the republic, and the immense wealth which
was thrown into the hands of the leading citizens, re-
versed this movement, and changed the government
back again from a republic to a monarchy. As a singular proof of the nullity of the mere form, without a
corresponding substance, and in confirmation of some of
the remarks made above, it may be added, that, for a
long time after this latter change, the republican system
was retained in name; that the people regularly voted
in the Domitians and the Neroes, with the same formal
freedom with which they had elected in better days the
Scipios, the Catos, and the Tullies. I have not room
here for a full development and illustration of these
important truths, but I trust that they are sufficiently
obvious to be admitted without much argument; as they

are in fact very generally acknowledged by all competent judges.

Applying these principles to the subject under consideration, we have every reason to deduce from them the most satisfactory and cheering conclusions, in regard to the stability of our present form of government. We find established in fact, in our country, a distribution of property corresponding to the distribution of formal political rights; with sufficient exactness to give them effect and entire security. It is not necessary, for this purpose, that there should be a precise arithmetical identity in the number of acres or of dollars, that measures the possessions of every citizen; but that there should be, in this respect, a complete equality of rights, and that inequalities in fact should not be excessive. In every town, country, and district, in the United States, there are a few persons considerably wealthier than their neighbours, and some in poverty and actual distress; but the number of both is comparatively small, and the mass of property is distributed in nearly equal shares among a third class of persons, holding at different points of the scale an intermediate station between the two. The mass of property carries with it of course the mass of political power, and thus neutralizes the influence, which the very rich would exercise over the very poor, and which, if the proportion of the number of these two classes to that of the whole community were other than what it is, would throw into the hands of the former the government of the country. Since, therefore, the form of our government corresponds with sufficient exactness to the poli-

tical condition of the people, we have all the security
for its continuance, that any nation can possibly have
for the permanence of its political institutions. In bad
governments, which suppose a vicious state of property,
this security is itself imperfect, because in such cases
the physical force of the society is opposed to the property, and although the latter element possesses every
advantage in the contest, the former may perhaps succeed. In a good government like ours, where the distribution of political rights corresponds not only with
that of property, but also in the main with that of actual
physical force, the security is every way complete. If,
in addition to this, the extent and position of the state
protect it, as with us, from the danger of foreign conquest and of accidental internal commotion, it possesses
all the guaranties of a long and glorious term of existence that are consistent with the instability of human
affairs.

Having thus taken a general survey of the various
elements, that make up the constitution of this country,
in the large and proper acceptation of the term; having
next analyzed this constitution and endeavoured to discover the great internal springs that move the machine;
having afterwards examined the foundations of this
system, and pointed out the firm basis upon which it
reposes and is likely to repose for centuries to come;
having found in every branch of the inquiry the fullest
cause of satisfaction with the present and high hopes
for the future, it is natural to cast a look backward on
the progress of events, by which we have reached this
point, and to mark the signal favours with which pro-

vidence has distinguished us at every period of our history. What a concurrence of independent, and, in some respects, apparently adverse circumstances were necessary to the establishment of this republic, and its advancement to the state in which we now see it! It was necessary that the first settlements should be made, as they were, upon a territory remote, but not too far from Europe; large, but thinly peopled, enjoying a temperate climate, and a fertile, well watered, but not too luxuriant soil. It was necessary that the settlers should be precisely what they were, civilized but not effeminate; pious—if you please, fanatical, for in many cases a little excess is the best security against deficiency; sages and scholars according to the learning of their age, and yet accustomed to toil, danger, privation, and hardship of every description. It was important, if not essential, that they should have been persecuted for their love of liberty, since persecution only could have given to this passion its proper intensity; and yet that they should have sprung from the freest country in Europe, in order that they might carry with them the usage as well as the theory of freedom. It was important that the settlements should have been the independent work of individuals from the middling classes, and have owed little to royal or noble patronage, since in this way only could our youth have been preserved untainted from the poison of aristocracy, and the pure republican principle been permitted to unfold itself in full vigour. It was also essential that the first emigrants should establish themselves in a number of separate colonies, that a foundation might thus be laid deep and

broad for the future stability of a federal union; and
that those separate colonies should be held together by
some loose bond of connexion, like that of the imaginary
right of sovereignty in the king of England, that they
might be secure from internal dissensions. When the
moment at last arrived for throwing off this foreign
thraldom, it was indispensable to our success, that there
should appear amongst us such a group of distinguished
political and military characters, as have rarely lived
together in any age or country. It was further necessary, that, out of this illustrious group, some one person
of the military class should be sufficiently conspicuous
above the rest, by a singular combination of talent, wisdom, and virtue, to acquire and retain the confidence,
without alarming the jealousy of his countrymen. It was
highly important again, in contributing to the easy and
early acquisition of our independence, that the hearts
of the arbitrary monarchs of Europe should have been
favourably inclined towards a cluster of infant democracies, and especially that France should have lent us,
as she did, the most timely and effectual aid: And
finally, when, after our independence had been achieved, our political institutions were found to require improvement, it was necessary that there should appear,
in a younger generation, another group of powerful,
wise, and virtuous spirits, to co-operate with the remaining revolutionary patriots in this salutary work.
Such is the series of fortunate circumstances succeeding
each other, through a long course of years, which were
either absolutely necessary or highly important, and

which in fact have concurred in the formation of the political system of this republic.

Of this succession of events the last in order, viz. the successful formation of the federal constitution, is the one to which we may, perhaps, with justice, attribute the greatest importance, as it was the indispensable condition, without which we should have lost the benefit of all the others. It may not be unnatural, therefore, by way of conclusion to our remarks upon this branch of the subject, to bestow a moment's attention upon the characters of the principal persons, under whose influence this instrument was formed and adopted, and upon the circumstances under which they acted. Although this period followed so nearly that of the conclusion of peace, it was still not precisely the race which achieved the revolution, that took the most active part on this occasion; but, as I have just intimated, a younger generation, the worthy imitators and rivals of their generous fathers. Of the leading patriots of the revolution, John Adams and Jefferson were abroad; Franklin was too old to lead in such an enterprise, but still did his part; Patrick Henry and Samuel Adams were opposed to innovation; Washington from his previous habits was less adapted to enter into the details of a new political arrangement; some of the others, and in particular Mr. Jay, co-operated efficaciously; but the labour, the responsibility, and, on the whole, the ultimate honour of establishing the new constitution, devolved upon a different class of persons, of which Madison and Hamilton may be considered as the representatives and leaders. These two illustrious friends and benefactors of their country, afterwards attached by circumstances to different political parties, were both at that time in the flower of life, neither of them being much over thirty, and they entered on the task which then engaged the public attention, with the ardour that belonged to their age and a maturity of judgment that would have done honour to a riper one. President Madison is the person, who will probably be ultimately recognized, as far as the title can be given with propriety to any individual, as the author of the federal constitution. It would give me pleasure to do full justice, according to the extent of my power, to his services; and to dwell at length upon the beautiful union of high intellectual qualities and accomplishments, with all the most amiable private virtues and graces, that have marked, throughout, the career of this eminent statesman. But the respect due to living characters prevents me from enlarging on the subject. Long may this objection continue to operate! long may this illustrious sage and patriot continue to enjoy, in his elegant and learned retirement, the cheerful recollection of a glorious and useful life, and the affectionate respect of his grateful countrymen! Over his great co-operator in the establishment of the constitution, an untimely grave has long since closed. He fell, not entirely without his own fault, but on the whole by a fatal accident, in the fullness of his power and the freshness of his honours, at the moment when he seems to have been looking forward, through some intervening period of public calamity, which he appears to have anticipated, to some higher political career than any upon which he had before entered. On the character of

Hamilton, public opinion has been much divided; and
few men have been alternately the subject of more decided praise and reprobation. Such is the common lot
of the great in active life. A period of more than twenty
years, that has passed since his death, and which in our
country is equal to a century elsewhere, has consigned
him to the roll of historical personages; and the people
who are now enjoying the benefit of his services, and
who suffered but little, if at all, by his faults and errors,
such as they were, are now disposed to regard him with
an eye of favour, and to pay him an almost unmingled
tribute of admiration and gratitude. Without going
precisely to this extent, an impartial observer may well
be allowed to speak of him, as one of the greatest, best,
and most useful men, that the country has produced.

Hamilton possessed a mind of the highest order, and
was capable of succeeding in every thing he chose to
undertake. It may perhaps, however, be conjectured,
that the natural bent of his disposition was for active
and especially for military life. We find him rushing
to the field, at the opening of the revolutionary war,
though just escaped from infancy, entering the army at
the age of sixteen or eighteen as a captain of artillery,
recommending himself immediately by his activity and
intelligence to the confidence of Washington, in whose
family he lived through the war as aid, and finally commanding with success one of the attacks on Yorktown,
in the decisive action that brought the struggle to a
close. This was a glorious career for a youth of his
age, and exhibited a taste and talent for military pursuits so strong, that we might naturally have supposed

it to be exclusive, and inconsistent with any love or
aptitude for civil and political occupations.   Instead of
this, however, no sooner were the labours of the camp
at an end, than we find him engaging with equal ardour
and distinction, in that of the senate and the forum.
He was a member and a leading one of the congress of
the old confederacy, but soon perceived the defect of
this system, and bent his mind to the discovery and
application of a remedy.   If Madison, from having
advised the first steps that were taken towards the
adoption of the present constitution, may, as I have
said above, be justly called its author, Hamilton, on the
other hand, was if possible still more zealous and industrious, in maturing its details and urging its adoption.
His influence with Washington, who appears to have
wavered for a moment in making up his mind upon the
constitution, was no doubt of material service in persuading him to approve it, and then to give it the
weight of his authority, which finally secured its adoption. These labours and successes would have been enough
to fill the life and establish the fame of any man; but to
fight the battles and found the government of the country, were only introductory steps in the grand career
of Hamilton.   We next find him at the head of (what
was at that time) the most important department of the
administration, not pursuing the lazy course of a beaten
routine, but organizing, establishing, discovering, new
modelling, creating every thing.   He found the country bankrupt, paid its debts, and left it possessed of
unlimited credit; he found the people poor, presented
them with a capital of a hundred million dollars to begin
with, and carried wealth into every body's coffers but

his own. Having thus settled the nation, and converted the chaos of the finances into a piece of clock-work, that has gone ever since without winding up, our political Hotspur (taking the name in a good sense) found the situation too quiet for him, and we next behold him figuring, after a few months' study, and no practice, in a post, at which few arrive without twenty or thirty years of steady preparation and effort. I mean at the head of the New York bar. In this field of unremitted and honourable labour, he continued to flourish, till the day of his untimely death, hardly less distinguished as a legal advocate than he had been before as a soldier and a statesman; confidentially consulted by the government; regarded as a leader by one political party, and admired and respected by the other; the delight of his friends and an honour to the country. Such was his habitual activity, that it was a mere episode, in the regular course of his labours, to arrange and organize the army that was raised in 1798. Notwithstanding the extraordinary variety of his pursuits, he never seems to have failed, or even to have fallen short of a high degree of excellence in any of them. If he wanted any thing, it was perhaps the finished elegance of manner as a writer and speaker, the attainment of which was in fact hardly compatible with the hurried course of his life. His writings exhibit a sound and judicious train of thought, expressed in perfectly plain and unpretending language; and this manner is, no doubt, on the whole, very suitable to the nature of the subjects he treated. But good taste would admit, and even at times, perhaps, require rather more point and polish, not to say correctness, than we always find. His eloquence, according to report, was also vigorous and cogent, rather than persuasive. There are few traces in his works of extensive reading or habitual and profound meditation, which were indeed inconsistent with his education and habits. His thoughts are rather the spontaneous results of a powerful, sagacious, and original mind, practical in its tastes and pursuits, and always directed intensely to the subject in hand. Notwithstanding these deductions, if such they may be called, (but how can any one man be expected to possess every valuable quality?) Hamilton is, perhaps, the most remarkable example, that has ever been seen, of an union of various and opposite talents. Combining the financial skill of Pitt, (applied, however, to far better purposes,) with the strong argumentative eloquence of Fox, rising as a legislative politician far above all names in English history,* to a level at least with the greatest lawgivers of ancient times, superadding to these merits a decided military turn, which with a proper field for its exercise would have made him one of the greatest captains of his day, he possessed all the talents that belong to practical life, in all its highest

---

* The most eminent theoretical politicians of modern times have not added much to their renown, by their attempts at actual legislation. The constitution prepared by Locke for South Carolina is an acknowledged failure. Bentham's ready made legislative wares have not yet found a purchaser, although the Cortes of Portugal, and lately the government of Colombia, have shown some disposition to bid. The praise given to Hamilton in the text will not, I trust, be considered extravagant, although I should not think of comparing him, as a scientific political philosopher, with Locke, Hume, or Burke.

and most honourable spheres. To say that he did not add to these the powers and accomplishments that belong to the academy, is only to say that his life was public and not academic.

When we look merely at his astonishing and various talents, it must be owned that such a character is somewhat dangerous in a free state. First rate capacity, unwearied activity, boundless ambition, directed by a passion for military life, an impetuous temperament, and a private morality that savoured in some points of the tent rather than the tabernacle, this was a combination of qualities, which has undoubtedly been accompanied in most other cases with a want of public virtue, and has accomplished the ruin of many a flourishing republic. It is, therefore, the more honourable to the character of Hamilton, that he exhibited no appearance of any such deficiency, and that, on the contrary, his talents and activity were uniformly exerted for the general good. The elevation of his character raised him far above the baseness of pecuniary corruption, and ought to have cleared him even from the suspicion of it. His purity, as secretary of the treasury, was however, called in question, under the influence of high party excitement, and I need not say came out unsullied from the trial. If he ever gave any reasonable cause for suspicion, it was, perhaps, when he exhibited so strong and eager a desire to prolong the war with France in 1799; but this may well be attributed to mistaken views of state policy. He has been accused of attachment to monarchy; but a closer scrutiny of his character may lead us to conclude, that what he loved was not monarchy, but military command; and having

done more perhaps than any other citizen of his age,
first, to shake off the government of a king, and then
to establish a purely democratic constitution, he could
hardly be suspected with reason of a fondness in the
abstract for monarchical institutions. It has been
rumoured, however, that he acquired and expressed
towards the close of his life a strong distaste for *democracy;* that he anticipated a domestic war between the
two political parties, and expected to take the military
command of one; that he cherished high ambitious projects for himself, upon the successful termination on
which he calculated of his new career, as commander
in chief of the federalists; that if these expectations
had been realized, even supposing his intentions to
have been at this time patriotic and disinterested, his
natural impetuosity would have made his dictatorship
very dangerous to the liberties of this country; and
finally, that such anticipations are of the nature of
those prophecies, which have a tendency to effect their
own accomplishment. But these are all idle rumours
resting wholly upon hearsay; and the slight foundation
of real fact, that may perhaps be mixed up in them,
might doubtless be explained in the most satisfactory
way. They should not be allowed, for a moment, to
cloud the unsullied reputation of this great public
benefactor. As a private man he constantly exercised
the highest moral virtues—a sublime disinterestedness,
a generous frankness that knew no disguise, because it
never dreamed of mischief, and a warmth of heart that
urged him to unwearied activity in the service of his
friends, as well as his country. Some few slight ble-

mishes soiled this noble character; but who would think of recording them against the blooming hero of Yorktown, the nursing father of the constitution, the founder of the credit of his country? When he died, there was a general burst of anguish and despair, little inferior to that which accompanied the funeral of Washington. Every one seemed to feel that the beauty of Israel was fallen upon his high places. Who can have forgotten the melting eulogy, in which Fisher Ames poured out his tender soul like water, over the ashes of his friend?

To Madison and Hamilton, therefore, is the country indebted, more than perhaps to any other two men, for the plan of our present federal government, and the first arrangement of its details. To persuade the people to adopt it was a new and still more difficult task, in which they also laboured with unwearied zeal and signal talent. Nor ought it to surprise us that the constitution, when first submitted to the people, should have met with great opposition. The adoption of it accomplished, as I have already observed, a complete revolution in the government of the country. Had this taken place without commotion or resistance, the fact would have proved the inattention of the citizens to their most important interests, and not their good sense or public virtue. Nor are we to suppose, however highly we may now think of the constitution, that the anti-federalists acted from vicious motives, or were even in all cases ill informed or perverse. They were in fact, on the contrary, the party, which had in its favour the presumption of right, because they defended the existing state of things against innovation. This is always a plausible argument; and they had besides the popular pretence of asserting the rights of states and individuals, against the encroachments of government, another golden topic. Nor did they want authority to back their reasoning. On the contrary, the weight of names, with one single great exception which probably turned the scale against them, was perhaps on the whole on their side. Take for example Virginia and Massachusetts, which had always been politically and intellectually the leading, as they are the oldest states in the union. In Massachusetts, setting aside John Adams, who was then in Europe, the two most distinguished revolutionary worthies in the state—what do I say? the only two patriots in the country whose zeal had obtained for them the singular honour of proscription, Samuel Adams and John Hancock—were against the constitution. The latter persisted in opposing it to the last; and it was with great difficulty that the former was ultimately persuaded to give it a reluctant support. On the other hand, who were the Parsonses, the Kings, the Ameses, and others—its principal partisans? Men of yesterday—young lawyers, before unknown to the country. They gave proofs no doubt of eloquence, talents, and book-learning; but were these qualities, however precious in their way, to counterbalance the mature wisdom, the rich experience, the tried patriotism of the incorruptible fathers of our liberty? Look now at Virginia; a young barrister of about thirty years of age, popularly called Jemmy Madison, comes forward, and proposes to his fellow citizens to abandon a part of their individual and state rights and submit to a

general government, possessing large and because untried of course unknown powers; to acknowledge a
single ruler under the name of a president, the extent of
whose authority future experience alone could determine. The proposition was, it must be owned, not very
palatable, and might well alarm a people less sensitive
on the subject of state prerogatives, than that of the
ancient dominion. Under these circumstances, the
oldest and most respected of the revolutionary patriots,
the man who was the first in all the country to raise
the cry of independence, Patrick Henry himself, then
governor of the state, tells them, in the same familiar
voice, sweeter than music, that was never known to
deceive, that never lisped a sound which was not as
pure and true as the word of inspiration, that Jemmy
Madison, though a clever and honest young man, is
wrong; that the innovations he proposes are dangerous;
that, under the name of a president, he is imposing
upon the country a tyrant in disguise, who will place
one foot on the border of Maine, and the other on the
farthest extremity of Georgia, and then—farewell to
liberty!—Is it singular that in such a conflict of authorities and opinions, the people of Massachusetts and
Virginia should have been divided, and that a strong
party should have been opposed to the new system? It
is evident, on the contrary, that the only wonder is,
how, in this state of things, which existed substantially
throughout the union, the federal constitution could
have been adopted. The force of truth, the pressure
of the immediate inconveniences resulting from the
vices of the old system, the unwearied activity of the
friends of the new, and above all the authority of

Washington, must be well considered, before we can realize the possibility of this salutary reform.

It is almost superfluous to say, that of all our revolutionary statesmen, no two were less obnoxious to the suspicion of interested motives, than Patrick Henry and Samuel Adams. Their very names are significant of spotless integrity and a singleness of heart, that looked exclusively as well as devotedly to the public good. It is a pleasant thing to turn away the mind for a moment, from the hollow professions and the ill disguised selfishness of some of our loudest contemporary patriots, and to let it repose upon the pure virtue of these excellent men. " I am not worth buying," was the reply of Adams to the British emissary, who invited him to fix his price, " I am not worth buying, but, such as I am, the treasury of England would not pay for me." Finding that he would not fix his price, the British fixed it for him, and offered a reward for his head. " Oh what a glorious morning is this," exclaimed the noble proscript, on the day of the battle of Lexington, nothing daunted by the prospect of the gallows. Not many years before, Sir Robert Walpole had publicly affirmed, that he knew the price of every patriot in England, and could command their votes whenever he chose to come up to it. Samuel Adams proved to his successor, that this was not the case in America; and in this difference, lay the secret of our success. The corrupt and selfish may laugh at honesty and call it enthusiasm; but it gives to talent an influence that nothing else ever can, and commands the respect and admiration even of those who want it. The honesty of these two celebrated patriots was not, however, of that rustic cast, which excludes the graces of manner. The language of the simple Virginian farmer melted like honey from his lips, and was alternately endowed with a Ciceronian charm, that captivated all hearts, and pointed with a passionate emphasis, that struck down opposition like thunder. We knew this before by tradition, and the elegant pen of his biographer has given ample confirmation of it. What presence and power of mind, in his well known check to the murmurs of the tories in the assembly of Virginia, "If this be treason, let them make the most of it." Samuel Adams was a ripe and accomplished scholar. He had formed his taste as well as his character, upon the finest models of antiquity, and was the most polished writer of his day in America. Are we, therefore, lightly to charge these tried friends of the country with selfishness or faction, because they did not perceive the necessity of the new constitution? Are we even to regret it, since their opposition proved ineffectual? It may boldly be said, that it was natural for the wisest and best men of the day, as these undoubtedly were, to take, in their position and at their age, the part they did. They had devoted the freshness of their youth, the maturity and vigour of their riper years, their whole being in fact, all the strength and wisdom that God had given them, to procure for the country the state of things which it was now proposed to change. Was it for them, when they had reached the ordinary term of human existence, to begin a new and contrary course of action, and to undo what they had been all their lives so laboriously doing? Surely not. Much as I admire the constitution, much as I rejoice that it was adopted, I confess that I like these sterling old hearts the better for opposing it, and for sticking fast to the text of state sovereignty, and the old confederacy, in defiance of what they doubtless thought a wanton and headstrong spirit of innovation.

It is, therefore, by no means necessary to suppose, as some have heretofore unadvisedly and rather unkindly done, that the anti-federalists acted entirely upon factious and selfish motives. They were doubtless in the wrong; but looking at the question as it then presented itself, they had great reason, high authority, and in fact much actual truth on their side; for in this as in all other cases of revolution, there was a conflict of rights and of principles, which no argument could reconcile, and nothing but force or authority could settle. A recurrence to force would have been in other words a civil war; and where was the weight of authority to be found, that could counterpoise that of the ablest and most respected revolutionary patriots? The thing must have appeared at the time impossible; but by one of the signal blessings of providence, which have marked so often the political career of this country, there dwelled amongst us an individual possessing, in the love of the people, in their gratitude for his services, and their conviction of his wisdom and virtue, such means of influence, as enabled him to interpose at the critical moment, the *dignus vindice nodus,* first to procure the adoption of the constitution, and then to give it, by accepting the presidency, the indispensable advantage of going quietly into operation, under the auspices of a general public favour. The age of Washington placed him at a middle point between the two parties; and his character qualified him fully to decide for himself upon the question; while his immense popularity, the bound-less and deep devotion with which he was worshipped, as it were like a god, throughout the country, rendered his opinion, whatever it might be, decisive with multitudes and very imposing in the minds of all. When we perceive with what difficulty the constitution was carried, even under the sanction of his recommendation, and with a fore-knowledge that the untried power of the presidency would be committed, in the first instance, to his unspotted hands and blameless heart, it can hardly be supposed that it would have been adopted under other circumstances. To him therefore, in the last resort, are we indebted for the constitution as well as independence. Never was an individual blessed before with such repeated opportunities of doing good, on so vast a scale, and never before was the blessing of providence, in this respect, so fully justified by the conduct of the subject. Never was the triumph of pure unadulterated virtue, over all the other principles that influence the march of human affairs, so complete, as in the whole military and political career of this incomparable man. Virtue was the basis of his character, and the secret of his talent, his wisdom, and his success. Without military instruction or experience in war, it made him a consummate general. Without extensive reading or scientific habits, it made him a profound political philosopher, and it gave him, without intrigue or effort, the undisputed empire of his country. Those who, on the testimony of their own hearts, deny the reality of virtue, must find the history of Washington an insoluble enigma; and those who, believing in this divine principle, are yet tempted to doubt its efficacy, in determining the course of events in this world, may observe the success of Washington and be satisfied.

Such, in a general view, were the circumstances that attended and occasioned the adoption of the constitution. The division into parties, which was then created, continued for a long time, under various modifications and changes of names, to distract the country; and has only yielded, within a few years, to the progress of time and events. Some traces of it still remain; but much has been done to obliterate them by the magnanimous policy of the present chief magistrate of the union; and this, with other circumstances of a different character, will probably, ere long, efface them entirely. It would neither be agreeable nor useful to enlarge at present upon this unfortunate but not dishonourable chapter in our history. I turn at once, in preference, to the fairer field of inquiry which offers itself in the great and interesting subject of our policy foreign and domestic.

CHAPTER IV.

The United States of America.—Internal Situation and Policy.

THE most important subject for consideration, in the political situation of every country, is the constitution or form of government, and this, in reference to the United States, has been cursorily treated in the preceding chapter. Next to this in interest are the great subjects of making and executing the laws, that is, of applying the theory of the government to practice. These operations are often comprehended under the single general term of administration, and the leading principles on which they proceed are called collectively the policy of a country, which, according to the nature of the objects immediately contemplated, divides itself into the two great branches of foreign and domestic. The former of these is the one which comes more directly within the scope of the present essay, and it will be considered somewhat fully in the subsequent chapters. As the limits of the work will not permit me to enter into a complete development of both, I shall confine myself for the present, to a few brief suggestions, upon one of two interesting questions connected with the latter. The object of the domestic policy of every government, in its most general expression, is to promote the welfare and improvement of the people, by all the just and constitutional means within its power; and considered in detail, it presents the two important questions, what measures will tend to produce these effects, and what are those which come within the legitimate action of the government. It is obvious that both will admit of various answers, according to the economical and political situation of different countries. Laws, that would be useful in some nations, may be pernicious or ineffectual in others. Measures, that would be oppressive in a republic, may be constitutional and just in a despotism. A correct and thorough knowledge of the character and condition of the people is, therefore, the basis of all judicious proceedings in the administration of a government, as in the formation of it; and the application of this knowledge to practice must be directed, by a just notion of the general tenets of political science and of the particular institutions of the country. These are the solid qualifications of a good legislator, without which eloquence and even logic, however successfully they may recommend their possessor to the public favour, will never enable him to accomplish the public good.

As the leading principle of our government is the sovereignty of the people, the genius of it, as respects its internal operation, must necessarily be to leave the greatest possible latitude to individual action. In a despotism, every thing which the ruler believes to be of public advantage may be rightfully done. In republics the magistrates exercise a delegated power, defined and limited by written instruments, which form in clear cases, their exclusive rule of conduct. In doubtful or discretionary cases, the administration of such governments must conform to their spirit, and contemplate the maintenance and extension of liberty. If this rule were inconvenient in practice, or injurious in its effects upon the moral or economical interests of the people, the fact would prove, not that the rule was erroneous, but that the government itself was thus far bad. If, on the contrary, the same rule which is prescribed by the nature of the government is also found to be the most advantageous to individuals, that could be adopted, it follows that the natural operation of the government is highly beneficial and the government itself good. Such is fortunately the case with us. The maxim of leaving the greatest possible liberty to individual action, which the character of our institutions enjoins, has also been declared by the soundest philosophers, and is now generally received throughout the world, as the one most conducive to the public wealth and prosperity. *Laissez nous faire,* was the well known answer of the French merchants to Colbert, one of the ministers of Louis XIV, who sent for them to inquire, what they wished him to do for the advancement of commerce. This laconic reply was quoted and commented on, with high approbation, by Dr. Franklin, in a short and pithy essay, which did much to make it popular. It was afterwards adopted by Adam Smith, as the basis of his treatise on the wealth of nations, which has long and deservedly been regarded as the text book of political economy. Finally, the governments of Europe, which had pursued for centuries an opposite system, have yielded to the force of truth, and are fast relaxing the shackles, which an unwise policy had imposed on private industry. The course recommended by the genius of our government, is therefore, in this respect, precisely the same, which the lights of experience and reason also counsel; and there is little doubt that, under the influence of such a combination of powerful motives, it will always be in future, as it has been hitherto, pursued with undeviating steadiness.

The general operation of this principle, in practice, is to limit the internal action of the government to the maintenance of existing rights, and to entrust to every citizen the care of improving his condition and providing for his comfort, in the way that suits him best. The community secures to each of its members the enjoyment of the fruits of his labour, but leaves him wholly to his own discretion, in regard to the mode of applying it and consuming its products. On this system, the preservation of the public peace, the administration of justice, civil and criminal, and the collection of the revenue form the principal objects of domestic policy; and such in fact they are and always have been, in the theory and practice of our government.

There have been, it is true, some remarkable deviations from this course, especially as respects the great and interesting subject of education. The instruction of youth, which, on this principle, is a matter exclusively of individual concern, has always been in every part of the country a standing object of legislation; and the opinion that it should be so considered, is evidently gaining rather than losing ground among us. Mr. Jefferson, one of the firmest assertors of the doctrine of individual liberty, devoted the greater part of his time and attention, during the last years of his life, to the establishment of a university, under the patronage of the state of Virginia, and in one of his last published letters to Major Cartwright expresses a strong wish for the institution of schools, under the authority of government, in all the civil divisions of the state. Schools of this kind have always existed in New England, and the good effects, which are generally thought to have resulted from them, seem to justify a deviation in this respect from the theory of the government. It would be possible, perhaps, to mention other instances, in which similar deviations have been or might be made with advantage, but it would lead me too far, to pursue the subject into all its details. Suffice it to say, that as a general rule, every thing but the three great objects specified above, and especially every thing connected with the application of labour to economical purposes, is abandoned entirely to the discretion of the individual citizen.

But the same sound and enlightened views of political economy, which lead to the establishment of this great principle, also indicate one great exception to it, which in most countries admits of an application not much less extensive than the rule itself. The same policy, which enjoins it on governments not to attempt to interfere by legislation with the course of private industry, makes it their duty to remedy by legislation the evils that have arisen, from preceding injudicious attempts of this description. They are not only bound not to make new laws on these subjects, but they are bound with proper caution, and in the exercise of a just discretion, and a due regard for vested rights and interests, to repeal such as have been made before; and where a mere repeal of the law is not sufficient to remedy the mischiefs it has occasioned, to do this in some other way. When war, for example, which is a state of things proceeding from the act of government, disturbs the natural direction of private labour, the principle of the greatest possible liberty of individual action loses its virtue, and can never recover it until a natural state of things had been restored, by another act of the government, exerted in making peace. When the merchants of the United States, previously to the late war with England, complained of the restrictions imposed upon their labour by the non-intercourse and embargo laws, it would have been thought mere mockery, if the government had answered, that the received doctrines in political economy did not admit of legislation for the encouragement of private industry, and that trade would find its level. The merchants would have replied, with great propriety, that they could not enjoy the benefit of the principle, until the government had first restored, by a new law, the natural state of things which they had disturbed by a former one. In the same way, if one of the starving labourers in England should represent to the minister, that his wages did not enable him to buy bread for himself and his family, it would neither be humane nor wise in the minister to answer, that the value of bread is regulated, like that of every thing else, by the amount of labour employed in producing it, and that the government have no means of changing the laws of nature, which they did not enact. The labourer might well reply, that if the government would repeal the corn laws and the taxes, he would undertake to be responsible for the consequences of the laws of nature. Legislation on economical subjects, however unwise for the purpose of effecting positive good, is, therefore, in many cases, not only wise but absolutely indispensable, as a remedy for existing evils and abuses. This principle is perhaps not so much an exception to that of individual liberty and the *laissez faire* policy, as a development and application of it. The government must not only let the citizen have his own way, but if he has unwisely and unjustly been taken out of his own way, it must put him back again, before it can require him, with propriety, to take care of himself. Nor is the negative act of repealing the existing law always sufficient. When the vicious consequences of it have become habitual, it is often necessary and of course politic, to counteract them by positive enactments of an opposite kind. When the mouths of the rivers in Holland are obstructed by ice, they break down the dykes that form their banks, and inundate the whole country. In this case, it is necessary, in order to remedy the mischief, not only that the obstruction should be removed and the old channels opened, but that the new ones should be dammed up. And so it may be at times with the course of industry. If, in consequence of injudicious laws, it has been driven into a new and unnatural direction, it may be necessary, in order to restore a natural state of things, not only to revoke these laws, but to enact others which may check the fatal habits to which the former had given rise. If a government had been sufficiently unwise to prohibit its subjects from owning ships, and had thus thrown the whole commerce and navigation into the hands of foreigners, it might be expedient, upon the adoption of a better system, not merely to repeal the old prohibition, but to counteract its consequences, either by prohibiting entirely the entry of foreign vessels, or by levying upon them and their cargoes a heavy tonnage and discriminating duty; and so of other analogous cases.

The field of this remedial legislation on economical subjects (as it may properly be called) is in most countries a very extensive one; and considering the imperfection of our nature, and the scanty share of wisdom that is habitually applied, throughout the world, to the purposes of government, there is room to suppose that it will not very soon be exhausted. Existing abuses are perceived, and the duty of reforming them is felt; but the new law, modified as it is by the passions, interests, and theories of the legislator, for the time being, though different from the old one, is not always better. Posterity will hardly believe, that it has been seriously contemplated as a relief for the present distresses of the labourers in England, not to abolish the corn laws and diminish the taxes, but to abolish the poor laws and restrain marriage. In this way nations that have once been cursed with a bad constitution and laws, move round for ever in a vicious circle, out of which (morally speaking) there is no possible exit. Such is now the case with almost all the governments of Europe. Their institutions were formed in a barbarous age, and correspond, in general, very correctly, especially in their economical regulations, with the date of their origin. The errors and abuses inherent in them are now (in some countries at least) distinctly perceived, and strong efforts are making in the way of reform; but it still remains to be seen whether the disease or the remedy will prove to be the greater evil. The United States are in this respect more favourably situated than any other Christian nation, because their government was established more recently, and was originally modelled, in general, upon the soundest notions of the most judicious practical philosophers. With us there is almost as little occasion for repealing old laws on economical subjects, as for enacting new ones. When Voltaire, after publishing his commentary on Corneille, was asked why he did not prepare a similar one on the works of Racine, he replied, that there would be nothing to do, but to write at the bottom of every page, *Pulchre, bene, optime.* The task of a commentator on the economical system of the United States is nearly the same. There are, however, one or two questions of an interesting kind connected with the subject, which have been at times matters of controversy, and upon which I shall venture to propose a few suggestions.

Agriculture and commerce are the two branches of industry, which have hitherto flourished most amongst us; and the signal success with which they have been prosecuted, has been doubtless owing, in a great measure, to the absence of the injudicious and oppressive restraints, which have been imposed upon them by authority of government, in most other countries. Agriculture, which constitutes in every nation the ultimate source of wealth, has been treated in most, as if it were a thing to be discouraged rather than favoured. The

basis of the legislation of all parts of Europe on this subject, until very recently, and of most at present, is to
limit the property in land to a few persons, and to em-
barrass the circulation of it from one to another as much
as possible. This system establishes an impossibility
physical and moral, that the land should be cultivated,
voluntarily condemns a great part of it to perpetual
sterility, and diminishes of course, to the same extent,
the population, wealth, and prosperity of the state. It
is sustained, for the purpose of effecting certain political
objects of a very questionable character; and so rooted
are the prejudices of the European statesmen upon this
subject, that in France, a country which by the effect of
revolution had once been fairly delivered from the system, the dominant party are at this moment striving,
with all their power, to bring it back, have already in
part succeeded, and will probably in time succeed entirely. The same abuses were extended by the Spanish
government to their American possessions, but were happily never introduced into the United States to such a
degree, as to take deep root, and all traces of them have
with us been long since exterminated. This difference
is the principal cause that can be assigned for the different progress of the Spanish and British colonies, the
former having been, in most other respects, quite as well
administered as the latter, and in some much better.
The new Spanish American governments have already
adopted new principles, in regard to the tenure and
transfer of land, which, with the freedom of trade that
also results from their change of situation, may be expected to produce, as soon as the present convulsions

shall be over, a very rapid increase of population, wealth, and general prosperity.

Agriculture, therefore, having always been with us entirely free from the trammels imposed upon it by the injudicious interference of government, neither requires, nor would, on sound principles of political economy, admit of any aid from direct legislation. Commerce is nearly in the same condition. It is true that, under the colonial system, this branch of our industry was hampered with some restrictions; but there was still sufficient latitude left for the development of the strong natural inclination of the people towards this employment; and they exhibited, even before the revolution, an aptitude for navigation and a boldness and success in its most hazardous and difficult departments, which excited the admiration of the old world, and were publicly declared, by so good a judge as Burke, to leave all parallel behind them. The revolution removed the shackles of the colonial system, and opened to our merchants and navigators the trade of the world. A judicious discriminating duty in their favour diminished the danger of foreign competition, and, although the country has lately shown a willingness to relinquish it, probably produced in its time no inconsiderable good. Finally, the political events that occurred soon after in Europe, singularly aided the progress of commercial enterprise amongst us, and gave us, after a while, a sort of pre-eminence in this branch of industry, and the arts connected with it, over all other nations. No economical regulations are therefore wanted with us for the direct encouragement of commerce and agriculture; both which, under the salutary influence of a wise political system and great natural advantages, have flourished and are still flourishing beyond all precedent.

There is, however, one way in which the community have it in their power to exercise a very beneficial action on the progress of both these great departments of labour, and that is, by opening and maintaining an easy communication between the different parts of the country, by roads and canals. This is, evidently, more than almost any other, a matter of common concern, because it interests the people exclusively in their social capacity, and therefore (although it does not come directly within the scope of either of the three great divisions of our domestic policy alluded to above) has always been regarded with us, and in every other country, as one of the functions of government. Government ought, however, to regulate its proceedings in this respect, as it naturally does, by the course of individual enterprise; because communications become necessary and convenient, only in proportion as the country is explored and settled. This power has, in the United States, been always exercised by the people, through the concurrent instrumentality of all classes of their political agents, in the local, general, and state governments. The municipal, city, and county authorities throughout the union, regularly lay out streets, build bridges, and open town and county roads. Roads of greater extent, and canals, are habitually undertaken either by the state governments, or by companies incorporated under them; and communications of a national character, which pass through several different states, have been in repeated

instances established or aided by the general government. This mode of proceeding is so perfectly natural
in all its parts, and so entirely consonant with the form
and genius of the government, that it seems at first view
surprising, how the propriety of it should ever have
been called in question. It has, however, as is well
known, been doubted by many very able and judicious persons, whether the general government possesses
a constitutional right to exercise any agency whatever
in the matter; and in the various discussions that have
taken place upon this subject, some distinctions have
been made, which would do honour to the keenest and
most practised casuist. It has been said, for example,
that the formal specification in the constitution of the
right of congress to establish post-roads, does not give
them a right to lay out such roads, but only to designate,
among the roads laid out by the states for other purposes, those which shall be used for the carriage of the
national mail. Again it has been said, that the general
government has the right of applying money to the
making of roads and canals, but not that of making them
itself; as if any body ever supposed that the president
and two houses of congress were to turn out and work in
person on the highway, as a part of their official duty.
But the controversy on this subject, which was at one
time carried on with a good deal of activity, has of late
almost wholly subsided, and the points in dispute appear
to have been settled (in the only way in which contest-
ed points are ever amicably settled) by the lapse of time,
and the gradual subsidence of the feelings in which the
difference had its origin. The general sentiment of the

country is more decidedly in favour of forwarding, in every possible way, and by the exercise of every species of rightful power, the noble work of facilitating communication among the citizens, and thus encouraging at once the progress of industry, in its three great branches of agriculture, manufactures, and commerce. The will of the people has been fully declared on this subject, and their agents, who generally regard their will as the only legitimate source of power, will probably feel no difficulty hereafter, excepting about the best means of carrying it into effect. The development of the spirit that now prevails amongst us, respecting this matter, and which has produced already the most magnificent results, may well be considered as one of the most fortunate events in the history of the country.

Of the three great branches of industry, therefore, agriculture and commerce, being already in the most satisfactory state, and having long since been relieved from the effect of all the restraints that were ever imposed upon them, neither require nor would admit of any aid from government, other than that to which I have just now alluded, and which results from facilitating the communications between the different parts of the country. Manufactures, the other principal department of labour, are somewhat differently situated. They have never flourished, as they naturally ought to have done, in proportion to the success of agriculture and commerce; and as their comparative failure has perhaps been owing, in a great measure, to the prohibitory system enforced upon us, while colonies, by the mother country, and its consequences, it is here, if any where, that the remedial legislation on economical subjects, which I mentioned before as being often necessary, might be resorted to with profit. The old restrictions have, it is true, long ceased to exist; but if the habits generated by them still remain and are found too inveterate to be conquered by the mere healthy action of natural causes, it may be necessary and politic to counteract them by positive measures, which would otherwise, and considered in themselves, be at variance with just principles and with the rights of individuals. As this question is perhaps the most interesting and delicate one, connected with our domestic policy, it may be proper to treat it somewhat more in detail.

Agriculture is the first object of attention with most new colonies, and they find their advantage, for a considerable time after their establishment, in exchanging the surplus products of the earth, for the manufactures of older countries, instead of attempting to work them up at home. In the natural course of things, however, the increase of population would pretty soon effect a change in this particular, and would render it more profitable to manufacture, on the spot, first the coarser and most necessary articles, which on all accounts should be made in every country for home consumption, and gradually those of mere convenience and luxury, to which the soil and climate might be favourable. The British colonies, that now form this republic, had been established and had flourished for a century and a half, at the period of the separation, and ample time had thus been afforded for the growth of manufacturing industry; but the system, on which they were governed, ordained and enforced a rigid monopoly in favour of the products of the mother country, and absolutely prohibited all manufactures whatever in the colonies. Hence the enterprise and industry of the people were wholly directed to the cultivation of the earth, and the exchange of its products for the fabrics of England. It is only, therefore, within the last half century, that the general causes which regulate the economical situation of a country, have had opportunity to produce their natural effect in ours; and during the greater part of even this period, the political condition of the world has imposed an effective check, upon the growth of manufactures, nearly as complete as that created by the previous colonial restrictions. While the war of independence lasted, the country was of course in a state of disorder, and no progress could be made in any branch of industry. Several years of peace elapsed, before the people recovered from the impoverishment and exhaustion produced by the struggle, and after reforming and finally settling the government, began to find opportunity to attend to business. The new disposable capital, created precisely at this time, by the funding of the national debt, gave a great impulse to industry, and a rapid progress would naturally have taken place in domestic manufactures. Just at this period, however, the war broke out in Europe, and threw into the hands of our merchants a monopoly of the carrying trade of the world. The new capital created by the funding of the debt, was also principally in their possession; and it was a matter of course, under these circumstances, that they should employ it in extending their operations, in

the branch of industry to which they were accustomed. They accordingly entered, with prodigious activity and enterprise, into the field of commercial speculation which was thus opened to them, and most of them
realised very large and rapid profits. No event perhaps could have occurred, more favourable, on the whole,
than this, to the industry of the country ; but the first
effects of it were felt exclusively in commerce and agriculture ; and while this state of things lasted, (which
was up to the time of the non-intercourse and embargo
laws,) manufactures continued, of course, in nearly the
same quiescent state as before. The restrictive system,
and the war with England, which followed it, discouraged commerce, and gave an active spur to manufactures, which was felt at once. Establishments of all
kinds started up like mushrooms, during this short period ; but were mostly ruined again, in consequence of
the immense supplies thrown in, immediately after the
peace, by the British. The distresses resulting from this
check, cast a temporary damp upon the business, from
which it has been since gradually and slowly recover-
ing ; so that there has been in fact no period, from the
first foundation of the colonies, up to the present day,
or at least to the last five or six years, in which there
has not been some powerful political cause, constantly
exercising an influence against this particular branch of
industry. Under these circumstances, it is just as natural that manufactures should not have flourished among
us, as it would have been singular, if there had been
nothing extraordinary to prevent them. It is therefore,
I imagine, to these, and not to economical causes, as

some have supposed, that we ought to attribute the low state of our domestic fabrics. It is true, that the wages of labour are higher with us, than in Europe; but this circumstance, which operates with equal force in navigation, has not prevented us from taking the lead of all other nations on the ocean; nor are the wages of labour at present one of the heaviest items, in the cost of the production of most of the articles, which we receive from Europe and especially from England. The difference would be more than counterbalanced, in most cases, by the expense of transportation; but when the political situation of a country holds out an immense bounty, in favour of the investment of capital in a particular way, it will necessarily take that direction, although there may be other modes, which would afford a real and equally sure, but smaller profit.

The political causes alluded to having now ceased to operate, we may reasonably expect an early and rapid advancement of our manufactures. The return of peace, although it removed the restraints on foreign commerce that existed during, and for some time previous to the war, has not restored to our merchants the monopoly of the carrying trade of the world. This employment, therefore, instead of affording opportunity for the investment of additional capital, will not hereafter occupy all that was engaged in it before. In the meantime, the payment of the national debt, which is now going on with rapidity, is constantly disengaging large amounts of property, which must be re-invested, in one form or another. It is said that, in the single city of Boston, no less than seven millions of dollars have been paid off in this way, in one year. As neither commerce nor agriculture hold out at present very flattering prospects for new investments, and as manufactures, on the other hand, if there be any truth in reasoning and experience, must afford large and constantly increasing profits, these immense sums will naturally, for the most part, take this direction. We find accordingly, that, within the last five or six years, manufactures have advanced with astonishing rapidity, in all the northern part of the union, and especially in New England, which will probably be, in the end, their principal seat. Upon returning lately to this country, after an absence of five years, I was not less astonished than delighted to witness the visible signs of this progress, and to find flourishing villages and even considerable towns springing up, as if by enchantment, on spots that were recently uninhabited. At Lowell, in Massachusetts, where there were not, if I am rightly informed, more than one or two dwelling houses in 1820, I found in the spring of 1825 a population of fifteen hundred souls, wholly engaged in manufactures; and it was the opinion of persons, who had the means of judging correctly, that ten years would add another cypher to the number. Similar results may be observed at Weare, Springfield, Dover, Somersworth, and various other places; and in short, the spirit that produced them is active through the whole country. The skill and judgment with which the establishment at Waltham has been conducted, and the large profits that have been constantly obtained there, have done much and in the best way, to encourage this spirit, and give it a proper direction. The founders of that establishment, though

governed, no doubt, immediately by an enlightened regard to their own interest, may well be considered as
public benefactors.

It is difficult, indeed, to estimate too highly the benefits that will result to the union, from the rapid progress
and great extension which we have now reason to expect in this branch of industry. They are so important
and various, that it would demand an entire work to give
a proper development of them all, and I must therefore
content myself, at present, with a hasty indication of
some of the principal. The political advantage of a
more independent position, as respects foreign nations,
will be justly considered as of no small value, by those
who recollect the inconveniences that arose from a different situation, during the late war with England, but
is inferior in magnitude to those of an economical character, upon which I proceed to make a few remarks.

In every community, the wants of the people are regularly supplied by the co-operation of the three great
branches of industry, in proportions determined by the
degree of civilization. The three classes of labourers,
which are respectively engaged in them all, derive their
subsistence from the products of agriculture, and must
receive their share alike, whether they dwell within or
without the country. If they all reside together, as
constituent parts of one community, they consume at
home the products of the labour of the whole, and the
population is then in its natural state. If either live
abroad, it still consumes the same amount as before of
the products of the community, for which it works, and
the population of the latter is of course regularly smaller

in the same proportion. If we suppose, for example, (what is perhaps not exactly the case) that the three classes of labourers are regularly equal in number, then a community that receives its manufactures from abroad, will be less populous, by one-third, than it would be if they were all supplied at home. Beside this, the labour required for exchanging the products of the two classes of workmen, now belonging to two distinct communities, will regularly divide itself between them, and the agricultural country will thus lose half its commercial, in addition to the whole of its manufacturing population. The distance at which the exchanges are made, being now greater, it requires a greater amount of labour than before to effect them, or, in other words, to carry on the necessary commerce; so that if this branch of industry before occupied a third of the labourers, it will now occupy more. On this first and simplest view of the effects on a community of the absence of domestic manufactures, there is, therefore, a loss of more than half of the natural population. But the natural population of every country is the true measure of its wealth, property, and political importance, and a community thus situated, sustains, in each of these respects, a positive loss of half its natural advantages. But this is not all. The labourers thus lost swell in the same proportion the population of some other country, by necessity one with which the losing people had a close relation. If the elements of wealth and power belonging to the two countries be naturally the same, and their relative force of course equal, one now gains and the other loses more than half of their amount, and their relative forces become as three and one. Thus, (on this supposition) the absence of domestic manufactures deprives a country of half its positive and two-thirds of its relative importance, degrades it of course from its rank among the nations, and places it at the mercy of powers, to which it is naturally equal, and with which it has the closest connexion.

It is commonly said indeed, by those who are less sensible of the importance of domestic manufactures, that there is in such a case only a fair exchange of values; that if one community supplies agricultural and another manufactured products sufficient for the consumption of both, and they divide between them the labour of effecting the exchanges, the result will be precisely the same as if each produced exclusively for itself; that there will be neither gain nor loss on either side, or at worst no loss but the waste of commercial labour, resulting from the increased distance at which the exchanges are made, and that this will probably be found to be more than counterbalanced by some accidental advantage; for that if it were not, the arrangement could not take place. Such is the argument, upon which the anti-manufacturing party rely, as a full defence and justification of their system. Their reasoning would in fact be sufficient for their purpose, if it were true that the agricultural labour of a manufacturing community is regularly diminished, in the same proportion in which it supplies foreign countries with the products of arts. It will be found, however, on the contrary, on examination, that in the case supposed, the exchange that takes place is wholly to the advantage of the manufacturing, and at the expense of the agricultural community.

It is necessary, in fact, before a community can export manufactures to any considerable extent, that its agricultural population should have reached its natural limit, which is determined in every country by the extent of the territory, taken in connexion with the political institutions and the state of civilization. Until that time arrives, manufactures naturally follow agriculture, and the home market is so much the more profitable than the foreign, as to prevent any great exportation. It is only when the population has reached its natural limits, and the home market afforded by it is supplied with manufactures, that exportation begins. We find accordingly that all the great manufacturing and exporting communities have always been states of limited territory and dense population. Now the extension of manufactures and commerce, that takes place in a country after its population has reached the natural limits, is all clear and positive gain. There is no diminution, but on the contrary an increase of agricultural labour, since there must be an improvement in the home market for its products, at least equal to the charges of importing them. In this respect, therefore, there is no loss. On the other hand, every labourer employed in preparing manufactures for foreign markets, and maintained in turn by the labour of foreigners, is a new citizen acquired by the state, who could not exist in it without he were thus employed, and the profits of his labour are a clear addition to the national wealth. In this way a nation may extend its population, wealth, and political importance, almost indefinitely, and may even build up, upon a narrow basis, a positive power sufficient for a time to awe the world.

Compare, for example, the present situation of Old and New England. Their extent of territory and other natural advantages, including the character of the people, are nearly the same. New England contains above a million inhabitants, and old England about twenty millions, and the difference between the wealth and political importance, belonging to them respectively, is at least as great. The principal reason of it is the superior extension of industry, chiefly in the two branches of manufactures and commerce, that has taken place in the mother country.

In an agricultural community, which receives its manufactures from abroad, the state of things produced is precisely the reverse of the one just described. While there is no diminution of agricultural labour in consequence of the export of manufactures, there is, on the contrary, in the agricultural community, which receives them, an actual diminution of manufacturing labour to the same extent. In one case population, after reaching its natural limit, goes on increasing, in exact proportion to the extension of industry. In the other, it is not permitted to attain its natural limit, but is reduced, as I have shown above, to less than half of its proper amount. Every individual who comes to maturity, after it has arrived at this artificial boundary, is compelled to emigrate, and is lost to the country.

It is sometimes thought, that if manufactures imported from abroad can be sold cheaper than similar articles made at home, there will be of course a profit in importing them, equivalent to the difference. If this could in fact be done, it must be by the result of some accident, since the charge of importation must always raise the price of the foreign article. But admitting the fact, let us examine, for a moment, the supposed advantages of obtaining manufactures from abroad, at a somewhat reduced price. Let us imagine, for example, that we get them at half the cost; that is, that instead of giving one-third of the products of the agricultural labour of the community in exchange for them, we obtain, by procuring them from abroad, an equal quantity for one sixth. In this case, there will be an economy of one sixth of the labour of the community, which will operate in one of three different ways, by occasioning either a diminution of labour, an increase of consumption, or an increase of population, in the same ratio. But the absence of domestic fabrics which produces this benefit, also produces a standing positive loss to the community equivalent to more than one-half of its labour and resources for the time being. If then we set off the gain against the loss, the result will be, not that we really gain anything, in consequence of the superior cheapness of the foreign article, but that we lose something less. If it were possible to obtain our manufactures from abroad for nothing, our population, wealth, and political importance, would then be precisely the same as if we made them at home. On every supposition excepting this, which is of course absurd, the want of domestic manufactures occasions a positive loss, corresponding with the value of the labour required for supplying them.

These principles, incontestable I apprehend as general truths, are of course modified in the case of each particular country, by the circumstances in which it is placed, and have hitherto had little or no direct application to the United States. Although we have received our manufactures from abroad, the extent of our territory and the scantiness of our population, in proportion to it, have thus far prevented us from sustaining, in consequence, any considerable loss of wealth or political importance. There has been, no doubt, a diminution of domestic manufacturing labour, corresponding with the amount of manufactures imported; but the labourers withdrawn from this branch of industry have not been obliged to quit the country, but have all been taken up by agriculture, and the population has on the whole increased as rapidly, as it could have done under any circumstances. Our case, therefore, forms an exception from the general rule, and the reason is, because our population has not yet attained its natural limit. For the same reason, the greater cheapness of the foreign article, which in general does not occasion any actual profit, but merely some alleviation of a standing positive loss, has been with us a source of real gain, because in our case there is no positive loss resulting from the same cause to set off against it. In stating the above principles, I have, therefore, had it in view, rather to elucidate the general theory of the subject, (which is necessary for a correct understanding of the exception as well as the rule,) than to apply them directly to the case of our country. But even with us there are several very serious inconveniences attending the present state of industry, which I shall now briefly recapitulate; and which, as the agriculture of the country has already obtained as great an extension as we need for the present to wish, make it extremely important, that labour should be directed in future, as much as possible, to the channels of manufactures and internal commerce.

The first and most obvious of the inconveniences alluded to, is the waste of commercial labour, produced by carrying across an ocean three thousand miles wide, the bulky agricultural products, that must be given in exchange for the manufactures we import, and bringing back the latter in turn from the same distance. This waste would be attended, in general, as I have stated before, by an actual loss of half the commercial population naturally belonging to the country, because the labour of effecting exchanges between communities thus situated, would regularly divide itself between them. But the singular aptitude of our citizens for the pursuits of navigation, has thus far left, in their hands, almost the whole of this branch of industry, and has prevented us from suffering, on this account, any actual loss. On the other hand, the waste of labour, which is incontestable, may fairly be considered as more than counterbalanced, first by the profit resulting to the community, from the greater cheapness of the foreign article, and secondly by the encouragement which a flourishing and extensive commercial navy affords to the public naval establishments, which are indispensable for the protection of our national rights and honour. The distance from which we receive our manufactures, considered merely as creating an extension of foreign commerce, may therefore be viewed, under all the circumstances of our case, as a positive advantage rather than an evil.

The great real economical inconvenience, resulting from the present state of things, is the uncertainty of all speculations, founded on the supposed situation of distant markets, and the constant fluctuation which is thus introduced directly into commerce and indirectly into the whole industry of the country. The home market is, in general, fixed and certain. Its extent may be calculated, and the probable increase or diminution of demand foretold with sufficient exactness. Nor is it materially affected by political accidents. Foreign commerce, on the contrary, is a sort of game in which fortune exercises at least as much influence as prudence and skill. All calculations connected with it, are not only more or less uncertain at the time of their inception, but are continually liable to be defeated by events that may intervene before their results can be realized. The whole capital invested in this pursuit, and with it the happiness of its owners and their families, lies at the mercy of political events, or in other words, of the caprice and violence of foreign powers. We cast our bread upon the waters, but whether in this case it ever returns again after many days, is a matter of chance. When we have covered the sea with our products, a wanton belligerent (and some war is always going on in one quarter or another) issues a decree, and sweeps the whole into his own coffers. We remonstrate—negotiate—go to war perhaps—possibly, after the lapse of twenty or thirty years, obtain some partial satisfaction. In the mean time, the unfortunate individuals who were plundered, have seen their prospects blasted for life, and gone down in sorrow with their wives and children to the grave. No associations can stand the force of these fatal shocks. Banks and Insurance companies sink under them like private fortunes. The only effectual remedy, is the one employed by England, of maintaining a public navy sufficiently strong to command the ocean and defy attack from any quarter; but the burden which such an establishment imposes on private industry, makes the remedy nearly as bad as the disease.

Independently of the violent attacks to which the capital employed in these exchanges is exposed, the mere circumstance of dealing with foreign markets at a distance, creates a disastrous uncertainty in the whole business. In a time of war, the most extensive European and colonial markets are thrown open to our flour and provisions; and our cultivators extend their enterprises in all directions, for years perhaps in succession. Peace comes at length, and all these markets are hermetically sealed. Flour falls from ten or fifteen dollars a barrel, to three or four, and ruin stalks at large through the fair plantations of the United States. Again a panic is felt in England, on account of a supposed deficiency in the supply of cotton actually on hand, and the value of the article takes a sudden rise. Our speculating merchants, incapable of estimating the correctness of the opinion that occasions it, go on buying for exportation at extravagant prices. Immense supplies arrive in Europe. In the mean time the imagined deficiency is found to be of little or no importance. The market is overstocked and the merchants are ruined. Finally we are forced ourselves, into a war with England, and

the usual supply of foreign manufactures is checked.
Immediately large amounts of capital, following the direction which they would naturally take in time of
peace—were it not for the very peculiar circumstances
in which our country had been placed—are invested in
domestic establishments which are to make up the deficiency. Every thing goes on prosperously until the
war comes to a close. Within a few months after, our
markets are inundated with British goods, cheaper than
we can make them, of equal quality, and our manufactures are involved in their turn in one common ruin.
It is in this way that the fluctuations incident to these
distant and uncertain exchanges, reach successively all
the great branches of industry. The effects I have described are not accidental, but the regular consequences
of the state of things which produced them, and will
continue to recur from time to time as long as this state
shall last. No foresight, prudence, or probity, furnishes
the means of avoiding them; and so extensive with us
have been the disasters they have occasioned within the
last ten or fifteen years, that there are probably very
few individuals in the country who have not felt them
within the circle of their own immediate connexions. It
is true, that wherever there is hazard there is also gain
as well as loss, but one result is hardly less pernicious
than the other, though in a different way. Large and
sudden fortunes, whether considered in their effects on
the party immediately obtaining them or on the community, are fatal to good morals and regular habits of
industry. These, on the contrary, are promoted by a
course of trade, which, when carried on with honesty

and judgment, produces slow and moderate but certain profits; and such is the one which naturally takes place, where the three great branches of industry furnish each other with a reciprocal home market for their respective products.

The constant and ruinous fluctuation, which the want of domestic manufactures introduces into the whole economical concerns of the country, is therefore the first great practical evil it occasions, and is itself one of sufficient magnitude to make us anxiously desire, on this account alone, a different state of things. But this inconvenience is not the only one. In the preceding remarks, I have supposed throughout that the quantity of manufactures consumed in the country is the same, whether we import them from abroad or make them at home. But this is probably far from being the case; and another unfortunate effect of the same cause is a greatly diminished consumption, attended with a corresponding injury to the civilization and general welfare of the people.

The necessity of this result is easily seen. The exchange which regularly takes place between the two classes of agricultural and manufacturing labourers, is that of the means of subsistence for the products of art. The cultivator feeds the manufacturer, who supplies him in turn with articles of use and comfort. But this exchange can never take place to any great extent, excepting where the two classes are situated in the neighbourhood of each other, and belong to the same political society. Provisions are too bulky, and in most cases too perishable, to bear transportation from one quarter of the globe to the other. If not consumed on the spot where they are raised, they cannot be consumed at all. Or even were it possible to surmount this difficulty, it is, and always will be, the standing policy of most countries to interdict their exportation. Such is the existing situation of things as between the United States and Europe. What then follows? Our cultivators have in most parts of the country, and in the usual state of commerce, nothing to offer in exchange for foreign manufactures, and of course no means whatever of obtaining them. The whole manufacturing population of the old world is represented in each separate precinct of our territory, by a few shop-keepers; and the amount of agricultural products consumed by their families is the only reciprocal demand upon a county or township of our cultivators, created by their whole consumption of European fabrics, which under these circumstances must of course reduce itself to nothing. In some particular sections of the union, the inconveniences of this state of things are partially relieved, by an extensive cultivation of the materials employed by the European manufacturers, which will bear transportation on account of the great profits obtained by working them up, and which, not being the growth of Europe, must of course be admitted. These articles, principally cotton, with some other agricultural products, such as rice and tobacco, to which our climate and soil are more favourable than those of Europe, pay for the foreign manufactures which we in fact consume. The transportation is effected by the navigators of the eastern and middle states, who in this way obtain a share of the return cargo; but the cultivators throughout these vast and populous regions, and through the whole western country, have nothing to offer in exchange for foreign manufactures, excepting the provisions of the ordinary kinds, which the caprice of foreign powers from time to time allows them to export. Their consumption of foreign articles must therefore, as I have said, be extremely small; and if they have no domestic manufactures in their neighbourhood, they are compelled to live without a knowledge of the arts, or an enjoyment of the comforts of life. But it is the extent of this knowledge and enjoyment that forms the distinction between a civilized and uncivilized state of society. A community thus destitute of indigenous productions, and excluded from an intercourse with foreign markets, has a constant tendency to decline into rudeness and barbarism. This tendency has in our case been counteracted in a great measure, by strong moral causes; but the only effectual and permanent remedy is to remove the principle of evil, by establishing domestic manufactures. It was, therefore, with great reason that Mr. Jefferson, in one of his private letters, written in 1822, declared his strong sense of the expediency of bringing the producer into the neighbourhood of the consumer. When in any county, township, or province containing four or five hundred families of cultivators, there are found a proportional number of families employed in manufactures, commerce, or professional business, there is then a sure and steady market for the products of all, and all are supplied with the articles of comfort and luxury which are essential to civilization.

and to the enjoyment of life. Prices must of course be fair, whatever they may be, and it is of little or no importance, whether they are or are not the same as on the other side of the globe. If a cultivator in the western country obtains from his neighbours in exchange for a part of his grain, good clothes and furniture, and a good education for his children, of what consequence is it to him, whether he gives for these comforts and blessings more or less grain than they cost in Europe? He cannot send his grain to England to buy clothes and furniture, nor his children to be educated. His wants must be supplied by his neighbours, who will consume his provisions in exchange for what they give him, or not at all. If they be not supplied, he loses the sense of moral dignity that results from a civilized mode of living, ceases to produce any more grain than what is necessary to furnish him with bread and whiskey, sinks into idleness, and dies a drunkard; while his children, growing up without education, of course follow his example. Every article of use and comfort which he can get at home for his surplus products, is therefore so much clear profit to him, although it cost him twice as much as a similar one is worth in England, France, or China.

Such in general are the respective results of the absence and presence of domestic manufactures upon civilization and happiness; and these principles apply with full force to the case of the United States. The loss of population and political importance which regularly follows from the want of this branch of industry, is, as I have observed above, prevented with us by the

great extent of our territory, which admits of a constant
extension of agriculture corresponding with the increase
of population; but this remedy brings with it another
disease of a different kind, which should not be overlooked in a general review of this subject. I mean a
necessity of the continual emigration of the young and
active part of the community, from the settled to the
unsettled parts of the country. Emigration breaks up
the family circles, and with them the natural sources of
happiness and virtue. It is easy, no doubt, to put a good
face upon a thing of this kind, and when the manly
New Englander mounts his dearborn to seek his fortune
in a distant wilderness, he recollects that he is a son of
the pilgrims, and that it is not for him to pretend to be
homesick, or to give way to despondency. He wears
his usual honest smile as he proceeds upon his journey,
and has his characteristic joke, wherewith to entertain
his fellow traveller or chance companion; but there is
much faintness of heart at bottom. If in the ardour and
inexperience of youth he had exalted his imagination
with brilliant visions of some fancied distant good, and
sets off in the expectation of finding an earthly paradise
ready planted to his hands on the banks of the Wabash
or the Missouri, he may feel, perhaps, but little regret
at the moment of parting. But he soon finds how much
he has deceived himself. Could he even obtain an immediate and easy possession of all the abundance he expected, his golden dreams would still not be realized,
because no advantages of fortune would ever make up to
him for the loss of home. But this is far from being the
case. His paradise proves to be a wilderness inhabited by

angels carrying tomahawks and scalping knives, his castle in the air a log hut, and his lot for life unremitted labour, ill-health, and severe privation. It is impossible to imagine (under a good government) a more difficult existence than the one he leads. In the midst of all this he finds that he has left his heart behind him. His friends at home, on the other hand, are not slow in discovering that he has taken theirs with him. If only one were missed out of a large family, the loss might be borne; but when Joseph is not, and Simeon is not, and they take away Benjamin also, the case grows serious; and however the aged parents too, on their side, may assume an aspect of indifference and go tranquilly about the business of life, they feel internally, as the Patriarch said, that all these things are against them. The sacrifice is nothing less on both sides, than that of the whole charm and beauty of existence. Nothing can ever make up to either party for the loss of those relations, which were endeared to them by the recollections of childhood and youth, and were intended by nature as the proper corrective of the many bitter drops that are mingled in our mortal cup, even when best tempered. Nothing can replace to the young the associations that surround the venerable beings to whom they are indebted for life, and who watched over them in their helpless infancy. Still less can any earthly substitute compensate the old for the absence of the grateful care and attention of their children. Those of us who have been abroad for comparatively short periods, and with the cheering prospect of return constantly before us, could give some account of the misery of these separations. What then must it be when they are perpetual? Nor let it be thought that these considerations are of too refined an order, to be applicable to the concerns of common life and to the feelings of the mass of the people. Men in this respect are all alike. Natural affection is as pure and as strong (to say the least), in the poor man's dwelling as in that of the rich. It is the only compensation which the former has for the supposed advantages of the latter, but it is one which if enjoyed is sufficient. It is the principle of goodness, and without goodness (as Lord Bacon says) man is a busy, mischievous, wretched thing, no better than the vermin. It is the internal fountain of all true happiness, and when this fails or throws up bitter waters, there is no remedy left but religion—that is, death.

These unpleasant results are remedied in a great measure, by the establishment of domestic manufactures. They are the natural absorbents of the increase of population which naturally takes place under a good government. They check at once, all emigration to distant parts. The family circles remain unbroken, and the happiness and virtue of the people unimpaired. Every succeeding generation obtains, with an equal amount of labour, a more abundant supply of the means of subsistence than the preceding one, and life is of course growing constantly easier and easier to all from year to year. The arts are steadily improving; and this by an internal process, that brings with it no danger of the introduction of foreign tastes and opinions. The society enjoys the natural benefit of a good government, and finds itself in a state of progress and

expansion, corresponding with the condition of growth
in the human body, and attended like that with an active movement and a sort of joyous exultation, that
seems in both cases to pervade and animate the system.
A community thus situated, will naturally in time enlarge its geographical limits; but this process will take
place slowly and gradually, so as not to produce any
violent interruption in the individual relations between
the members, and of course without the unpleasant consequences that arise from emigration to distant parts.
Such are the effects of an extension of domestic manufactures, proportional to that of the other branches of
industry; and it is therefore a great pleasure to me to
be able to add, that such appears to be the condition to
which the United States are now rapidly approaching.

If the justice of the above remarks appear, as I think
it will, sufficiently obvious, it will hardly be necessary
to refute in detail the vulgar error, that manufactures
are of immoral tendency. I have shown on the contrary that their influence, moral as well as economical,
is in the highest degree favourable. Labour in fact
of all kinds, is known to be the parent and guardian of
good morals, and this must be supposed true of manufacturing as well as other kinds of labour, at least until
the contrary be proved. The only argument that is
ever alleged in support of a different opinion, is founded on the wretched situation and depraved character of
the workmen employed in some of the manufacturing
establishments of Europe and especially England. But
is there no part of the world in which the labourers
employed in agriculture are also a depraved and miser-

able race? Look at Russia, Poland, and Turkey, not to mention the West Indian islands and our own southern states. The wretchedness and depravity of a part of the manufacturing population of Europe, are owing to vicious political institutions and bad management, and under similar circumstances a population employed in agriculture or commerce is neither happier nor better. It appears probable indeed, that manufactures have under good management a better moral effect upon the persons engaged in them, than the other branches of industry, for the precise reason that is sometimes made an objection to them ; I mean that they bring men together in large masses. Such collections have been supposed to generate naturally bad habits ; but in this respect a distinction must be taken between collections of independent individuals and of families. When men or women are taken from their family circles, which are the natural mode of their existence and the only one consistent with virtue and happiness, and brought together in large masses as independent individuals, it has been found that no severity of discipline will prevent abuses. This has been, and still is seen habitually, in the cases of armies, crews of ships, monasteries, and colleges for education. In all these establishments, it is usual to employ unwearied diligence and all imaginable means for the maintenance of correct habits, but it is very rarely, if ever, that the object is completely attained. But where the family circles are kept entire, large collections of men are under the influence of all the motives that ordinarily produce good conduct, increased by the effect of the extension of social communications that take place in such circumstances. Now this is the state of things in most manufacturing establishments, which naturally bring together the persons employed in families, because in most of them the labour of men, women, and children, is needed in various proportions. No other condition of life is equally favourable to the maintenance of a family among the labouring classes, and of course to their happiness and virtue. And even in those manufactures where men only are employed, their fixed position and regular profits hold out at least as powerful inducements to the formation of family connexions, as any that are offered by agriculture and commerce.

We find accordingly that the morality of our well conducted manufacturing establishments, instead of being objectionable, is probably superior to that of any other portion of the community. I have been told by a person intimately acquainted with the state of the cotton manufactory at Waltham, from its commencement, that among the several hundred persons of both sexes, mostly young, who had been employed there for ten or fifteen years, a single instance only of irregular intercourse had been discovered. Intemperance and the vices punishable by law were unheard of. Compare this statement with what is known of the morals, I will not say of our colleges and cities, but of our sequestered country towns. The last are doubtless much superior in this respect to the cities and towns of most other parts of the world, but the purest of them contain a larger portion of alloy, I fear, than Waltham. I am aware that it would be rash to expect that all or the average of our

manufacturing establishments will be as well managed
as this; nor is it necessary that they should be in order
to establish the point in question. It may be remarked
however, that no establishments can flourish long or become permanent, but such as are well managed, and
these will of course determine the average state of morals among the persons employed in this branch of
industry.

There is perhaps rather more plausibility in the objection sometimes made to the introduction of domestic
manufactures, that the labour they require is of a less
healthy and agreeable description than that of agriculture. It is said to be a hard thing to take young men
and women from the pure air, varied occupations, and
simple pleasures of a country life, and immure them
for ever within four stone walls, where they are stunned
by a deafening din of machinery, and condemned to
perform some single operation from one year's end to
the other. But if we adopt the principle of interdict-
ing all employments excepting the one which is the most
eligible on all accounts to the individuals engaged in it,
it is evident that there can be no exchange of products,
and that the whole machinery of social life, which is
moved by this single spring, must come to a stand. The
less inviting occupations are for the same reason more
lucrative, and thus afford to those who practise them a
solid compensation for their comparative inconveniences.
Every employment, however, has its bright and dark
side. A sneering satirist would find no difficulty in
drawing a sufficiently repulsive picture of the three noble professions of divinity, law, and medicine, all of

which exercise so worthily the highest faculties and best affections of our nature, and which form in our country (as they might do every where) the Corinthian capital of society. As respects the point in question, no one certainly can be a greater enthusiast than I am, in regard to the beauties and delights of the country; but in reasoning on the subject, it is necessary to avoid illusions, and we shall be mistaken if we suppose that the common cultivator connects with rural sights and sounds, all the fine associations that are attached to them in the mind of the poet. If the present Laureat of England, who has described so feelingly, in his Espriella's Letters, the wretchedness of an ill-managed manufacturing population, had realized the golden dream of *Pantisocracy* in which he formerly indulged, when it was the height of his ambition to drive his own team up and down one of our villages; or as he expressed it himself,

> The tinkling team to guide
> O'er peaceful freedom's undivided glade,

he would probably have found that driving a team of oxen, or even keeping a flock of sheep, when it becomes the regular occupation of life, is not a whit more poetical than superintending the movement of a water-wheel or a steam engine. If, upon a fair comparison, we allow that agricultural labour is perhaps more agreeable and probably more healthy than any other, we shall also, I think, be satisfied that a manufacturing population is the one best situated for social enjoyment, and the one (of mechanical labourers) that will take the highest rank in the intellectual scale. The workmen are brought nearer together, and are able without inconvenience to see each other oftener, whether for purposes of improvement or pleasure. If their labour be somewhat monotonous, their seasons of repose are proportionally regular, and might be diversified with recreations and useful exercises of the most various kinds. We have seen of late the practice of attending scientific lectures at the hours of leisure, introduced among the operative mechanics in England, with great success and benefit. These as occupations for the evening, might be interchanged with assemblies for dancing, theatrical representations, and other innocent forms of social recreation; so that on the whole a daily round of objects, including those subservient to labour and enjoyment, might be brought before the mind of the manufacturing labourer, as various at least as those which regularly present themselves to the cultivator, and perhaps in the main not less agreeable. We may therefore conclude with safety, that there is little or no force in the objection made to the use of domestic manufactures, on account of their unfavourable effect, whether on the morals or the happiness of the individuals engaged in them. I have shown before that their influence on the community at large is in both respects extremely beneficial.

I have been led to treat this point rather more in detail than I should otherwise have done, because I was anxious to exhibit, in what appears to me its true light, the nature of the change that is now rapidly taking place in the industry of the country. It is desirable and important that the public should form a correct opinion of the effects of the progress of manufactures amongst us; and instead of looking upon it, as some have done, with apprehension, should regard and receive it as a blessing of Providence. The question still remains whether it be the duty of the government to encourage this progress by direct legislation; and if so, what new laws would be most expedient for the purpose. But these are matters that can only be discussed with profit in great detail, and which I must omit, as well for want of space as of the necessary materials. Most of the general principles that are applicable to them have been hinted at above. If the absence of domestic manufactures be owing in a great measure, as I have supposed, to political causes and the habits generated by them, it comes within the regular province of government to apply a remedy. The care of determining the nature of this remedy and of conciliating the encouragement of one branch of industry, with a just regard for the rights of individuals, whose property is invested in others, and for the general welfare of the union, belongs and may be trusted with safety to the wisdom and experience of congress.

Such are the few observations which the limits of the present essay will permit me to offer upon the topic of our domestic policy. But before I finish this chapter I shall be excused, I hope, for adding a single remark, upon the organization of the executive department of the government. Although the internal affairs of the country are incalculably more various, more weighty, more essentially interesting than the foreign relations; although the legislative and judicial departments of the government are almost wholly occupied with business of domestic origin, all of which requires in a greater or less degree the co-operation of the executive; although the people have uniformly manifested a wish to occupy themselves with their own concerns rather than those of other nations; notwithstanding all this, it so happens that there is no department of the executive branch of the government exclusively devoted to this great and paramount object. Our foreign relations, though by general acknowledgment of much inferior concern, employ two whole departments, the war and navy, and almost wholly the two others; for the only active business of the treasury is to levy the duties on our foreign commerce, and the principal occupation of the secretary of state to superintend the negociations with foreign powers. The remnant of time that is left to the departments of state and war, from the pressure of their more immediate business, is all that can now be devoted, by the executive branch of the government, to our domestic concerns. One would think that pride, if not policy, would induce a nation so jealous as the United States have always been of their dignity, rights, and interests, to reserve at least one executive department for home.

CHAPTER V.

*Spanish America.—Political Condition of the New
States.*

I HAVE dwelt at some length, in the first chapter of
the present work, on the important effects of the emancipation of Spanish America upon the present state and
future prospect of the whole civilized world. I have
said that this event, putting as it does the last finish to
the new form of political existence of our western continent, which was commenced by the liberation of the
United States from the yoke of Great Britain, completes
in one of its principal parts the development of a new
universal system, and must be regarded as one of the
leading circumstances, in the most interesting crisis in
the fortunes of Christendom, that has occurred since the
first establishment of the European commonwealth upon
the ruins of the Roman empire. I shall have occasion
hereafter, to recur to these considerations, and to state
them a little more at length. The present chapter will
be devoted to a few remarks upon the causes, immediate
and remote, of the struggle for independence in Spanish America, the historical events that have marked its
progress, and the present condition of the new governments that have been established in the different parts
of that immense region.

It would be taking a very narrow view of the nature of this struggle, or of that which preceded it in our country, to look merely at the particular events, which determined the period when these great revolutions occurred, and the circumstances that attended them. The general causes that fix the substantial character of the movements, that change from time to time the appearance of the world, though less obvious for the moment, are of far more real consequence. We are not to suppose that the patriotic zeal of our noble ancestors was so strongly excited, by the mere necessity of paying a half-penny too much for a pound of tea; or that Hampden was stung to madness by the thought of losing a few shillings under the name of ship-money. These were the forms under which a vicious political organization made itself felt in the mother country and in the colonies, at the time when the people in each were able and willing to assert their rights; any other exercises of the same authority occurring at about the same time would have produced the same effect. As respects the revolution in Spanish America, the particular events that determined the time and mode of its recurrence, were the troubles of the mother country, and the usurpation of the Spanish throne by a foreigner. When the whole empire threw off, by a simultaneous movement, the yoke of France, every separate kingdom and province assumed for the moment, and under the emergency of the case, the right of self government, and the American colonies were not less justified in so doing than the different parts of the peninsula. Peru and Mexico being placed in the same circumstances, possessed of course the same political rights with Castile and Grenada. There was, therefore, this peculiar circumstance attending the commencement of the Spanish American revolution, which favourably distinguishes it from almost all others, that it was not even in form illegal. In this respect it stands on even fairer ground than ours; for although our fathers always affirmed that they only claimed the rights of Englishmen, and were probably sincere and perhaps correct in this, there was nevertheless much to be said on the other side; and the government constantly professed to exercise nothing but a legal authority. In the other case there could be no dispute or difference of opinion; and the South American revolution, up to the time of the re-establishment of the king of Spain in 1813, was in no way tainted with the least suspicion of illegality. In the meantime the Americans had been naturally led, in the exercise of the functions of self government, to form new relations with each other and with foreign powers, and to accommodate themselves in various respects to a new position, in which they had been placed by events beyond their own control. Whether, under these circumstances, they were bound even in form to return to their allegiance, upon the king's return to his dominions, is a question, which few perhaps would venture to decide at once in the affirmative. The rights of one man over another depend upon the relations between them, and if one of two parties wrongfully change an existing relation, he cannot of course take advantage of his own wrong to acquire new rights. But if an existing relation be altered, without the fault of either party, their respective rights and duties are then determined by the new relation and not by the old one; and this was the state of the case between the king of Spain and his American colonies. It may fairly be doubted therefore, whether, from the time when the first movements which took place seventeen or eighteen years ago up to the present day, these colonies can be charged, in strictness, with illegal resistance or formal rebellion against the just authority of the parent country.

But however this may be, the substantial justification of their continuance in a state of independence, after the re-establishment of peace in Spain, was no doubt the same with that of our revolution; I mean, the inherent vice of the relation in which they were supposed to stand to the crown. In both cases, the mother countries claimed and exercised the right of imposing, in their own interest, various restrictions upon the inhabitants of the colonies, which were not imposed upon their European subjects, a circumstance which rendered the connexion between them even more objectionable than it otherwise would have been. But independently of this, it was in itself a thing unnatural and inexpedient, that communities situated at such immense distances from each other, should pretend to act together for the purposes of government as one body politic. A connexion of this kind, formed and growing up by accident, could not fairly be considered as binding on either party; and had an amicable proposition to dissolve it been made by either, it is not easy to see upon what just ground the other could have refused. We have seen in fact an arrangement of this kind actually taking place, during the last year, between Portugal and Brazil. At all events, it is just as certain that a separation, compulsory or peaceable, will in all such cases occur sooner or later, as that a fruit that has come to maturity will either fall or be plucked from its parent tree. It must also be allowed, on the other hand, that governments which had claimed and exercised for centuries dominion over vast provinces or rather empires in embryo, under the name of colonies, and whose pride at least is interested in preserving all their ancient rights and dignities, can hardly be expected to surrender such possessions without a struggle. However plain might be the law of nature, and even the dictates of policy, passion and prejudice would inevitably hold a more persuasive language, and govern for a time at least in the councils of almost any nation on the globe; and the more a nation thus situated was under the influence of routine and precedent, the less likely would it be to make a virtue of necessity and yield with a good grace. Great Britain, for example, might be expected to acquiesce on such an occasion much more readily than Spain, as in fact she did. When we look at this subject, under a general point of view; when we consider the vast extent of the American continent, and the prodigious development of population, wealth, and power, which is going on upon it, with a sort of impulse unknown before in the annals of our race; when we think how comparatively short a period must place the nations that inhabit it far above those of the old world, in all that constitutes material, intellectual, or moral greatness; and that it is the chosen and destined theatre of an improved civilization, which will cast a new and glorious light upon the character and prospects of mankind; when, I say, after dwelling for a while on these high contemplations, we recollect the feeble state of the European countries, from which these colonies emanated, and especially the notorious decrepitude and wretched imbecility of Spain, it seems like absolute madness for such a power, to pretend to master this mighty movement and direct it in its own interest. The account of such pretensions sounds like the vulgar stories of witchcraft, in which the beautiful and gifted spirits of a better world are represented as obeying the orders of an earthly mistress, for no better reason than that she is the ugliest and the weakest creature in the parish. Such, in fact, is the nature of the present contest between Spain and her ancient colonies. Unfortunately, however, we know that it is impossible for Spain or any other government similarly situated, to view such a struggle in its proper light. The mother country can see nothing in these brilliant youthful states but graceless children. Their natural effort to separate and acquire independence, when they have reached maturity, is a sin against legitimacy. The king is bound in honour and in conscience to transmit his hereditary dominions undiminished to his successor. Power is gone, but pride remains; and the government, rather than publicly acknowledge a fact, which no individual of common information in any part of Christendom would venture to question, which no member of the government would himself in private undertake to dispute, will consent to any sacrifices, endure the most ruinous privations, and in one word consummate the ruin of a country. How happy it would be for Spain, if her

European allies, who know very well how to interfere in her affairs when any mischief can be done, who can cover the peninsula with troops whenever any point of their own is to be carried, whose armies even now garrison the capital and constitute the only effectual support of the present rotten and wretched system, would for once exert themselves a little to promote what they feel and own to be the real good of this ill-fated nation! Delicacy it seems forbids. A strange kind of delicacy this, which allows them to invade a kingdom, under different pretexts, every ten or fifteen years, and carry on the government as it were in the king's name, but does not permit them to adopt, in his name, a measure which, as they confess, is the only one that can save him from ultimate ruin. Is this delusion or hypocrisy? whatever it may be, it is fatal enough to the Spanish nation, and well illustrates the truth of their own proverb— Save me from my friends and I will save myself from my enemies.

The history of the struggle for independence in Spanish America is, upon the whole, highly honourable to the character of the inhabitants of that region. It has been more tedious, more bloody, and more marked by vicissitudes of fortune, than ours; but this difference was naturally to be expected from the difference in the particulars of the two cases. The contest was carried on, in the first place, upon a much more extensive field, and by a much larger population than that of the United States at the time of the revolutionary war. These circumstances increased the probability of a successful result, but rendered it more difficult to establish a concerted system of operations among the several states, which has in fact never been completely effected up to the present day. With us an organized concert existed long before the war commenced, and was ready to be brought into action for military purposes, from the first moment when the exigency of the case required it. The Spanish colonies again were not accustomed to the business of government and legislation, which is in part a matter of routine and mechanism, and thus far can only be learned by experience. This experience they were yet to acquire, at the very moment when they wanted it most, and when they were worst situated for obtaining it. We on the contrary have had, from the beginning, our great and general courts, our assemblies and councils, our caucusses and town meetings, our orations and our newspapers. Faneuil Hall had rung for fifty years in succession, with the indignant eloquence of Dr. Cooke the father, and Dr. Cooke the son, before its echoes replied to the nobler voices of Otis, Adams, and Quincy. Our governors, from the time of Andros, who was forcibly deposed in 1688, down to that of Hutchinson, who was compelled to flee the country, had led the life of martyrs and confessors; and our ancestors had been for more than a century in constant training for the act of revolution. The habits of the Spanish Americans were also much less military than ours. After the first conquest of the country, they had had no troubles with the natives, and had never taken part in the wars of Europe, or been engaged in quarrels with each other. With us, on the contrary, the savages were never subdued until they were exterminated, and our forefathers were compelled to carry on with them a perpetual war of life and death. The musket and the broadsword were their constant companions; battles, wounds, conflagrations, and death, were familiar things. By constant exercise and practice, they appear to have acquired a relish for military life and the manly virtues which it brings into action. Remote as they were from Europe, they never failed to engage with ardour in the wars of the mother country, and wherever they were engaged, they acquitted themselves with distinction. The men who had taken Louisburg and fought with Montgomery at Quebec, were at no loss when called on to defend their firesides and their families. Another great distinction in our favour and against the Spanish colonies was the respective strength in each of the royalist party; with us, at least in the northern section of the country, the tories were a small and feeble portion of the people, and found it necessary to emigrate *en masse* at the opening of the war. The nobility and clergy of the mother country had neither part not lot amongst us, and the government had none of the usual strongholds and defences in which kings are accustomed to entrench themselves, for the purpose of making head against the aggressions of the people. In the Spanish colonies, there was a regular and powerful aristocracy, which possessed most of the land and with it the effective political power, and which adhered in general to the royal cause. The clergy declared almost unanimously for the king. When we consider the immense influence of this body, in every part of the Spanish empire; when we take into view the wealth and power of the nobility, the scantiness of the free white population, and the inefficiency of all the rest of the inhabitants, it becomes almost wonderful how the independent party have succeeded. Finally, the cause of liberty did not obtain in South America, as it did with us, the encouraging assistance of a generous foreign ally. The first monarch in Europe lent his countenance to us, as early as the fourth year of the war, and, before the sixth, three or four of the leading powers were fighting on our side. The Spanish colonies had carried on their weary struggle ten or twelve years, before the United States even began to exhibit any signs of sympathy. It was not till the end of their third lustrum of agony and blood, that a single European power would acknowledge the fact of their actual existence, nor has any foreign nation, European or American, yet consented to depart in their favour from the line of strict and relentless neutrality.

Under all these circumstances, it is, I repeat, rather to be admired, that the Spanish colonies should have been able to achieve their independence at present, than that the war should have been much more tedious, bloody, and doubtful than ours. It is true that the enemy with whom they had to contend, was entirely different in resources and character from England; and this was one of the principal advantages which served as an offset to all the inconveniences and dangers of their position. Could the Spanish cabinet have employed a financial and naval power equal to that of Great Britain, to sustain the strong party they had in America, the present struggle must have proved ineffectual, and the emancipation of the colonies have been delayed for an indefinite period. But though Spain has done quite as much as could have been expected from a kingdom so feeble and helpless, distracted too at the time by revolution and foreign war, she was of course incapable of acting with the spirit and vigour, which alone could have ensured success. It must nevertheless be considered as highly honourable to the independent party, that with so many obstacles to conquer, and so few resources at their disposal, with every thing to contend with at home and little or no help from abroad, they have accomplished, in about sixteen years, a revolution which gives a new form of existence to eight or ten powerful nations, changes the political condition of half a continent, and affects the fortunes and prospects of the world at large, more powerfully than almost any event that ever occurred.

But although I am ready to do full justice to the merit and the talent of the actors in this great movement, I am not yet prepared to go quite so far, as some very judicious persons have somewhat indiscreetly done, in exalting their pretensions. I have heard it said, for example, and that too by our own countrymen, not only that a seat in the congress of Panama was the highest and most honourable post that any living individual could occupy, but that this assembly would be the *first,* that had ever asserted the rights of man against tyrants and oppressors. Mr. De Pradt indulges in the same course of thinking, and in his late pamphlet on this congress makes no scruple of placing Bolivar far above Washington. I confess that I am quite at a loss to perceive any rational grounds for these strange exaggerations, nor do I believe that the statesmen and generals of Spanish America, or their countrymen for them, would dream of putting forward any such pretensions. Viewing it as certain that they have established their independence, they have done no more in this than the authors of our revolution; and if they had in some respects greater difficulties to contend with, their struggle was also proportionally longer and more doubtful than ours. But the great and glorious distinction, that belongs to our fathers, is that of having set the example to our brethren in the other part of the continent. Between the merit of conceiving and directing a difficult, apparently a desperate enterprise, and that of imitating this enterprise, after it has been triumphantly carried through by others, under similar circumstances, the distance is infinite. I say not this, for the purpose of depreciating the just reputation of the revolutionary worthies of the south. They have done nobly what they had to do, and have done, I believe, all that mortal man could have done in their position. It is not their fault that our fathers were earlier on the stage; but are these on the other hand to be deprived of their proper glory, because their actions have been copied by others? As to those who represent the congress of Panama as the first assembly, that ever undertook to resist the unlawful pretensions of government, I would ask them whether they have forgotten a meeting that was held at Philadelphia more than half a century ago, for precisely the same object; whether they have never read a celebrated declaration made by that meeting, which has not only served as a pattern to all the subsequent declarations of a similar kind, but which, to say the least, will bear a comparison both as to matter and manner with the best of them; the publication of which, according to the best European authorities, opened a new era in the history of the world. Thus much may be well said, upon the comparative merits of the revolutionary worthies of North and South America, as respects the great work of achieving independence, in which the latter as well as the former may be supposed to have completely succeeded. But it should not be forgotten, that the acquisition of independence was only one and perhaps not the most difficult of the exploits of our fathers. After obtaining this prize, they had to prove that they were worthy of it, and that they possessed the wisdom and virtue necessary for forming and administering a government. In this second undertaking they acquitted themselves in such a way, as to excite the admiration of the civilized world, and the lapse of half a century has confirmed from year to year their claims upon the veneration and gratitude of their countrymen. I am willing to believe, that the Spanish Americans will also meet, in this particular, with equal success, and to admit that what they have already done in this way is highly honourable to them; but all their political establishments are still as it were in embryo, and experience only can enable us to decide upon their value. Should they prove in fact to possess the same consistency and practical excellence with ours; should our neighbours in the south be able to shew us fifty years hence, a confederacy or a cluster of confederacies as flourishing as ours is now, we may then admit and with pleasure, that they have successfully imitated our example. But we can never admit that the disciple is greater than the master: or that we are to undervalue the master because he happens to have a worthy disciple. Whether some of the Spanish American states have not imitated even too closely the mere external form of our institutions, is a point which I shall presently have occasion to discuss; but waving this for the present, and allowing to the legislators of these states all the credit to which the most ample success will entitle them, I cannot but think that the Rivadavias, the Guals, and the Salazars, may well be satisfied, if the great award of posterity shall ultimately place them on a level with Franklin, Adams, Jefferson, Hamilton, and Madison. To discover how a thing can be done, and to do it after the discovery has been made, are two very different things. We know the anecdote of Columbus and the egg; and without descending to so trivial an illustration, we may well say, that if it required the genius of Columbus to explore the way to the new world, something less was necessary to follow him there. Few imitators stand in a better relation to their models than Virgil to Homer; but in the temple of fame, where Pope has placed them both, the Mantuan occupies a lower seat, and looks up with reverential awe to his mighty prototype:

> On Homer still he fixed a reverent eye,
> Great without pride, in modest majesty.

It would be easy indeed to support by classical authorities, a theory not very flattering to the reputation of imitators, but to this extent I have no wish to go. The Spanish Americans have proved sufficiently that they are not to be ranked with the *servum pecus.*

The same remarks may be made upon the respective pretensions of Bolivar and Washington. The attempt to compare them is wholly premature. Bolivar is still in the midst of his career; and although I have no disposition whatever to cherish the doubts respecting his future conduct, which the enemies of liberty affect to entertain; although I feel the fullest confidence that he will justify the hopes of the world, and terminate as he has commenced, the glorious mission which has been allotted to him, it is nevertheless too early to award the prize before the race is run. Long as he has laboured in the cause of his countrymen, and much as he has done for them, he has one thing left to do, more difficult, if we may judge at least by its rarity, than all the rest; and without which all the rest will go for nothing and worse than nothing. He has yet to show, that he knows the difference between true and false greatness, that is, between true greatness and a hoop of gold cr a wooden seat covered with velvet. After subduing hostile enemies, he has yet to subdue (if he is unfortunate enough to feel them) the impulses of irregular ambition; and this is the achievement which Cicero, in his splendid but unhappily wholly unmerited encomium on Cæsar, declares to be the one which raises a man as it were above the level of humanity. The enemies of liberty in Europe, who judge of others by the consciousness they have of their own base and sordid sentiments, generally laugh at the idea that Bolivar will ever resign his

truncheon and descend to private life. For my part I
see no reason whatever to suspect him. His whole conduct, as far as I am acquainted with it, has been patriotic
and disinterested, and affords the happiest prognostics
of his future course of life. When he shall have justified, as I have no doubt he will, these high expectations,
we shall be able to pronounce a favourable opinion on his
general character, and to class him with the few great
commanders in free states, who have been at the same
time heroes and friends of their country. Even then,
however, before we can compare him with Washington,
he must have rendered the most important services to
his fellow citizens in the foundation and administration
of their civil institutions, must have rescued them from
monarchy, as he had redeemed them before from foreign bondage, must have held out to them the graceful
and edifying example of a private life corresponding in
dignity and purity with the glory of his public career,
and finally must have brought his earthly course to an
honourable end. Death, says Burke, canonizes a great
character, and we may add death only; because nothing
else can give us complete assurance, that the greatness
we admire will be kept up without failure or fault to the
last. To accomplish all this may not be so easy as Mr.
De Pradt, whose pen sometimes outruns his judgment,
perhaps imagines. All this, however, must be done,
before Bolivar can claim the honour of being a worthy
and successful student in the school of Washington.
Greater honour than this he need not wish, and can
never under any circumstances aspire to. To place him
at present above his illustrious master, is merely an idle

exaggeration, and argues a very inadequate conception of the characters of both. In general the world and even his own countrymen have been somewhat too prone to raise up rivals and equals to our incomparable hero. Bonaparte was at one time the Washington of France; Iturbide in his day was a Washington. Riego and Quiroga rose in a few months from the rank of lieutenants to be the Washingtons of Spain. The name of the father of his country is too honourable a title to be lavished upon every bold adventurer, even in a cause apparently just. The world had been created nearly six thousand years, before the appearance of the first or rather the unique Washington, and it would be singular if half a dozen more should spring up like mushrooms within twenty years of his death. I would not be understood, however, to confound the name of Bolivar with those of the other pretenders to distinction, whom I have just mentioned. Should the close of his career correspond with its commencement, he will no doubt stand more nearly on a parallel with Washington, than any other character recorded in history.

It is not my intention to recapitulate here in detail, or to comment at length upon the military events of the Spanish American revolution. These are in their nature sufficiently public, and it is my object to note the moral causes and effects of these and other such movements, rather than to write their history. This will furnish a splendid subject for the Livies and Humes of future ages. I shall confine myself at present to a few remarks upon the political institutions of the nations that have been formed out of the ancient Spanish colonies:

and shall consider what arrangements would have been most suitable to the new condition in which they found themselves, and how far they have succeeded in solving the problem which that situation presented.

The leading principle upon which the Spanish colonies have proceeded, in organizing their political institutions, appears to have been a desire to copy as far as possible those of the United States. They have all adopted the system of representative democracy, and the forms in use with us of a single elective chief magistrate and two elective legislative bodies. They have also in general followed our model in regard to the manner of choosing these functionaries, the duties that are respectively assigned them, and even their names. Three or four of the new states have also introduced the federal principle, which seems to have its partisans in some of the others. Where this feature exists, the resemblance is complete. In the others the absence of it occasions a considerable divergence; but even here the imitation is very direct. Brazil also, with the variation of its hereditary chief magistrate and senate, has been evidently copied from the same original, and not without a marked attention to the federal feature, which forms one of its principal peculiarities. Throughout the whole of these vast regions, it is only in Paraguay that we find the government resting on a wholly different basis. In that province, as far as we are acquainted with its institutions, which is very slightly, we have reason to suppose that they are the same which were established by the Jesuits, and which vary essentially, not only from those of the United States, but of every other christian country. I shall say a few words respecting them before I leave this subject.

As respects the others, however, the plan of copying directly and minutely, as well in their essential principles as their internal forms and names, the institutions of the United States, is too flattering to our national pride, not to be considered at first view as plausible and judicious. It must be owned too, that the example of an experiment attended with such brilliant success, was certainly seducing; and it would ill become me to intimate, that any other or better mode of proceeding could possibly have been discovered. We ought not, however, to be so blinded by partiality for our own government, or for those who have done us the honour to copy it, as to forget that the legislators of Spanish America, in imitating so closely the works of our patriots and sages, have not precisely followed their example. They too had successful and plausible models before them, and they borrowed from several of them such parts as they approved; but they did not act upon the principle of copying immediately, closely, and throughout, the form of any government before established. It may be said indeed, and with great truth, that there was at that time no existing government so well fitted to serve as a pattern in legislation as ours is now; but it should also be remembered, that the material virtue of a good constitution is its conformity to the condition of the people, who are to be governed by it. Now the fact that a certain form of government has been attempted with extraordinary success, in one nation, instead of proving that it would be equally successful in all others, furnishes *prima facie* evidence that it would not; because we know that hardly two nations can be mentioned, whose condition is not in some important respects materially different. However beneficial a particular institution had been found in other countries, it would be necessary to ascertain, before it could be copied with safety, that the mode of operation would be precisely similar; and there is still, in this plan of legislation, the inherent danger, that you can never be quite sure that your observations have been complete and correct; and mistakes on these great subjects are of lasting consequences and often irremediable. These considerations are so important, that prudent men have generally thought it safer to adopt as the leading principle in legislation, that of maintaining the existing state of things; and where alterations are suggested by particular circumstances, of not extending them much farther, either in conformity to abstract notions or foreign examples, than the occasion itself requires. This appears to have been the principle that was acted upon by the founders of our institutions. The great object of the revolution was independence, and the acquisition of this was considered as the proper remedy for the evils attending the old system. The separation from the mother country left, however, certain blanks in the latter, and the principal object of our legislators seems to have been to fill these, in the manner corresponding most nearly with the spirit that prevailed in other parts of our institutions, and for the rest to maintain these institutions as they stood. They introduced a new method of designating the governors and councils of the several states, the one in use before having become impracticable, and they substituted a new principle of union among the states, for the old one of a common allegiance to the king. In most other parts, they left every thing in the main as it was. Some years later, this new principle of union was found to be defective, and a second generation of patriots and sages, as I have said before, introduced another; but they too made no further innovations in important matters, and with this improvement, the venerable fabric of our institutions was left once more in its primitive state. Had the legislators of Spanish America imitated, in this respect, the *example* of our statesmen, instead of copying their works so minutely as they have done, I am not sure that they would not have taken a wiser and a safer course. The one they have pursued would be perfectly justifiable, only on the supposition, that there existed a strong similarity between the respective situations of the people in the two divisions of America; and it is therefore reasonable to conclude, that the Spanish American lawgivers proceeded upon such an opinion. It may also appear presumptuous to differ from them in regard to this point; but I confess that as far as we are acquainted abroad with the character and condition of our southern neighbours, I am not able to discern this striking resemblance; and I think I see, on the contrary, differences in some very important matters, which would hardly be consistent with the easy and successful operation of the same institutions in both.

If we look, for example, at the state of property, which forms in all countries the most important feature in the condition of the people, we shall find that it was entirely different in North and South America. Our fathers, when they took into their hands the government of their country, found the property in substance equally divided. They found the whole population virtually independent in their circumstances, enjoying the necessaries and comforts of life, and possessed of the intelligence and virtue, which naturally accompany so advantageous a position. They also found them in regular and habitual exercise of extensive political rights. Upon this basis, it was easy to erect the fabric of a free representative government; and it is, as I have stated in a preceding chapter, the conformity between the system thus established and the condition and character of the people, which resolve themselves ultimately into the state of property that constitutes the real and substantial security which we have of the durability of our present institutions. In Spanish America, on the other hand, the property appears to have been very unequally divided, and to have been held exclusively, in immense masses, by a few persons. As a necessary consequence, the comforts of life, intelligence, and industry, (the principle of virtue,) were distributed in the same way, and the mass of population had never enjoyed or exercised any political rights whatever. Is it possible that a free and popular government erected on such a basis can be permanent? Far be it from me to affirm the contrary. I only say, that this basis is essentially different from that which existed in the United States; and that if the same institutions are also expedient in Spanish America, it must be for reasons other than those which recommended them to us. It is true that laws have been already made in most, or perhaps all of these new states, which provide for the equal division of property among all the children of the same parents, and thus open the way for the gradual subdivision of the large masses which now exist. This is no doubt just and proper, supposing a popular government to be established; but it is still nothing else, than an attempt to reconcile and accommodate the state of the people to a form of government, introduced in conformity to abstract notions or foreign examples. Now the principle adopted by our legislators, and which is generally considered a much safer course, is to take the state of the people, as you find it, and to regulate your form of government accordingly. In this way you secure, for the time being, an easy and quiet administration of the public affairs; and if improvements are necessary, they are subsequently introduced without much danger, under the name of laws. On the other hand, if the form of government is essentially at variance with the state of the people, it can never go into quiet operation, still less become permanent; and the adoption of it is a mere signal and occasion for fresh revolutions.

It may be said, indeed, that liberty is a principle in itself so valuable, that wherever a new government is to be established, it should be made at all hazards free and popular; and as no one is more decidedly attached to popular forms than I am, so no one can be more ready to admit and to insist, that they should be introduced as universally and as rapidly as possible. But the friends of liberty, if they expect to carry their point, must be prudent and judicious, as well as hearty in the cause.

Of what advantage is it to set up a shadowy phantom of popular government, merely for the sake of seeing it vanish in smoke after a few weeks, months, or even years? Does this in good earnest encourage and promote the great object, or do in any way any good whatever? In the United States, we hold nearly two millions of blacks in domestic slavery, while our senate chambers are daily echoing with our fervent protestations of zeal and affection for freedom under every colour and aspect! And reason good, for it is one thing to love liberty, and another to love desolation, slaughter, and universal uproar, which would be the consequence of a simultaneous and general emancipation of the blacks. Any measure, therefore, and most of all a measure so momentous as the establishment of a new constitution of government, is not necessarily politic and expedient, merely because it is favourable to *liberty,* that is, to the absence of restraint upon individuals. The absence of restraint in itself is a good thing, but the absence of all restraint would be, in other words, the absence of all government, and would of course afford no basis for any institutions. Restraint to a certain extent is every where necessary, and the degree to which it might be admitted, must be determined, as I have stated above, by considering not merely abstract notions and foreign examples, but also the state and condition of the people. The institutions which may be recommended by the former, can only be established with safety as far as they are also consistent with the latter. Any attempt to introduce others, however beautiful in theory, and however beneficial elsewhere, is dangerous. To say that it will certainly be ruinous or greatly injurious to the nation that makes it, would be going too far; because we know that Providence often modifies the working of general causes, so as to bring good out of evil. Dangerous and imprudent such attempts certainly are, and it is the practice of men and nations who pretend to wisdom, before they invoke the special intervention of Providence, to exercise in the first instance, with the greatest possible effect, the power and means which the same Providence, operating through the general laws of nature, has placed at their disposal.

It appears, therefore, rather a doubtful point, whether the establishment in Spanish America of governments, as popular as that of the United States, was a measure recommended by the character and condition of the people, and of course whether these governments are likely to be equally durable and successful with ours. The same remarks apply with the same or greater force to the attempts which have been made or are making, to organize some of these states on the federal principle in imitation of our union. In this respect, as in the other, the legislators of the south, in copying the works of our ancestors, have overlooked the spirit in which they were executed, or rather have exhibited an entirely different one. The sages and patriots who framed our institutions, were the representatives of a number of entirely independent communities, and, acting as such, they assumed the federal principle as a part of the existing state of things, which was to form the basis of the social fabric, and serve as the *substratum* for such additions as were necessary. They had before them some very brilliant examples of governments arranged in a more compact manner, and the general notions prevalent at that day were rather against the expediency of attempting the federal principle on a very large scale. Notwithstanding this, our ancestors adhered firmly to their wise and cautious plan of building on the existing foundations; and adopted the federal principle in a form before unknown in any other country. Spanish America was also parcelled out into a number of wholly independent provinces under the names of kingdoms and captain-generalcies. But these never seem to have contemplated the plan of a confederacy. A union substantially similar to ours, was therefore never even thought of in the south; but some of these provinces have undertaken, in organizing their separate governments, to subdivide their territory into independent states, for the purpose of afterwards re-uniting these states on the federal principle. To say that this proceeding was injudicious and unwise, would be premature at least, and perhaps incorrect. It is certain, however, that it does not correspond with the conduct of our legislators, whom our southern neighbours apparently intended to follow. It corresponds, on the contrary, with what their conduct would have been, if instead of assuming the existing divisions into states, as a part of the basis on which they were to build, they had attempted, from deference to received opinions and foreign examples, to abolish this division and establish a consolidated government. If the several clusters of United States which have been formed in Mexico, on the river La Plata, and in Upper Peru, present an external semblance of our union, the principles that led respectively to the establishment of them, are not only different but directly opposite; and the case affords a singular example of the danger of direct imitation. To imitate directly the brilliant and successful work of another hand, is in fact in most cases the surest method that can be taken of becoming an original, in some other much inferior in order.

If then, it may be asked, the institutions of the United States were not suitable to the condition and character of the Spanish Americans, what others would have suited them better? What forms of government would have coincided sufficiently well with the existing state of property and civilization, to be durable and permanent? These are the great problems which it was and may be again the duty of the legislators of the south to solve, but which I am far from pretending to be able to solve for them. No foreigner probably possesses the information respecting the political situation of these immense regions, almost unknown abroad, which would justify even a suggestion of the nature of the institutions that would suit them best. We know negatively, that certain things did not exist there before the revolution; that, as I have stated, there was not the equality of property and the division into independent states, that were found with us. We also know that to adopt the existing state of things as the basis of every new political organization, is the safest principle that can be acted upon, and is in particular the one which was followed by our forefathers. Even this rule, however, may not be without exceptions, and we may perhaps conceive of a state of things so entirely rotten and vicious. that nothing can be made of it; of a political edifice so completely dilapidated, that no part of it can be built upon, and that the whole must be removed and the ground swept clean, before a new construction can be undertaken with advantage. Such may have been the case in Spanish America, and it is therefore not certain, although the presumption is perhaps against them, that our southern neighbours have not done in every respect the best they could. My object in the preceding remarks has not been so much to censure their proceedings, as to show that although they have copied the external forms of our institutions, they have not borrowed, and could not possibly, in this way, borrow their spirit, which lies in their conformity to the condition of our country; and of course, that the successful operation of these constitutions with us affords little or no assurance of what their effect will be elsewhere, and under other circumstances.

Without, however, pretending even to suggest an opinion as to what forms of government would be most suitable to the condition of Spanish America, much less to speak with decision on this subject, it is not very difficult to perceive that there was one important element of political power, at their disposal, which did not exist at least to the same extent and in the same shape with us, which they have certainly not entirely neglected, but of which they might perhaps have taken greater advantage than they have done, in forming their institutions—I mean *religion*. It has been made by some an objection to the constitution of these new states, that they have adopted an established religion, and that in

some of them the exercise of any other is prohibited under severe penalties. This latter clause is undoubtedly
injudicious, at variance with policy as well as common
humanity, and directly detrimental to the purpose which
it is meant to promote. But as respects the former,
instead of blaming the Spanish Americans for having
done too much, I should rather be disposed to think
that they had done too little; and that the religious establishment, which they did not create, but found
already existing in full vigour, deeply seated in the
faith, affection, and habits of the people, might have
been employed, with great propriety and utility, as the
mainspring and principal basis of the new political institutions. It does not belong to my purpose to state in
detail what would have been in this case the modes of
legislation and administration, or the names and functions of the principal magistrates. These are matters
comparatively unimportant in all governments. But on
this supposition, the great rule of assuming the existing
state of things as the basis of the new fabric would have
been observed, and at the same time an element of
power been brought into action, not inferior perhaps in
beneficial potency to any other, and amply competent
to keep in motion the machinery of any constitution.

Religion, wherever it can be employed in this way,
seems in fact to be the proper corner stone of every
political fabric; the theory of the natural separation of
of church and state, which grew up at the time of the
reformation, and has since gained so much currency
that the Catholics themselves have found it necessary to
admit it, has in fact no foundation whatever in truth,

and is one of those popular errors, or rather abuses of language, which become universal for a time from some accidental misconception, and, when this is removed, are again rejected with equal unanimity. Such at no distant period will be the fate of this theory; for how can it be said, with a shadow of plausibility, that the state, which is a body politic or political person, declaring and enforcing the laws for the general good, is entirely different from the church, which is the same body politic or political person, declaring and enforcing the same laws for the same purpose, under different sanctions. Morality, or natural law, which is the basis of all legislation, considered in its origin, is the system of the relations established by the will of God among the individual members of the human race. The state declares it to be the law of the land, and enforces it by judicial process. The church declares it to be the law of God, and to be provided as such with appropriate rewards and punishments. It is evident that both these functions are exercises of the sovereign power; and unless we suppose a complete *imperium in imperio*, or two distinct governments in one community, it follows that the church and the state are not only not to be considered as naturally independent of each other, but that they are in their nature and should be in fact not merely united but identical. The unity, or in other words the existence of government, requires that in every community the controlling power in religion should be held and exercised by the same persons who also hold and exercise the controlling power in politics. In this case the church and the state concur in recommending the same duties, and what is even more important, if possible, the laws are enjoined upon the public as religiously obligatory, which they really are. Where this is not the case, there is not only a continual danger or rather moral certainty of collision between the two distinct lawgiving powers, that is, in one shape or another, of civil war; but the laws emanating from the government lose the advantage of a religious sanction, take no hold upon the minds or hearts of the people, and are looked upon as mere rules of practical expediency, which may be violated without impropriety, by any one who is willing to suffer the penalty. As the obligation to obey the laws of the state, results in fact from their supposed conformity to the laws of nature, that is the will of God, and as the knowledge of the true character of this obligation produces a stronger disposition in the public mind to obey the laws, than any other consideration that can be presented to it, it is evidently in the highest degree politic and useful, to make the connexion between the government, that is morality as declared by law, and religion, as apparent as possible. Where the reality of this connexion is fully established in public opinion, it would show a great want of true statesmanship not to make use of that opinion as an element in the constitution of a new political society.

Of ancient states Rome is the one, in which the natural alliance between religion and government was most distinctly perceived and turned to the best account.— "However highly we may value ourselves, Conscript Fathers," says Cicero in one of his addresses to the senate, "it is certain that we have not exceeded Spain in population, nor the Gauls in corporeal vigour, nor the Carthagenians in shrewdness, nor the Greeks in art, nor even the other Italians in love for the native soil; but in piety, religion, and the one great science that all human things are directed and governed by the will of God, we have gone beyond all other nations." Lord Bacon makes no scruple of attributing to this difference the elevated policy and consequent success of this illustrious republic. " Never," says he, before quoting the above passage, " never was there such a state for magnanimity as Rome." Peculiar circumstances, which were hinted at in the former part of this work, and which I have not room to enlarge upon here, prevented the reality and great advantages of the union of government and religion from being perceived, in the principal states of modern Europe, and in fact, as I have said above, exalted the contrary principle of the natural separation of church and state into a sort of received axiom, especially among those persons who affected an independent and popular way of thinking on political matters. These states have experienced in consequence, in greater or less degrees, both the inconveniences which I have mentioned above, as results of this axiom applied to practice. They have been and still are distracted by dissensions between the two lawgiving powers, and have lost the advantage of founding their legislation on the firm basis of a direct religious sanction. The two countries in which these inconveniences have been least felt, and in which the political arrangements on this subject, though not perfect, approach most nearly to the correct ideal model, are England and the United States.

In England the king, who represents in his person the sovereign power of the nation, is also the head of the church; so that the unity of church and state is complete, and the system thus far theoretically perfect. By this arrangement, one of the two practical inconveniences above indicated, to wit, that of collision between the two lawgiving powers, is wholly avoided. Nor has the advantage of investing the laws with a religious sanction been entirely overlooked, since Christianity has been declared by the competent authorities to be parcel of the law. But as the unity of church and state was declared in England by Henry VIII., more for the purpose of escaping from the partial supremacy of a foreign prince, than from a perception of the essential correctness and expediency of the system, it has not been turned so much to account as it might have been, nor perhaps has the full virtue of the law maxim above stated been distinctly appreciated. In the United States, the sovereign power in religion as well as politics resides in the people, and here again the unity of church and state is complete, the system theoretically perfect, and the practical inconvenience of collision between the two lawgiving powers entirely avoided. With us too Christianity is parcel of the law, and the state is therefore, to a certain extent, consecrated (in the language of Burke) by religion. But with us also, this arrangement was the result of causes, other than a distinct perception of its essential value, though different also from those which introduced it in England. In this country it was the result of the general prevalence of the common opinion, alluded to above, respecting the natural separation of church and state. However singular it may seem, that the universal belief in this principle, and, as our legislators supposed, the practical adoption of it, should have produced, in fact, the directly opposite result of a perfect unity of the two lawgiving powers, it is nevertheless certain that this was the case. Our ancestors denied that religion had any concern with government, and therefore kept it entirely out of the hands of the political agents of the people. The controlling power on this subject remained, of course, like every other not specially granted, with the people itself, which in our country, where the people is the acknowledged sovereign, is its proper place, on the system of a unity of church and state. But as this system was thus introduced by a sort of accident, its real value has not been generally felt. No attempts have been made to improve it to the greatest possible extent, and the laws have hitherto wanted the advantage of a direct religious sanction. In this important particular, therefore, the position of England and the United States is nearly the same. In both the general theory of the constitution on the subject of religion is perfect, and in each it will perhaps be found expedient to introduce some new practical arrangements, whenever the public opinion shall be prepared to receive them with approbation. This, however, will not happen in our day.

In Spanish America the public opinion, on this whole subject, was diametrically opposite to what it was and still is in this country; and was as much in favour of a powerful intervention of the religious principle, in the machinery of government, as it would have been with

us against it, if such an idea had been for a moment entertained and suggested by any one. In Spanish America, such an intervention was in perfect conformity with
the long established order of things; and the new constitutions might have been consecrated by a direct
religious sanction, without the least innovation upon
received opinions, or rather in perfect accordance with
them. If then religion be in general the natural foundation of law and government, if it had long been
established as such in Spanish America, and if this state
of things was approved by the undoubted verdict of the
public faith and feeling, why not maintain it as the basis
of the new institutions, and build upon it such additions
as were necessary, instead of going abroad to borrow
another principle? I speak with great diffidence on this
subject, as every one is bound to do, in criticising the
government of a foreign nation; but it seems to me, I
confess, that religion should have been made by the lawgivers of the south, the principle in forming their political creations, in the same way that liberty was with
us; and I think that in pursuing this line of conduct,
they would have imitated much more perfectly the proceedings of our legislators, than they have done, because
they would in that case have acted in their spirit
instead of copying the form of their works. Whether
a government formed upon this basis would or would not
have been for practice as good as ours, is a question
which we need not undertake to determine. Religion
and liberty are both excellent things, founded in truth,
dear to the wise and good of all countries, the sources
of our happiness and the basis of our hopes. To be

able to employ either of them as the corner stone of the
social fabric, is a piece of good fortune that ought to sa-
tisfy the ambition of any community.   To inquire for
any practical purpose, which is preferable as a principle
of government, would be to suppose that either might
be adopted with equal facility, which is certainly not
the case in Spanish America, and probably never was
or will be in any country on the globe.   If the question
be asked in reference merely to theory, it may be answered that as principles of government each have peculiar advantages. Liberty defines the law with greater
certainty, and religion enforces it with more effect.—
Liberty is enterprising, restless, sometimes turbulent,
and not unwilling to look for occupation beyond the
limits of her own territory.   Religion on the contrary,
abides in peace, and is bent on maintaining it abroad and
at home.   Liberty is better suited to the youth of nations, and religion to their riper period; and that people
perhaps would be the happiest of all, which should be
established and grow up under the auspices of liberty,
and then in the progress of years pass, by a natural and
easy gradation, under the dominion of religion; the
case of nations being different in this respect from that
of individuals, with whom religion, though always indispensable, is more especially beneficial as a rule of conduct in youth.   As principles of government, the two
however are not inconsistent, because the law of nature,
whether published as the will of the people or the will
of God, is still the same; and sanctions, in the latter
case, all the just rights of individuals, as in the former
it still appeals, though indirectly, to its divine origin,

as the proper source of its obligatory character. But without carrying any farther these general considerations, which, as I observed above, have no immediate application in practice to this or any other case, it is sufficient to observe, that in omitting to adopt as the basis of these new institutions, the one of these two principles which was placed at their disposal by the existing state of the country, and attempting to introduce the other, in deference to the example of a foreign nation, they have, I fear, unnecessarily resigned a great positive advantage, and exposed themselves, to say the least, to great eventual danger. It may be thought by some that all the virtue of the religious principle will be secured by an established church; but it is much to be feared, I think, that such an institution standing in connexion with others belonging to a different order of political forms and principles, will be a source of weakness rather than of strength. It may well be doubted how far an established church, if at least it correspond at all in form with those already existing in other countries, can be reconciled with a government of a wholly popular kind. The supremacy of the pope and his pretensions to appoint the principal ecclesiastical dignitaries, would hardly consist with the sovereignty of the people, and their consequent inherent right to exercise, either in person or by delegates, every function belonging thereto, whether political or religious. Considered under this point of view, the objections that have been made to the adoption of an established church, as a part of the new political institutions in Spanish America, are by no means without foundation.

Paraguay, as I have already remarked, is the only section of this vast region in which an attempt appears to have been made to employ the religious principle as the main engine of government, but we know too little of the general situation of that country, and in particular of the form of the institutions now existing there, to be able to say how far they are likely to succeed, and still less whether they would be a proper model for imitation in other parts of America. The Jesuits, by whom they were founded, were not deficient in sagacity or instruction; and the country, while under their direction, appeared to flourish. The situation of it, since it was taken from their hands, is in a great measure unknown and will continue to be, as long as the present rigorous system of exclusion is enforced against foreigners. This feature in the government of Paraguay we may venture unequivocally to condemn, whatever may be the character of the rest. It is probably, however, a measure of temporary policy, adopted with a view of counteracting the contagious influence of the revolutionary movements going on in the neighbourhood. But whatever may be its object, it makes it impossible for the moment to obtain any accurate information of the state of this very peculiarly situated community, and of course to dwell at any length upon the nature of its institutions. Doctor Francia, who is now at the head of them, seems to be a man of a powerful character, but his history is very little known and his intentions seem to be obscure; at least the state papers to which his name is affixed, are evidently drawn up on purpose in a style better fitted to conceal his views than to explain them. We must leave him and his government as enigmas to be solved by the progress of years and future events.

If these general observations upon the political institutions which have been established in the several parts of Spanish America are at all correct, it follows of course, that there is no necessity of examining in great detail those of each distinct section. They are all copied from one common model, resemble each other very nearly in their external form, and are alike liable to the objection that they have little or no foundation in the condition and character of the people. Reasoning on general principles, it is of course impossible not to draw the conclusion that they are destined to undergo many very important changes, before they settle down into a fixed and permanent shape. We are not to suppose, however, that because there is a probability of the recurrence of such changes, the political situation of these countries is desperate; that the objects for which they have been so long struggling are unattainable; or that they are destined to return to their ancient subjection to Spain. Their independence may be regarded as a settled thing, settled as well by the imbecility of Spain, as by the power and resources of the new states. There is, therefore, no chance of their future subjugation by this or any other foreign state. They will in all probability be left entirely to themselves as regards the formation of their governments, and will have an opportunity of founding, new modelling, and improving, until they shall have placed them at last upon their true and natural basis. If, as there is room to suppose, they have not perfectly succeeded in their first attempts, the fact is neither singular nor very alarming. Every thing is yet in a state of revolution, and it is at this moment as easy and familiar a matter in all these countries to found or reform a constitution, as it is in a long established government to pass an ordinary law, or to publish a royal decree. The best advice that foreigners can give them is to abjure all foreign influence and example, and to act as much as they can for themselves, upon a careful and correct view of their own internal situation. With this counsel and the heartiest wishes for their ultimate success, we must leave them in the hands of the great disposer of human affairs.

In the empire of Brazil an attempt has been made to accommodate the liberal political institutions of England and the United States to a condition of society still less fitted to receive them, if we are rightly informed respecting it, than that of most parts of Spanish America. The popular provisions of the new system may, therefore, be considered for a time at least, as a dead letter. The only substantial thing about it is the crown and the military force at the emperor's disposal. But even this institution of royalty, unsupported as it is by tradition, and foreign to the feelings of the new world, can hardly be looked upon as very stable; and the Portuguese, as well as the Spanish division of our continent, is probably destined to undergo various revolutions, before it settles down under a fixed and lasting government. In the course of these events, it will not be surprising if the Emperor Pedro should have occasion to repent of the premature stirrings of his youthful ambition; and should look back with some regret to his quiet little patrimony on the banks of the Tagus, where his ancestors had reposed in peace for centuries, and where the banner of England over them was fear if not love.

The observations in the preceding chapter on the domestic policy of the United States, apply without alteration to the Spanish and Portuguese sections of the continent. I shall therefore proceed at once to the consideration of the foreign policy of this our western world, which naturally divides itself into two distinct heads, the international relations of the two Americas, and the policy of both, as respects the rest of Christendom. I shall devote a chapter to each of these subjects, and shall then in another make a few brief remarks upon the popular and interesting topic of the congress at Panama.

CHAPTER VI.

European Colonies in America.

THE authority of Europe, which prevailed half a century ago over our whole western world, is now acknowledged only in the comparatively desolate and uninhabited although extensive regions, north of the limits of the United States, and the islands in the Gulph of Mexico. It is also not difficult to foresee on the most obvious general principles, that these remaining possessions must sooner or later follow the fortunes of the rest, and become like them, in one way or another, independent of the mother continent. In a political system so young and vigorous as ours, the absorbing power is too great to permit these foreign substances to continue very long undisturbed within the sphere of its action, and they must ultimately be all taken up and assimilated to the mass. Considered, therefore, merely as European colonies, there is little to be said of them, except that they must after a while cease to be so. The time when this revolution will occur, the circumstances under which it will be effected, and the results that will follow it, are matters so completely uncertain and conjectural, that it would be useless to speculate upon them at any great length. I shall accordingly confine myself in the present chapter to a few very brief and superficial observations.

The British possessions that overhang our whole northern border, and the Spanish islands which lie so near our southern coast, and would in powerful hands command the outlets of our western waters, are now the principal appendages remaining to Europe in this part of the world, and are especially those in regard to which the people of the United States have a right to feel the strongest interest. The former are probably destined to pass a longer term of colonial dependence than the latter. The principle of adhesion between a metropolitan government and its remote dominions, depends very much upon its own strength and resources. While the ruling state preserves its greatness, the colonies naturally continue to acknowledge its authority. Our revolution, in this as in almost every other respect, was an exception from all known rules. When, on the contrary, the vital spirit ceases to animate the central organs of the body politic, it cannot of course be very active in the extremities, and the latter must either fall off or be abandoned by the power that before protected them. It was thus that in the declining period of the Roman empire these very British islands begged, and begged in vain, to be treated as a subject province, and were compelled to receive with reluctance and *groans* the boon of independence. Since that time the state of things has materially changed, and such is now, and probably may be for two or three centuries to come, the political power of England, that her distant appendages will scarcely attempt or even desire to change their position. Her greatness, however, being founded principally on foreign commerce, and not sustained by a corresponding territorial basis, must of course undergo a somewhat rapid decline, and the time when this shall happen will be the period, for the scattered and heterogeneous possessions of this queen of the ocean and mistress of islands to assume respectively an independent life. The Canadas, the East Indies, New Holland, the Cape of Good Hope, and the rest of the colonies, will then separate their fortunes, and severally provide for their convenience and safety, in the manner which may appear to each most expedient.

It is not impossible that at this epoch, whenever it may arrive, the British colonies in North America may voluntarily connect themselves with our republic. I say not this because I feel as a citizen of the United States any wish for territorial extension, still less for actual conquest in that quarter. Should these provinces, when they shall separate from the other portions of the British empire, erect themselves into an independent nation or nations, they would then be as regards the United States in the situation of weaker powers in the neighbourhood of a stronger; and this relation might well be considered as at least equally flattering to our pride with the other, if not more so. But looking merely to the operation of general causes, it can hardly be doubted that it would be the policy of these colonies, considered under every point of view, commercial or political, to form a part of our union, rather than to exist in a separate state. It would also, for the most obvious reasons, be our policy to assent to this connexion, whenever it might be by them spontaneously proposed. A result of this kind is wholly independent of the possible course of events in any future contest with England. Had we subdued Canada in the last war, or should we do it at any time hereafter, we should of course restore it at the conclusion of peace, which would never be made upon any other basis than that of prior possession. While, however, the British empire retains its vigour, which, as I observed before, may probably be for two or three centuries to come, its distant appendages will doubtless adhere to it; and Canada may perhaps be one of the last that will fall off. It would, therefore, be wholly premature to enlarge upon the subject now. The events of future centuries may be left with safety to the care of future generations.

The separation of the Spanish West Indian islands from the mother country, is an occurrence probably much less distant. Spain has now reached in her course of decline and fall the period of weakness alluded to above, when a government naturally loses or abandons its remote possessions. Her feeble and distracted condition, as I had occasion to remark in the preceding chapter, is the circumstance that has principally favoured the attempts of the popular party in the colonies, and which still secures their independence. The same cause had previously induced the inhabitants of Cuba to assume a virtual sovereignty as respects their foreign trade, while they continued in form and name to adhere to the crown. In consequence of this arrangement they enjoyed most of the benefits of actual independence, without exposing themselves to the risks that might eventually grow out of even a successful effort to obtain it. How long this precarious and as it were provisional state of things is likely to last, and under what circumstances it will probably be changed, are questions of considerable interest to the people of the United States; but they are too delicate, on several accounts, to be treated here in detail.

The republic of Hayti, without belonging precisely to the class of European colonies in America, seems to hold its independence by a somewhat doubtful tenure, (the price that is to be given for it being not yet paid,) and may be considered with propriety in the same section. Notwithstanding the very questionable character of the late transaction with France, (which does, however, quite as little honour to that powerful kingdom as to its ancient colony,) the example of Hayti has been upon the whole of a nature to encourage the expectations of the friends of humanity, in regard to the capacity of the black race, for self-government and the arts and habits of civilized life. It would be difficult indeed to assign any sufficient ground for the supposition of an essential inferiority in this branch of the human family, or in fact of any real inequality among the varieties of the species indicated by their differences of colour, form, or physical structure. If (which may well be doubted) such a prejudice has ever prevailed among enlightened men, it is probably rare at present, and may be expected to become continually more and more so. There are no facts, as far at least as I am acquainted with the subject, which authorise the conclusion that any one of the several varieties of our race is either intellectually or morally superior or inferior to the rest, and there are certainly enough that attest the contrary. Each great

division of the species has had in its turn the advantage
in civilization, that is in industry, wealth, and knowledge, and the power they confer; and during this period of conscious triumph, each has doubtless been inclined to regard itself as a favoured race, endowed by
nature and Providence with an essential superiority over
all the others. But on reviewing the course of history,
we find this accidental difference uniformly disappear-
ing after a while, and the sceptre of civilization passing
from the hands of the supposed superior race into those
of some other, before inferior, which claims in its turn,
for a while, a similar distinction. As respects the immediate question, it would seem from even a slight examination, that the blacks (whether of African or Asiatic
origin) have not only a fair right to be considered as naturally equal to men of any other colour, but are even not
without some plausible pretensions to a claim of superiority. At the present day they are doubtless, as far
as we have any knowledge of them, much inferior to
the whites, and have been so for several centuries; but
at more than one preceding period, they have been for
a length of time at the head of civilization and political
power, and must be regarded as the real authors of most
of the arts and sciences which give us at present the
advantage over them. While Greece and Rome were
yet barbarous, we find the light of learning and improvement emanating from this, by supposition, degraded and accursed continent of Africa, out of the midst of
this very woolly haired, flat nosed, thick lipped, coal
black race, which some persons are tempted to station
at a pretty low intermediate point between men and

monkies. It is to Egypt, if to any nation, that we must look as the real *antiqua mater* of the ancient and modern refinement of Europe. The colonies that civilized Greece, the founders of Argos, Athens, Delphi, and so forth, came from Egypt, and for centuries afterwards their descendants constantly returned to Egypt as the source and centre of civilization. There it was that the generous and stirring spirits of those days, Pythagoras, Homer, Solon, Herodotus, Plato, and the rest, made their noble journies of intellectual and moral discovery, as ours now make them in England, France, Germany, and Italy. The great lawgiver of the Jews was prepared for his divine mission by a course of instruction in all the wisdom of the Egyptians. But Egypt, as we know from Herodotus who travelled there, was peopled at that time by a black race with woolly hair;* and the historian adds in the same passage, that these physical qualities were also proper to so many other nations, that they hardly formed a distinction. It appears in fact, that the whole south of Asia and north of Africa were then possessed by a number of powerful, polished, and civilized communities of kindred origin, differing among themselves in some points of their outward conformation, but all black. Ethiopia, a country of which the history is almost entirely shrouded in the night of ages, and of which we know little or nothing, except that it must have been in its day a seat of high civilization and great power, probably the fountain of the improvement of Egypt and western Asia, was inha-

* Euterpe, sec. 104.

bited by blacks. It then comprehended the country on both sides of the Red Sea, whence the Ethiopians are said by Homer to be divided into two parts. The great Assyrian empires of Babylon and Nineveh, hardly less illustrious than Egypt in arts and arms, were founded by Ethiopian colonies, and peopled by blacks. Hence it was a doubtful question, at a time when the historical traditions of these countries had become a little obscure, whether the famous black Prince Memnon who served among the auxiliaries on the side of Troy, at the siege of that city by the Greeks, was a native of Babylon or Ethiopia proper, and he was claimed as a citizen in both these places. Strabo tells us that the whole of Assyria south of Mount Taurus, (including, besides Babylon and Nineveh, Phœnicia, Tyre, and all Arabia,) was inhabited by blacks; but there seems to have been some mixture of whites among them, for the Jews fall within this region, and the Arabs of the present day, although dark, can hardly be called black. These, like the Medes and Persians, who were also white, were probably colonies of the white Syrians, described by the same author as dwelling beyond Mount Taurus, which had emigrated to the south. But Palestine or Canaan, before its conquest by the Jews, is represented in Scripture, as well as other histories, as peopled by blacks, and hence it follows that Tyre and her colony Carthage, the most industrious, wealthy, and polished states of their time, were of this colour. In these swarthy regions were first promulgated the three religions which have exercised the strongest influence on the fortunes of the world, two of which we receive as divine revelations; and, as far as human agency was concerned in it, we must look to Egypt as the original fountain of our faith, which, though developed and completed in the new Testament, reposes on the basis of the old. This consideration alone should suffice with Christians to rescue the black race and the continent they inhabit, from any suspicion of inferiority. It appears, in short, that this race, from the period immediately following the deluge down to the conquest of Assyria and Egypt by the Persians, and the fall of Carthage, enjoyed a decided preponderance throughout the whole ancient western world. It is true, that after thus leading the march of civilization for about two thousand years in succession, maturing the profound and solid wisdom of Egypt, founding the splendid but transitory fabric of Greek refinement, and assisting at the first communication of our holy faith; after inventing and carrying to a high degree of perfection, almost all the arts and sciences of which we are now so proud; after covering the banks of the Ganges, the Euphrates, and the Nile with miracles of power and skill, which have not only never been surpassed or equalled, but of which at present we can hardly conceive the possibility ; after modelling their civil and political institutions with such a masterly insight into human nature, as to fix through them, probably for ever, the stamp of their peculiar genius on the social organization of the world ; after effecting all this, it is true that they finally began to fall before the rising greatness of their own accomplished and vigorous pupils, and have been, with the exception (if we choose to rank the Arabs among them) of one later period of passing triumph.

(which lasted, however, for six or seven centuries,) during which they adorned the close of their high career with the wild and brilliant glory of the Saracen ascendancy, and produced a third religion, which, however inferior to the others, is the purest, next to them, that has yet been published,—have been, I say, with this exception, declining ever since, until they sunk at last below the level of the whites, where they have remained, as far as we have any knowledge of their condition, for several centuries past. This inferiority is likely enough to continue, and it is perhaps as improbable (though not more so) that the black race will ever revive the wonders of Egypt and Babylon, as that Greece will rear Epaminondas again, or the bees of Hymettus cluster in our time, on the infant lips of another Plato. Nations and races, like individuals, have their day, and seldom have a second. The blacks had a long and glorious one; and after what they have been and done, it argues not so much a mistaken theory as sheer ignorance of the most notorious historical facts, to pretend that they are naturally inferior to the whites. It would seem, indeed, as I have hinted before, that if any race have a right to claim a sort of pre-eminence over others, on the fair and honourable ground of talents displayed, and benefits conferred, it is precisely this very one, which we take upon us, in the pride of a temporary superiority, to stamp with the brand of essential degradation. It is hardly necessary to add, that while the blacks were the leading race in civilization and political power, there was no prejudice among the whites against their colour. We find on the contrary, that the early Greeks regarded them as a superior variety of the species, not only in intellectual and moral qualities, but in outward appearance. " The Ethiopians," says Herodotus, " surpass all other men in longevity, stature, and personal beauty." The high estimation in which they were held for wisdom and virtue, is strikingly shown by the mythological fable current among the ancient Greeks, and repeatedly alluded to by Homer, which represented the Gods as going annually in a body to make a long visit to the Ethiopians. Their absence upon this excursion is the reason given by Thetis to her son Achilles, in the first book of the Iliad, for not laying his complaints at once before the highest authority. " Jupiter," she tells him, " set off yesterday attended by all the Gods, on a journey towards the ocean, to feast with the excellent Ethiopians, and is not expected back at Olympus till the twelfth day." This was an honour which does not appear to have been bestowed upon any other nation. The epithet *barbarous*, which was frequently applied by the Greeks to foreigners in general, and which in our modern languages has an offensive signification, does not appear to have been used by them as a term of reproach. It may possibly have acquired that character at a later period, when the Greeks were really superior to all their neighbours; but the word seems to have been in the first instance a proper name, borrowed from some foreign, probably African dialect. It is still retained as the name of the north of Africa and its inhabitants, and may have been common at this remote period to the whole black race.*

Notwithstanding the present general inferiority of the Africans, we find even now, that the high intellectual spirit that once flashed out so finely in their sunburnt climates is not yet wholly quenched. Major Denham, in his late volume of travels, has presented us with several specimens of contemporary African poetry, which are hardly inferior to the sweet and lofty strains

---

* *Barbary* is a proper name for the north of Africa; and *Berebber* or *Barbar* for one of the distinct races that inhabit it, and are scattered thinly over its whole extent, from its eastern to its western extremity. It is conjectured by some competent judges, that they composed the original population of this region before its conquest by the Saracens. (See *Quarterly Review for March*, 1826, p. 520.) In the curious geographical memoir by the Sultan of Bello, inserted in the appendix to Major Denham's travels, it is stated that the Barbar formerly reigned in Syria. It would thus seem that at some remote period this name, according to the tradition of these countries, was common to the whole or a great part of the population of the southwest of Asia and north of Africa, which included nearly all the foreign nations known to the Greeks. The period indicated, is also the one in which the Greeks habitually employed the same term, to express foreign nations in general. A coincidence of this kind could not well be accidental, and there is, therefore, little doubt that the Greek word βάϱβαϱος is no other than the proper name Barbar. The etymology of this word has considerably engaged the attention of the learned. (*See North American Review*, Vol IV, p. 155.) As the explanation given above appears not only satisfactory but somewhat obvious, it is rather singular that it should not have been offered before.

of the ancient Monarch Minstrel. The dirge of the Fezzaneers in honour of their chief Boo-Khaloom will bear a comparison with the lamentation of David over Saul and Jonathan. " Give him songs ! give him music ! what words can equal his praise? *His heart was as large as the desert!* The overflowings of his coffers were like streams from the udder of the camel, bringing health and refreshment to all about him." An extempore love song, of which the major has inserted a translation, unites the tenderness and purity of the Canticles with something of the delicacy of imagery that distinguishes the poetry of Moore. The triumphal ode of the Sheik of Bornou, written by himself, upon his return from a victorious expedition against the Begharmies, is still more remarkable, and may fairly be considered as poetry of the first order. If such a thing were to be produced by one of the reigning sovereigns of Europe at the present day, we should not hear the last of it for twenty years. All these are the productions of Arabs, who seem to have had from the beginning a more poetical spirit than the other kindred races, though anciently inferior to some of them in most branches of art and science. Of the actual state of the negro nations that inhabit the interior of Africa, we knew little or nothing, until the late travels of Major Denham ; excepting that we civilized Christians had purchased and made slaves of a considerable number of persons belonging to them, and that these persons thus kidnapped and reduced to slavery, appeared to us who did not understand their languages, and could not of course converse with them, as a degraded and stupid race of men, incapable of writing epic poems, commanding armies, enlarging the limits of science, or superintending the government of a country. It is needless to add, that this reasoning proved the stupidity and degradation of those who thought it satisfactory, and not of the Africans. Major Denham and his enterprising companions have finally given us a glimpse of a part of the interior of this great continent. What new discoveries may be made in the immense region, that stretches from the lake Chad to the Cape of Good Hope, and which includes the ancient Ethiopia, once the most civilized part of Africa, we shall see hereafter. If it shall appear, as it probably will, that none of the black nations are now on a level with the civilization of Europe, the fact will of course prove nothing against their ancient attainments, or natural capacity for improvement. In stating these considerations in favour of what seems to be a just and humane view of this question, I would not be understood to intimate the opinion that the blacks are destined to recover, in America, the moral or political superiority over the whites, which they once maintained in the old world, or even to rival them in the arts of life. Their relative position is too unfavourable. The most that can reasonably be expected of them is, that when thrown by circumstances into the form of independent nations, they will show themselves capable of self government, and of profiting by the lessons and example of their neighbours.

It has sometimes been thought, that the vicinity of one or more independent black states would be dangerous to the internal tranquillity of our country; but the

experience of more than twenty years in the case of the
republic of Hayti, affords a practical refutation of this
opinion. There are even some positive advantages attending this circumstance, of no small consequence. A
flourishing and prosperous community of this description, would naturally attract from amongst us the free
blacks, who are found in the slave-holding states to be
troublesome members of society, and who would thus
obtain abroad an open and inviting field of action. A
natural drain of this kind would remove these persons
from our territory much more rapidly and effectually
than the laborious and expensive efforts of the Colonization Society, which, however well meant, can hardly
produce any important results, counteracted as they are
by all the motives that ordinarily affect the human mind.
The society invites the free blacks to quit a country
where they are comfortably situated, and emigrate to
another, where they are to encounter great hardships,
with no certain prospects for the future. It is obvious that
this must be from first to last a forced proceeding; and
the least difficulty about it, (though this is not a small
one,) is, that the society is under the necessity of defray-
ing all the expenses of this unnatural emigration. In the
other case, the emigration, being voluntary and spontaneous, would of course be executed at the expense of
the emigrants; and being the effect of powerful motives
operating in the ordinary way, might be expected to be
rapid and extensive. How far the abovementioned society is likely to accomplish the farther object of remov-
ing the slave population itself from our soil, is with me
a still more doubtful question, than that of its success with

the free blacks. When we consider the natural increase that takes place among the slaves, amounting to not less than thirty or forty thousand a year, and that the society have not yet made arrangements for transporting annually to Africa more than three or four hundred persons, it is easy at least to see, that their arrangements must be very much extended before they will even begin to approach the accomplishment of their purpose. Add to this, that a moderate and regular emigration has in general little or no tendency to diminish the population of a country, and the case will be found to be still more desperate. Finally, it may be questioned whether we ought to wish to remove from amongst us, if we could do it peaceably and easy, so large a portion of the working class. The political condition of the blacks is certainly far from being what we could wish it; but such as they are, they are nevertheless industrious and useful labourers, and the southern states would, I apprehend, suffer not a little from the loss of them. The expulsion of the Moors from Spain, and of the Protestants from France, for reasons not unlike those which are now urged for the removal of the blacks, have been commonly considered as among the most impolitic measures that ever were adopted, and a similar result obtained by a special operation *ad hoc* on the minds of the blacks, would be just as impolitic, though somewhat less violent and odious. It is needless, however, to argue against the policy of a scheme, of which the accomplishment is obviously and physically impossible. Our duty, as respects the blacks, appears to be in the first place, to make them as happy as we can in their present condition, and then to employ such means as may be most expedient for raising them by a slow and gradual process to a higher one. Of these means, one of the most important is to discourage in every possible way, the idea that any thing can be effected immediately and at once; and the Colonization Society, however respectable from the high character of its members and the purity of their intentions, produces thus far a great positive evil, inasmuch as it keeps up in the public mind an impression, that the situation of the slaves can be violently and suddenly altered for the better, by this expedient of emigration. This opinion engenders a morbid and mistaken sentiment in regard to the whole subject. Mr. King's proposition in the senate is liable to the same objection. In this as in every other project for political improvement, we must assume and build upon the existing state of things. Improve the character of the blacks, and emancipation will come in due time without an effort; whereas, by a premature zeal for formal emancipation, you destroy the possibility of improvement, and thereby defeat your own object. The society may perhaps effect some good by founding a colony on the coast of Africa, although even in this particular its efforts are liable to the same objection, which is made habitually with so much justice to those of our missionary institutions, that they employ upon a distant and uncertain object, a part of the time, funds, and good will of the public, for the whole of which there is ample occupation at home. While, therefore, we express our sincere admiration of the honest zeal and generous philanthropy of the members of this body, we may be allowed to wish that these most estimable qualities may receive a different direction, and be devoted to some of the numerous objects of great and undoubted utility, which our country offers in such abundance.

CHAPTER VII.

Foreign Policy of the two Americas.

In the first chapter of this essay, I described in a summary way the position of the American continent in the general political system of Christendom, and represented this system as consisting of three great divisions, the continent of Europe with its dependencies, the British empire, and our western hemisphere. I remarked that each of these divisions was organized and held together by a distinct political principle; that this principle was on the continent of Europe that of arbitrary government or legitimacy, in America that of popular government or liberty, and that the British empire, standing politically as well as geographically at a middle point between the two continents, was to a certain extent under the influence of both these principles, but that the present leaning, both of the government and the people, was in favour of liberty. I also stated very briefly, the manner in which the internal policy of the several sections of the system was affected by the operation of the principles, that respectively prevail in each; and remarked, that the effect of arbitrary government on the continent of Europe, was to discourage the industry of the people, and to produce a sort of torpor and stagnation in the body politic; that the opposite principle, which governs with us, was also attended with an opposite effect, and led to a universal activity and consequent prosperity throughout the country; and finally that England, as might be expected from her situation, enjoyed some of the advantages of the liberal principle, and experienced some of the inconveniences of the arbitrary one; and was also exposed, more than either of the others, to the peculiar evil of a constant and standing collision of opposite parties. I shall now proceed to make a few remarks, in the brief and cursory manner that suits the plan of the present essay, upon the mutual relations of these great divisions of the political system, and more immediately upon the policy of our section of it as respects the others. The same principles which constitute these divisions, and determine in a great degree their internal situation, will also be found to exercise a strong influence upon the character of the relations that exist between them. I shall first inquire what these relations are, as they actually exist at present, and then consider the causes that have produced them, and the modifications they may probably undergo in future.

The existing relation between the continent of America and that of Europe, (considering the latter as represented by the holy alliance,) is that of hostility actual in some parts and only virtual in others, but real and effective in all. Between the kingdom of Spain and the Spanish American nations, formerly her colonies, there has long been and is likely to be for a length of time to come, a state of declared and open war; and although all the foreign powers, European and American, have professed and in fact observed a fair neutrality between the belligerent parties, as regards any immediate participation in the contest, they have all exhibited, as far as they could consistently with such a position, their sentiments in regard to the points at issue, and have all attached themselves as it were, by community of principle and sympathy of feeling, to one or the other cause. This war forms, for the time being, the great question in general politics, and the inclination manifested by the different powers, in regard to it, determines their relations to each other and their position in the common political system. The United States (the only American nation not actually engaged in the war) evinced, by their early recognition of the independence of the Spanish American states, a disposition to take a favourable view of their principles and policy. This disposition was indeed openly professed in the declaration of President Monroe, that he should consider the interference of any other government in favour of Spain as an act unfriendly to us. The continental powers of Europe, on the other hand, have exhibited and continue to exhibit, as far as they can do it, consistently with the observation of a formal neutrality, a strong sympathy with the other party. Their advice, encouragement, and flattering prognostics in regard to the future, have no doubt done much to induce Spain to continue the war; and they would probably have assisted her with their military and naval forces, or in other words have engaged in the contest, on her side, had they not been aware, that, in that case, the United States and Great Britain would have taken part actively with the Americans. Even France, the only great continental power which pretends to a position partially independent of the alliance, and which has appeared in fact to exhibit, on this question, occasional symptoms of a divergent policy, has nevertheless in the main pursued the same line of conduct. The present ministers are somewhat irresolute, and if left entirely to themselves, would perhaps adopt another course; but the violent section of the royalists professes, without wavering, the faith of the holy alliance upon this subject, and completely neutralizes the better spirit of the cabinet. It appears, therefore, that the whole continent of America is enlisted either actively or virtually, on the side of the Spanish American states, in this momentous struggle, and in the same way the whole continent of Europe on the side of Spain. The existing relation between the two continents, is, therefore, as I stated above, that of real and effective hostility.

It is evident that a contest of this prodigious magnitude, involving so many different nations and such immense interests, extending over so vast a theatre, shaking the christian world, as it were, from Kamschatka to Cape Horn, and determining for a time the political situation of all its members, cannot well be owing to merely accidental and transitory circumstances of trifling moment, but must be the result of causes certainly powerful, and probably of permanent and essential interest. And we find in fact, upon examining the nature of these causes, that they resolve themselves (as was justly remarked by President Monroe, in the message above quoted) into the opposition that exists between the principles of government, that respectively prevail in the two great divisions of the Christian system, and have been already so often alluded to in the present work. The Spanish Americans are contending for independence and liberty, and the United States sympathize with them, because they have not long since passed through a similar struggle, by means of which they acquired and are now enjoying those great blessings. The continental powers of Europe sympathize with Spain, because their governments are all organized on arbitrary principles, and because they are naturally led, by this state of things, to disapprove the extension of liberal principles in any part of the world, and to apprehend the reaction of such extension upon their own subjects at home. In taking these different views of the subject, the two parties are no doubt equally honest, and both express their respective sentiments without disguise or scruple. But as there is now hardly an individual in the United States, who entertains on this subject the opinions of the holy alliance, the forms in which they are commonly advanced may not perhaps be familiar to the American public, and a simple statement of this, in the language of a believer, while it gives a more distinct notion of this mysterious creed, may possess in some degree the merit of novelty. The following article upon the subject is extracted from one of the leading ultra newspapers of Paris, which happened to fall into my hands at the moment of writing these pages. While it explains the opinions of the holy alliance on this subject, it may also serve to show how fully they are embraced by the fanatical party in France.

" It has been remarked in France," says a writer in the Quotidienne, " that *the people* have sent in their resignation; and it may now, perhaps, be added with propriety, that the liberal opposition have become emigrants. Tired of attacking in vain the thrones of Europe, they have set sail for the other hemisphere; where they are now contesting with the descendants of the commanders of Cortes and Pizarro, the claims of the latter to the territory conquered by their ancestors. From the summit of the Andes, liberalism is now proclaiming the rights of man and the sovereignty of the people, and having established republican governments in certain half savage communities, presents the work of her hands to the civilized nations of the world, as the perfection of wisdom.

" The same arguments have been urged in defence of the insurgents of America, which had previously been employed to justify the revolutionists of Europe. It was not, say their advocates, the ambition and turbulence of a few persons, but the irresistible force of circumstances, which occasioned these sanguinary struggles. A strange mode of reasoning this, no doubt, and one which, if admitted, would justify as well every species of excess. The colonies have also been compared to individual men, who are subject in their infancy to many restrictions, from which at a riper age they are exempt. It would be easy to show that this argument is also wholly inconclusive, and that what is true of the individual is far from being in every case true of the species. But waving this objection, we would willingly learn what these communities, infant or mature, have gained by changing their government, and whether they have not, on the contrary, lost every thing, by falling under the authority of a few aspiring leaders."

" It will perhaps be urged, that Spain had no other claim to America but the right of conquest, which now belongs to the insurgents; and this mode of treating the question would not be wholly destitute of plausibility, if the present possessors of the country were the native Americans, rising in rebellion against their old conquerors. But we all know, that instead of this being the case, the native Americans have taken no part in the insurrection, and that they are now fatigued with the war, and anxious for the return of the mild and peaceful government of Spain. Bolivar, Santander, Sucre, Bermudez, Montilla, Paez, and the rest of the republican chiefs, are either Spaniards or of Spanish descent. A singular sort of *patriots* these, by the bye, who renounce their native land and the blood that flows in their veins. But as respects the right of Spain to America, it does not here come in question, because, as we have said, it is not the natives who make the war. We are fully satisfied that they are all anxious for the restoration of the paternal government of the Viceroys, which they found much preferable to that of the modern dictators. It is natural in fact, that the Americans should be opposed to the new systems, considering the distracted situation in which they have placed the country. The cities have lost their splendour, the precious metals are monopolized by foreigners; European vessels rarely approach these shores, now infested by pirates, and where their cargoes are in danger; the port of Acapulco, formerly so much frequented, is now abandoned by all, except perhaps a few Englishmen. The population of Mexico, Carthagena, Caraccas, and Lima, is reduced a third; and such is the poverty of the new governments, that Colombia, the famous mother republic, has no means of paying the interest on her debt.

" It is thought by some that the independence of the Spanish colonies would be favourable to the maritime powers of Europe, inasmuch as it would open a new market for their products. But the experience of England proves the incorrectness of this opinion, however certain it may appear at first view. The British were the first to recognize the new republics, entered into contracts with them for exploring the mines, and obtained the concession of commercial privileges of great value. But notwithstanding these advantages, their commerce has been ruined in America, and it would not be singular, if they should now declare war against Bolivar. *There is little doubt in fact that they excited the insurrection of Gen. Paez, in order to chastise the government of Santa Fe for concluding a treaty of commerce with the United States.* Be that, however, as it may, England has evidently ruined instead of enriching herself, by monopolizing the commerce of Spanish America.

" It is added, that the Spanish American colonies are twenty times as extensive, in point of territory, as the mother country, and that their population is greater. If this be an objection, it might be urged with still more force against Great Britain, since the whole number of the inhabitants of the three kingdoms does not exceed twenty millions, and the colonies in India contain more

than a hundred. But it would be idle to attempt to reason with the liberalists on the subject of political economy. We all know that they are ready to sacrifice
every thing to their system, even the commercial prosperity of the nation, which they affect to admire so much.
Such is their stupid blindness, that they cannot foresee
that their doctrines tend directly to give to England a
monopoly of the commerce of the world. They are sworn
enemies to the industry of France, because they will
make no compromise with what they call their principles; but like idolatrous savages would immolate human
victims, if necessary, at the foot of the statue of liberty.
It is true that their doctrines have ceased to be popular,
but unhappily their threats and their sophistry are still
not without some influence on *the cabinets of Europe;*
which are not yet satisfied that the revolution, although
it has taken refuge on the other side of the Atlantic, is
a whit less dangerous to the old world, than if it had
remained there. Fortunately the American nations are
beginning to be weary of the anarchy which has been
given them in exchange, and are becoming impatient of
the yoke of the revolutionary chiefs. Colombia, of
whose power and perseverance we have heard so much,
is on the eve of civil war, and her coasts are menaced by
a squadron fitted out from that very island of Cuba, so
lately the destined object of invasion. Peru, which was
lost by treason, is shaking off the yoke; at least it is re-
ported in Europe, that Ferdinand VII. was declared in
that viceroyalty, immediately after the departure of
Bolivar for Panama; and this commander, instead of
presiding at the congress, will be obliged to carry on the

war in the province of Caraccas, which detests his authority, and which will probably very soon return to the government of the lawful sovereign.

"Thus there is a visible tendency in the communities of both the old and new worlds to work out their own salvation by themselves. It has perhaps been decreed by Providence, that the cause of legitimacy should never triumph, by its own power; that revolution should labour for counter-revolution; *rebellion be the principal support of lawful authority;* and that these are the appropriate means ordained by the Supreme Being for the welfare of kings and nations!!"

This will be found, I think, by the American public, rather an amusing specimen of *legitimate* politics. That the British government excited the insurrection of Paez, and will probably declare war against Bolivar; that the opening of new markets is not an encouragement to industry, and that rebellion is the natural support of lawful authority, are propositions, which are no doubt received as articles of faith by the adherents of the holy alliance, for they are certainly not much countenanced by merely human reason. Remark, too, the admirable consistency of the two first sentences in the last paragraph, and at the same time the highly flattering idea which they hold up of what is here called legitimacy. There is, it seems, a visible tendency in the communities of the old and new world to work out their own salvation. Good; but what next? It has been decreed by Providence, that legitimacy is never to triumph by its own power; or in other words, is never to work out its own salvation. The natural, or as it is here described

providential action of communities, and that of legitimacy, are, therefore, essentially different; and as the
former is the only correct description that can be given
of law and government, it follows that legitimacy is here
represented as opposed to law, that is, is illegitimate.
The word, as here misused, seems to mean a few reigning families. But what is this natural action which communities exercise, and which these supposed legitimates
cannot perform? That of working out their own salvation. The communities of the old and new world are,
therefore, lusty fellows, that know how to help themselves, while legitimacy is an overgrown changeling,
who must have his food put into his mouth. Legitimacy
has certainly great reason to be obliged to the *Quotidienne* for the compliment. Finally, what is this salvation which the communities are to work out? It consists
in divesting themselves of all political power, and en-
trusting it to this very helpless legitimacy, who is incapable, by the supposition, of exercising it. Such is the
sublime philosophy of the modern European doctors, in
the science of government. How poor to this the theory of liberty! how flat and unprofitable the reveries
of the Lockes, the Burkes, the Montesquieus, and the
Ciceros!

The leading French ministerial paper, which, like
the ministry it represents, has occasionally vacillated in
regard to the American question, and has published
some articles favourable to the independence of the new
states, contained, about the same time when the above
extract appeared in the *Quotidienne,* a short paragraph
which may also be cited as a sort of curiosity. It is

introduced, by a pretty indirection, with some remarks upon the weather and the season.

"The heat and dryness of the season," says the Etoile, " have excited apprehensions respecting the harvest, and at all events, the situation of England will be very critical during the next winter. It is easy to foresee that the severity of the weather will bring on troubles in the manufacturing districts, for it must necessarily be a long time before the industry of that country shall have recovered from the late shock. The radicals are as busy as ever, in reforming the government, and they have now the advantage, which they did not enjoy before, of finding a great number of popular harangues ready made to their hands, by the ministry, and especially Mr. Canning. They have but to alter a few names and phrases, such as Colombia or Spain into England, Cortes into radical provisional government, and Bolivar into Hunt, and these speeches will suit their meridian to a hair. Then they have only to found in some corner of Lancashire, a snug little government *de facto,* which Mr. Canning has instructed them to distinguish, with all the necessary precision, from one *de jure,* and they may then make war without scruple, and borrow money at pleasure from their friends on the continent, taking care of course, like their comrades in America, never to pay their debts."

What profound policy, and what fine pleasantry to season it! How ridiculous the position of poor Mr. Canning, detected by the *Quotidienne* in stirring up the insurrection of Paez, and declaring war (unbeknown to the public) against Bolivar, and now laughed at by the

Etoile, for playing into the hands of the radicals, and, notwithstanding his intrigue with Paez, making speeches in favour of this same Bolivar and the South American cause! How just the triumph of these more than Machiavelian wits over unhappy England, cursed with a new market for her products of more than sixteen million souls, and crushed to the earth by the wealth of the American mines! It must be owned that the logic and the humour of these writers are quite upon a par. It has hitherto been held, that those should laugh who win, and on this principle, the continental *graciosos* should have waited till they had beaten the other party, before they began to make merry at his expense. But they rather choose to imitate the non-combatant in Moliere, who returned good reasons for hard knocks. *Il me donna quelques coups de baton, mais je lui dis bien son fait.*

To treat this matter a little more seriously, the two articles quoted above, which express the sentiments of the two sections of the royalist party in France, the only country where there has been any prospect of the adoption of a distinct policy in regard to America, prove how completely the whole continent sympathizes with Spain. When I say that these articles express the sentiments and indicate the policy of the continent, I do not of course mean to be understood, that all the statesmen of the holy alliance would countenance, in all its details, the wretched sophistry of these paragraphs, which are, however, extracted from the most accredited journals. There are no doubt wiser heads in the committee at Paris and the cabinets of Petersburgh, Berlin, and Vi-

enna, than these editors, although the latter seem to
think almost as meanly of the cabinets of Europe as
they do of the patriots of America. The system of the
allies, as understood and explained by their most judicious partisans, reposes on a single principle, which is
also briefly stated in one of the above extracts. *The
cabinets of Europe,* says the Quotidienne, *are not yet
satisfied, that the revolution, although it has taken refuge on the other side of the Atlantic, is a whit less
dangerous to the old world, than if it had remained
there.* This is a rhetorical manner of saying that the
revolution is not less dangerous now than it was before,
and that the cabinets have not done what, in the opinion
of this writer, they should have done upon this supposition. This principle, therefore, of the supposed danger to which the monarchies of Europe are exposed, in
consequence of the success of so many revolutions, and
the establishment of so many republics in the new world,
is, at present, the basis of the continental system, in regard to our continent. It may be worth while to examine very briefly, how far their apprehensions are well
founded, and what would be the best measures which
the continental powers could adopt, in order to escape
from the danger, such as it is.

If several neighbouring nations, being in close communication with each other, were constituted and governed nearly in the same manner; and if certain abuses,
common to them all, had been remedied in one by a recurrence to the desperate expedient of a revolution, it
is easy to conceive, that the governments of the rest
would be alarmed, and not without reason. Then would

there be a real danger, on the common principle, that similar causes naturally produce similar effects, and that successful examples are the most powerful stimulants that can be employed, for bringing moral causes into action. In any other case the danger would be wholly imaginary. To suppose that the quiet of the established governments of Europe is threatened by the occurrence in a remote quarter of the globe, of revolutions in the state of communities differently situated, resulting from causes which could not by possibility exist in the old world, would argue a very keen sensibility on the subject of revolution in general, and perhaps a consciousness that there was something wrong at home. The direct and immediate object of all the revolutions that have taken place in America, is *independence of Europe.* What has this to do with the reform of any abuses that may be found or imagined in the governments of that part of Christendom? That Russia, for example, should be alarmed about her own tranquillity, because the colonies of Spain have shaken off the yoke, is about as reasonable as it would be for the United States to feel uneasy, because the Sultan of Turkey has suppressed the Janissaries, and introduced the obnoxious *nizam-jedid,* or to consider that their interest was involved in the question, whether the inquisition shall or shall not be revived in Spain. Where the situation of two countries is wholly dissimilar, when there is no pretext that the abuses reformed in one by revolution exist in the other, it is evident, that there is no reasonable ground for apprehension ; and this is precisely the case with the continental monarchies of Europe and the new governments of America. The establishment of them is no doubt the result of revolution, but it is of such a revolution as cannot possibly occur in the monarchies of Europe; for the plain and simple reason, that they are not colonies but independent nations. The only European nations, which might reasonably be expected to feel any alarm upon the subject, are those which possess colonies. These might very fairly consider as dangerous, the example of other colonies throwing off their allegiance to the mother country. It so happens, however, by a rather singular coincidence, that the only two European nations, now possessing colonies of any importance, viz. England and Holland, are precisely those which have exhibited the least apprehension upon this occasion, and have taken the lead in acknowledging the independence of the Spanish American states.

It may be said, however, that these new governments have all adopted republican institutions, and that the existence of so many republics, even in a distant quarter of the globe, threatens the stability of the monarchies of Europe. This is in fact the only account, at all consistent with common sense, that can be given of the supposed danger; but even this will not be found in reality much more plausible than the other. The continental governments of Europe either are or are not suited to the condition of the societies they respectively represent. If they be, they have all the security against revolution that any government can possess, and it would show a very great want of political sagacity, and a very pusillanimous temper, to apprehend any thing from the existence of other governments, established in other communities, differently situated, and a thousand leagues off. If they be not, if they in fact require reform, then they are no doubt in a critical position, and any movement, that may happen abroad or at home, is fraught with peril: but the source of the danger is the existence of the abuses, and not the example of the reform in another country. It is, therefore, not less certain than it is singular, that if we allow these governments the credit for sagacity and worldly wisdom, to which they are perhaps fairly entitled, and suppose them of course not to be ignorant of truths so obvious as these I have just stated, this alarm, which they are all so loud and eager in professing, about the existence of republican and liberal constitutions abroad, is neither more nor less than an *open confession*, that such constitutions would not be wholly out of place, on the continent of Europe. If such a person as Prince Metternich, for example, a statesman of great experience and talent, really believes, as we have reason to think he does, that the internal peace of the empire of Austria is endangered by the existence of republican governments in the United States, and in South America, it must be because he knows that the government of that empire, (though it could not be probably changed all at once to one of a republican form,) would admit of great improvement. Thus the very alarm that is now kept up, by the continental statesmen, respecting the existence of revolution and republicanism abroad, amounts to an indirect satire on their own policy, and a defence of the very proceedings and principles they mean to attack.

Thus far, however, the danger is no doubt real, and as long as the continental statesmen neglect and refuse to introduce in the empires they respectively govern, such political improvements as the condition of the people really requires, so long will the introduction of such improvements, in other countries, make it more difficult for them to sustain their present institutions. To this extent, the hostile position in which the continent of Europe is disposed to place itself, towards the new world, is, perhaps, the natural result of the existing state of things. The question still remains, however, whether the declaration of war, which the powers have openly or virtually made against the young republics of North and South America, was for them the true course. I am inclined to think that their policy, in regard to this subject, will be found to be nearly as questionable as their principles.

If a wise statesman felt that the government he was called to administer, required improvement, and that the necessary changes were recommended to the people by the example of other nations, he would no doubt make it his business to introduce them, as soon as possible, and would thus remove at once all uneasiness upon the subject. If a government were unwise enough to determine not to take this course, the next most plausible one would be to remove the dangerous example, that is, to counteract by violence, the attempts, which other nations might be making, to improve their institutions. This latter policy is completely Machiavelian in its character; it laughs at every thing like natural law and justice; but when it can be carried into effect, would no doubt, for the moment, answer the purpose. We have seen it in fact adopted with success, by the Austrian government, in the cases of Naples and Sardinia; and by France (under the instigation of the allies) in that of Spain. But to this reckless and unprincipled course of proceeding, success is essential; and to fail in attempting it, would make matters much worse than they were before. Here therefore, as it seems to me, lies the great political error of the arbitrary governments. Blinded as they are, no doubt, by prejudice, passion, and supposed interest, they can hardly be so blind as to imagine, that the continent of America can be brought back again, by a *coup-de-main*, to its ancient dependence upon Europe. Since the public declaration of England and the United States, they cannot but know that this is impossible. But in this case, every thing depends upon the probability, or rather certainty, of effecting the object by a *coup-de-main*. To engage with a country in a state of revolution in a war, of which the result is doubtful, and which will be necessarily tedious and difficult, instead of diminishing the danger, only renders it ten times greater and more pressing. It answered very well for the Austrian government to make war upon Naples and Sardinia, for changing their constitutions, because they had a moral certainty that they could, in each case, effect a counter-revolution in a single campaign. But does Prince Metternich, or Count Nesselrode, or any of their counsellors, believe that the same result can be obtained in Spanish America? Surely not. Why then Identify themselves with the cause of Spain, and by encouraging her to continue the contest, keep the attention of the world at large, and of their own subjects in particular, continually alive to the affairs of our western continent? While the war goes on in America; while it forms the pivot, upon which the general politics of Christendom are made to turn; while the marches, battles by sea and land, military and political mavœuvres, revolutions, constitutions, and congresses, which successively grow out of it, constitute the most interesting series of publications any where occurring, it is certain that all the active and stirring spirits in Europe will keep their eyes fixed upon the scene. Is this what the continental statesmen would naturally wish? If they will not remove the abuse in their own governments, and cannot remove the example of reform, the only remaining course which prudence recommends, would be to keep the latter out of sight. Instead of encouraging Spain to persevere in the war, they should rather persuade her to finish it as soon as possible. The American republics would then be quietly occupied, in the arrangement of their internal affairs; and the spectacle of durable and constantly progressive but noiseless prosperity, which we may reasonably hope they would all then present, would be much less likely to exercise a contagious influence on the fiery spirits of Europe, than the brilliant exhibition of political and military enterprise, which we are now witnessing, and shall continue to witness, till the end of the struggle, should it last half a century. It is the process of revolution, and not the quiet operation of republican governments, which is likely to excite imitation. A hundred aspir-

ing young men will be wrought up into a sort of passion, by the example of Bolivar, who would not even
think of reading through, from one end to the other, the
ablest state paper that could be written. The trophies
of Miltiades, as we are told in ancient history, would
not let Themistocles sleep o' nights; but many a true
patriot has found himself dozing, even in the day time,
over long financial and political reports and documents,
however important. And it is not the perusal of such
papers, or in general the silent study of the march of
established governments of any form, that tends to create a revolutionary fever at home or abroad. To favour
rather than discourage the conclusion of the present war
in America, would therefore have been the true policy
of the continental statesmen of Europe.

Their course, however, such as it is, was recommended
by the party feelings and habitual modes of thinking,
which prevail among them, and which are much more
universally followed as motives to action, than distant
views of general policy. It is therefore not to be won-
dered at, however much it is to be regretted, that they
should have yielded to considerations, which in most
similar cases are apt to govern. It can hardly be doubted, in fact, that they have exhibited what they think a
high degree of moderation and prudence, in not engaging openly in the war on the side of Spain. There is
little doubt that they would have gone to this length,
immediately after the occupation of that country by
France, had not the successive public declaration of the
United States and of England, given them to understand
that they would in that case have other enemies to con-

tend with, beside the new Spanish American states. The message of President Monroe, in which he signified the intentions of the United States, on this subject, excited a strong sensation throughout Europe; and if it did not entirely change the determination of the continental powers, induced them at least not to precipitate matters, and to proceed with great deliberation, in a course of policy which was likely to affect so essentially the aspect of political affairs. Whether the knowledge they had then obtained of the views of the United States, would of itself have ultimately defeated their projects, is perhaps uncertain; and the issue probably depended in a great measure on the part that should be taken by England. Could the continental powers have persuaded England to make common cause with them, in a crusade against the Spanish American governments, the apprehension of offending the United States might not perhaps have deterred them from engaging in the enterprise. They might even at bottom have felt a secret complacency, in the idea of involving the liberal institutions of the whole continent in one common ruin, and might not have realized, until they had ascertained by experience, the desperate character of the attempt. There is even reason to suppose, that some of the continental statesmen, endowed with rather more zeal than discretion, made at this time indirect overtures to the British government to co-operate against South America, and proposed, should the United States make themselves troublesome, to assist in reducing them again to their old condition of British colonies. But this was a policy, which no British statesman would have dreamed for a moment of adopting. The experience they had acquired during the late three years' war, had completely rectified their errors upon this subject, and dispelled some lingering dreams of future conquest, that perhaps until that period may have flattered the hopes of a few old fashioned tories. Even Lord Castlereagh was much too reasonable for this; but whether, if he had remained at the head of affairs, the British ministry would have declared so early, in a public manner, against the interference of the continent, and have followed up the declaration so promptly by a recognition of the independence of the new states, is, as I have stated in a former chapter, something more than doubtful. By a sort of accident, that may almost be considered providential, a ministerial revolution took place just at this critical moment, a moment when the fortunes of the Christian world, for centuries to come, depended, in a great measure, on the decision of the British cabinet, and this revolution was in favour of the cause of liberty and America. It brought into power a minister less committed to the continental allies by the previous policy of the government, more liberal and popular in his sentiments, and better fitted, by his independence and superiority of talent, to enter on a new and bolder course of action than Lord Castlereagh. The immediate consequence was a decided adhesion, by the British government, to the cause of Spanish America, and a participation in the contest, as far as it could possibly be carried, consistently with the fair observance of a formal neutrality. This additional weight turned the scale at once, with the continental powers, against the project of open interference, which till then they had probably not abandoned. It ought, as I have shown above, on every consideration of regard for their own interest or for that of Spain, to have induced them to use all their influence with the latter power, in favour of immediate peace. Instead of that, they unfortunately preferred the policy of encouraging Spain to continue the war, although they could not venture to assist her in it, and thus made this ill-starred kingdom the victim of their inveterate prejudices and empty terrors.

These considerations bring me to the other great point, in the international relations of the principal powers of the Christian world, and in the foreign policy of America, which is the position of the British empire as respects the two continents. It follows, from what has been remarked above, that this empire is now placed in a friendly attitude towards America, and in a hostile one towards the continent of Europe. The declaration in favour of the Spanish colonies, and the subsequent acknowledgment of their independence, produced a feeling of disgust and indignation in the cabinet of Spain, and in those of the principal continental powers, which was only prevented by the most imperious prudential considerations, from breaking out into open war. The dissatisfaction created by these measures was infinitely greater than that which was occasioned in the same quarters, by the similar previous proceedings on the part of the United States. The latter were so obviously the natural, we may say necessary, results of our geographical and political situation, that the public mind was every where prepared for them; and that they excited no surprise, and comparatively but little discontent, in the governments more immediately interested. England, on the other hand, was regarded as a sort of apostate from the common cause. She had been fighting the battles of counter-revolution, by the side of the continental powers, for thirty years; and all at once, in a quarrel which appeared to them to be only a continuance of the same long struggle, (as to a certain extent it in fact was,) they found her suddenly deserting their standard, and then, with hardly a perceptible interval, taking the field among the auxiliaries of the revolutionary party. It cannot be denied, that there was a good deal of inconsistency in these proceedings, on the part of England, and it probably appeared even greater than it was, to her old continental friends, whose habitual modes of thinking prevented them from realizing the powerful considerations, which recommended to the British government a new political course, while circumstances were nearly the same as before. The disappointment felt by these powers at seeing their projects defeated, was thus aggravated by the strong disgust, which an act of apostacy from selfish motives, real or supposed, uniformly and very naturally excites; and the feeling of reciprocal ill-will, which has ever since existed between the British cabinet and the other principal European governments, is perhaps as cordial as any one of the kind, that was ever masked under the outward form of alliance and friendship. The same proceedings produced of course a deep sensation of gratitude in the new American governments, and of approbation in the government and people of the United

States; who thus found the policy, in which they had led the way, sanctioned and sustained by the imitation of England, and the eventual danger, to which it might have exposed them, completely removed, by this imposing authority in their favour. In this way the existing political system was completed, in all its different parts; the independence of the Spanish colonies finally assured; the two continents of Europe and America left in a state of political opposition or virtual hostility, and the British empire recognized as an open and declared ally of the latter party. Such is the outline of the present international relations of the Christian world.

It has so happened, therefore, by a somewhat singular effect of the course of public events, that Great Britain and the United States, who but a few years since were at war with each other, upon grounds, as it then appeared, of a permanent and essential character, who for a long time previous had been in a state of continual and bitter collision, and had never since the war of independence, one may say, in fact, since the first settlement of the colonies, had a single moment of real cordiality, have now, without any sacrifice of pride or principle on either side, without concession and indeed without concert, been brought by the mere force of circumstances, into a situation of virtual alliance and amity, so deeply and broadly founded in the interests of both, and in the established political system of Christendom, that it cannot well fail to supersede all the old motives of contention, and to endure as long, perhaps, as the national existence of either. This relation is so far from having been the effect of any reconcilement of feeling,

between the countries and their governments, or of any
artificial arrangements, digested by leading individuals,
who might be supposed to rise above the low sphere of
national animosity, that it has taken place, as it were,
against the will of the parties, whose sentiments are
even now less friendly than their position, and who
seem to glare on each other with eyes of hatred and
suspicion, at the very moment when they are exchanging good offices of high importance, and taking the field,
in fact, together against a common enemy. It is known
indeed that the British government, though often re-
quested, has constantly refused, through the whole period during which this new relation has been growing
up, to act in concert with the government of the United
States. They declined the proposition made by the
latter, that the two governments should recognize, by a
simultaneous act, the independence of the American
states, although such a proceeding would have been
perhaps upon the whole even more honourable to them,
than to follow step by step, and at short distances, in the
course marked out and pursued by us. They also affected to consider as hostile to them, the declaration
made by President Monroe, that the American continent was no longer open for colonization, although the
obvious purpose was to discourage a cession by Spain of
any part of her American colonies to any other power,
a purpose that had already been distinctly and formally
avowed by England. There is, therefore, this rather
singular difference, in the form and spirit of the relations now existing between the British empire, and
the two continents respectively; that with that of Eu-

rope a feeling of deeply seated animosity is veiled by
a semblance of apparent good will, while in regard
to us, the new sentiment of amity has hardly yet begun
to beam out brightly, in the countenance of either party, through the sour and gloomy expression, which had
been so long worn by both, that it had become habitual
and in some degree natural. But this is a matter of
little consequence. The forms in this, as in most other
cases, accommodate themselves, after a while, to the substance ; and we have reason to expect that the two governments, after they shall have stood by each other
faithfully, for half a century, in regard to their most
important interests, will not refuse at last to exchange a
few civil speeches and good humoured looks. Mr.
Canning indeed, whose decision and talents have done
so much in fixing the new position of the British empire, in regard to the continent, has been also among
the first, to perceive the bearing of this position upon
the direct relations between that empire and the United
States. His address to Mr. Hughes, at the Liverpool
dinner, is conceived in the true spirit of these relations,
as they now exist. The tone being thus given by the
leading voices, the minor performers will of course in due
season join in the chorus; and it would not be surprising
if we should, after a while, be as much surfeited by the
gross adulation of the inferior British presses, and second rate politicians, as we have heretofore been dis-
gusted by their causeless and tasteless satire.

I observed, in a preceding chapter, that the new relation of political alliance and amity, which has been
established by the force of circumstances, between Great
Britain and the United States, was of such a kind, that

the latter power would have no reason to blush for its
position in this particular. It is in fact a relation, on all
accounts, equally honourable and advantageous to both
the parties. It coincides completely with the economical interests of both, which naturally lead them to entertain an active intercourse and commerce with each
other, and which were constantly sacrificed under the previously existing system of mutual hostility. Politically
viewed, it is also a perfectly fair and equal connexion.
The British islands, from their geographical situation
and comparatively small material resources, are hardly
safe from the influence of the continent, and require to
be sustained by some extraneous aid. They have accordingly sought and found such support in their immense commerce, their colonial establishments, and the
moral power which forms the natural accompaniment
and safeguard of both. By the help of these additional
resources, Great Britain has hitherto succeeded in
maintaining a completely independent position, and has
even at times exercised a powerful influence, in the general European system. But the new form which this
system has now assumed, in consequence of the great
political development of Russia, would have made it
difficult for England to hold her ground without obtaining on her side a corresponding extension of her commercial and extra European resources. This she will
in fact acquire, by the establishment of friendly relations
with the American continent. By forming this connexion, she becomes an active member of a vast political
system, which embraces, beside her own dominion and
dependencies, the whole western hemisphere; finds new

markets for her products, in regions where population and consumption are advancing, and will continue for centuries to advance, with almost miraculous rapidity, and thus realises the only augmentation of power, which she had reason to desire, or could in fact turn to account. America, on the other hand, has already derived and will long continue to derive the most important benefits from the accession of England to her cause. It served, as I have stated before, to settle the question of the interference of the continent, in the affairs of the south, and put the last seal to the independence of the Spanish colonies. The countenance of this great European power will also continue to be a protection to them against the danger of any future revival of the old project. The political benefits resulting to the United States from this cause, are chiefly indirect, but not the less real. It is now acknowledged, that we could not see with indifference the subjugation of our southern neighbours and allies, by the continental powers. Without pretending to decide precisely, what our policy would be, if such an attempt were made, we have certainly great reason to be gratified by any circumstance that prevents the occurrence of the crisis, and removes the eventual danger of a war. Such is the effect of the new position of England. We derive, also, from this state of things, the great direct advantage of finding a power with whom our relations were before of a difficult and delicate character, and whom we viewed, in the language of public law, as our *natural enemy*, converted by the force of circumstances, and without any sacrifice by us of pride or principle, into a firm friend and ally.

The benefits respectively derived by the two parties to this great political union, are therefore, for the present, very nearly equal. In the progress of future events, we may anticipate, that America will become every year more and more important to England, and that England, on the other hand, will gradually cease to render any essential service to America. Such is the rapid growth of our continent in population, wealth, and political power, that it must at no distant period be entirely secure in the extent of its own resources, not merely from conquest, which it is already, but from any apprehension or danger of attack. The adherence of Great Britain to our system will then be to us of no utility; while the same causes will render the connexion, in an economical point of view, to her constantly more and more valuable. Add to this, that while our continent is yearly developing new resources of every kind, it is altogether probable that the British empire will be gradually brought within smaller dimensions, by the successive falling off of its distant appendages, and will ultimately be reduced to its primitive possessions on the north-western coast of Europe. The United States, having thus become the most populous and powerful nation of English origin, will naturally take the place of the British islands, as the commercial and political centre of the English settlements in every part of the globe; while the original, but then exhausted parent soil, will lose her present high standing as a constituent member of the great system of Christendom, and finally sink into a dependency on the continent. But without dwelling too much, in anticipations which may appear to some to be dictated by national pride, rather than just political foresight, it is sufficient for our immediate object to remark, as I have done before, that the existing friendly relation between the British empire and the continent of America, is for the present at least, whatever it may be hereafter, equally, as well as highly benefical and honourable to both the parties.

Such, therefore, is the general outline of the present international relations of the Christian world, and particularly of our continent, in regard to Europe. This immense system is of course made up of a number of minor ones, each of which has its separate constituent and regulating principles, and its appropriate internal and external policy. The movement of some of these inferior spheres is, at present, in a high degree interesting and important. The war in Greece, in particular, is perhaps better fitted to excite the imagination and warm the heart, than any political event of modern times. It is filled with incidents and episodes of a strange and poetical cast, such as the adventures and character of Ali Pacha at the opening; the daring and successful enterprises of the Grecian Admirals; the romantic devotion with which Lord Byron offered up his heart's blood, as he had done before the first and finest fruits of his genius, in this sacred cause; the spectacle, quite unexampled in modern times, of the successful invasion of Europe by an African army; the appearance of Lord Cochrane upon this new theatre; and finally the suppression of the Janissaries and a complete revolution in the internal policy of Turkey. There is something dramatic in this series of occurrences, independently of

the intrinsic interest of a contest, that revives all the
charming associations connected with our classical studies, and in which our holy faith is painfully struggling
for existence on the same fields that witnessed its first
triumphs. It is no doubt true, that poetry has not much
to do with government, and that the Christian powers
would perhaps be hardly justified in making common
cause with the Greeks, merely as descendants of the
countrymen of Homer and Plato; but even statesmen
might reasonably take alarm at the unanimity with which
the self-styled true believers have rushed to arms, at
the first display of the *Sandjiak Sherif,* and might
justly enough apprehend the effect on Europe, of the
entire subjugation of Greece, and a thorough regenera-
tion of the Ottoman empire. It would, however, lead
me too far from my immediate purpose, to dwell at
length upon these considerations. Beside the war in
Turkey, there are also other episodes of much importance,
in the political action which is now proceeding. Such
are the immediate relations between the empire of Brazil and the kingdom of Portugal, the new constitution
that has just been adopted by the latter, and the influence of these events on the other continental powers, and
especially Spain; the respective positions of this latter
kingdom and France, as an occupied and occupying
country, and so forth. Of these international questions
of a secondary order, there are two, however, of paramount importance, and which have heretofore served at
times to determine the character of the general political
system of the day; I mean that of the extension of constitutional liberty on the continent of Europe, and that

of the maritime rights of neutrals. Both these subjects were treated at considerable length, in the former part of this work. The first has since been settled or thrown aside, as it were, by the complete ascendancy of arbitrary principles on the continent; and has ceased to be an object of contemporary interest, did it even fall within the plan of the present volume, which is more expressly devoted to America. The other has assumed a different aspect, in consequence of the additional importance which our continent has acquired in the political system, and of the altered position of England. It may be proper, therefore, in order to complete the view, which I have endeavoured to give, of the foreign policy of the two Americas, to add a brief survey of their actual situation and prospects, in regard to this question.

The glaring injustice and gross absurdity of the maritime pretensions of Great Britain were sufficiently exposed, in the preceding volume. These pretensions have never been defended out of England, excepting in a time of high party excitement, by a few individuals in our own country, and have been repeatedly denounced and condemned by all the Christian powers without exception. We may, therefore, fairly consider them as repugnant to the common sense and feeling of the world, and in opposition to natural law. The pertinacity, with which England has nevertheless sustained them, against the universal opinion of Christendom, is also perfectly well known, and this circumstance has at times exercised a decisive influence on the foreign relations of the United States. It served in fact, until after the close of the late war, to determine their position in the general system. This cause established between us and Great Britain a relation of virtual hostility, and had a strong tendency to involve us as her enemy, in any war in which she might be engaged. It also naturally established a relation of virtual alliance, between us and the continental powers of Europe, especially Russia, who had shewn, ever since the time of the armed neutrality, a strong determination not to yield to the maritime pretensions of England, and who had ample means for sustaining what she thought to be her rights. For the same reason, we regarded France and the other maritime powers of the continent as natural allies; and all these governments entertained, on their part, the same views in respect to us. This state of things furnishes the true key, to our foreign relations up to the treaty of Ghent. It accounts, in part, for the assistance which we received from the continental powers, in the war of independence, and for the sympathy we felt and exhibited in the fortunes of those powers, during their long revolutionary struggle with England; and it illustrates more particularly the causes, which produced the late war with that power, and which brought it to a close. The political events that have occurred within a few years, I mean the emancipation of Spanish America, and the change in the position of England, have fortunately very much reduced the importance of this question at least to us; but it is still not without its interest, and should be carefully kept in view and considered by every judicious American statesman.

Should a general war unhappily break out among the Christian powers, while the causes which now determine their international relations (and which have been concisely stated in the present chapter) shall continue to operate, it would necessarily be one, in which the United States and Great Britain would both be engaged, and on the same side. There would be of course in such a case no embarrassment, in regard to neutral rights, and this thorny question may, therefore, be regarded as adjourned, for at least half a century. In the mean time, such alterations will probably occur, in the position and relative situation of the two countries, as will prevent it from ever afterwards becoming a source of trouble. This result is one of the most agreeable consequences of the establishment of the present political system, and of its operation upon the interests of the United States. While the question of neutral rights formed the leading point in our foreign policy, it gave a sinister and gloomy aspect to all our future prospects. It was next to impossible in the nature of things, that after so much controversy, negotiation, and bloodshed, the respective pretensions of the two parties could ever be amicably reconciled. Their opinions had become with each articles of political faith, sanctioned by tradition, sealed by the blood of martyrs, and in which both parties acquiesced in a manner without inquiry. We went to war upon these points in 1812, and made peace again in 1814, without approaching to a settlement of them, and with the agreeable anticipation of being compelled to renew the struggle at the opening of the next war in Europe. Most happily for us they have since been settled, in the only way in which they ever could have been, by events that have diminished their practical importance, and connected our political interests with other questions of a different character.

The subject of neutral rights was still as delicate and critical as ever, at the time when the former part of this essay was published, and however hopeless the attempt, it was nevertheless natural to endeavour to find some means of adjusting it, in an amicable way. I then suggested a method of effecting this object, which would have removed the difficulty, and introduced at the same time an important improvement in the practical law of nations. I proposed that the two parties should take a higher ground, than any which had hitherto been occupied in the negotiations on this subject, and should agree to extend to the ocean, the principle which had long been admitted in warlike operations on land, of respecting all private property; and should prohibit the capture of it under any pretext whatever, whether by national ships or privateers. Such an arrangement would have set aside at once, and without any compromise of pride or principle on either side, all the questions which had heretofore been treated as doubtful, such as the rule of '56; that of *free ships, free goods;* the restrictions on colonial trade and impressment at sea. It also appears very easy to show, as I then endeavoured to do, that this innovation in public law would not only be productive of much incidental convenience in this respect, but is also imperiously demanded by a regard not merely for common humanity, but for ordinary consistency and plain good sense. The suggestion was treated as visionary, in some respectable quarters, but I have had the satisfaction to see it already produce im-

portant practical results, and am not without hopes that
it may yet do something, in co-operation with other more
imposing authorities, to effect the object in question.
President Monroe, in his next succeeding message to
congress, informed that body, that an arrangement of
the kind just mentioned had been proposed to the leading European powers, Great Britain, France, and Russia; and I have had the satisfaction to learn, from an
authentic quarter, that the suggestion I had offered on
the subject was taken into view, in determining upon
these proposals. They have not yet, I understand, been
fully successful with either of the powers; but it is conformable to the usual course of things, that such an innovation should be for some time under consideration,
and should be stated in various forms and quarters before
it is actually admitted. The president, in his message
to the house of representatives on the Panama question,
adverts to this subject in a manner suited to its high
importance, and consonant with the enlightened and humane views that distinguish the whole document. It
may in fact be very reasonably expected, that our sister
American states will readily join with us, in introducing
this principle as the basis of maritime public law, and
thus escape from the difficulties inherent in the subject,
on any other construction, and which have already begun to present themselves in our negotiations with these
powers. By some persons the remarks made on this
subject, in the work alluded to, and in the successive
messages to congress in which it has been mentioned,
have not been fully understood, and have been thought
to contemplate merely the abolition of privateering. But

while the practice of capturing private property at sea is in any way kept up, the abolition of privateering would be, as I remarked on a former occasion, injurious and not advantageous to the cause of humanity. Privateers are, on the present system, the natural defence of a weaker commercial power against a stronger one. The improvement contemplates that private property of all kinds should be respected by public as well as private armed ships, and would of course, if introduced, supersede privateering and the necessity of it. This interesting subject was ably treated by Mr. Livingston of Louisiana, in one of his speeches in congress upon the Panama question. His observations exhibited the same enlightened zeal in the cause of humanity, of which he had given so many proofs, in his previous legislative and political labours. With these distinguished modern names to support it, in addition to that of the great Frederic of Prussia, and our own Franklin, Jefferson, and Adams, who established it forty years ago, as between the two countries, by a formal treaty, I see no reason to despair that this salutary principle may be ultimately, and at no very distant period, sanctioned by the general consent of civilized nations as a standing rule of public law. I cannot refuse myself the pleasure of adding here a translation of the passage in the late authentic and valuable work by Dohm, upon the life of Frederic, in which he mentions the treaty just alluded to, between the United States and Prussia. It will serve to show that the importance of the rules established by it has been as highly appreciated by competent judges on the continent of Europe, as it has in this country.

After mentioning the fact of the conclusion of the treaty, (which appears to have been the last that was negotiated under the authority of Frederic,) and quoting the articles in question, the author proceeds in the following manner.

"On these grounds was the treaty in fact concluded. It was the last that was negotiated under the authority of Frederic, and it gave the first example of a high minded spirit of humanity, which has not yet been imitated even in theory, still less in practice, by any other power. Instead of this, we have seen on the contrary, the unavoidable horrors of war greatly augmented in these latter times, by the unnecessary and savage barbarity with which it has been carried on.

" Some persons have unjustly and vainly attempted to depreciate the merit that properly belongs to Frederic, and to the government of the United States, for establishing these humane rules, by remarking that there was at the time very little probability that a war would ever break out between the two nations. But the case, though doubtless improbable, was nevertheless possible; and was therefore precisely the one, for which it was most expedient and natural to provide a remedy beforehand. It can hardly be expected, that nations who are so continually engaged in war, that a peace between them, when it happens, is little more than a truce, will do much to mitigate the cruelty of its laws and usages. The example must be given by those, which from their respective situations are more amicably disposed towards each other. It may be added, that the treaty did not contemplate merely the case of a war between the parties, but also that in which one party should be at war and the other neutral. When at some perhaps very distant period, the manners of the Christian world shall begin to soften, and it shall become the sincere and earnest business of nations and their rulers to diminish, if they cannot entirely prevent, the horrors of war, it will then be remembered by posterity with pleasure and gratitude, that Franklin, Washington, and Frederic, were the first to entertain these humane notions, and to recommend them as laws to the observance of their respective countries."*

* The title of the work from which the above passage is extracted, is as follows : *Memoirs of my own Times, or Contribution to the history of the last quarter of the* 18*th, and the beginning of the* 19*th century, by Christian William Dohm.* It is written in German, and the first five volumes (which are all that have appeared) are wholly occupied with the life of Frederic, and the history of Europe during his reign. The author had been employed by him in the most important diplomatic and political affairs, and enjoyed his confidence and friendship in a high degree. He writes with great good sense and coolness, (though with a very decided partiality for his sovereign,) and also displays throughout, as in the above extract, a humane and upright character, which does equal honour to himself and to the monarch who knew how to distinguish and appreciate it. He is one of the few modern statesmen who are not Machiavelians by system, and proud of being thought so. The work is full of valuable information, which would be entirely new to the British and American public, and it is much to be regretted that it has not yet been translated.

As regards the immediate purpose of putting our relations with Great Britain on a better footing, the importance of the new principle in public law, here alluded to, has been greatly lessened by the subsequent events to which I have repeatedly adverted, and which have formed the main subject of the present chapter.

CHAPTER VIII.

International Relations of the two Americas.
Congress of Panama.

THE general principles that determine the international relations of the two Americas, have been necessarily stated in the preceding chapter. It has been
shewn that the position of our continent, in the political
system, is fixed by the nature of the institutions by
which it is governed; that as these institutions are the
same throughout the whole continent, the foreign relations of its different sections are of course similar; and
that they are those of virtual hostility to the continent
of Europe, and of amity with the British empire. A
community of interests, as respects the general subject
of foreign politics, naturally gives a friendly character
to the immediate intercourse between the two great sections of the continent. It only remains to show that this
relation has been, is, and is likely to be, in fact, of the
description which might have been expected. I shall
offer a few remarks in illustration of this point, in the
present short chapter.

On the old European theory, which supposes that all
neighbouring nations are as such natural enemies, the
relative position of the United States and the new

American governments, would have been by no means
of the most amicable kind. These governments, however distant some of them may be, are on the whole our
nearest neighbours, and the two most powerful of them
approach very closely to our southern and western
limits. The statesmen of Europe, reasoning, as they
habitually do, upon the Machiavelian principle, consider it accordingly as a settled point, that the natural
relation between the United States and Spanish America is that of hostility; and they will probably do all
they can in the way of intrigue and negotiation, to
give reality to this anticipation, and thus diminish the
influence of the American continent, on the general system, by bringing its different parts into collision with
each other. Little, however, need to be apprehended
from such efforts, if, as there is reason to suppose, they
are counteracted by the force of circumstances, and if
the natural relation of the different parts of America
be, as I have considered it, in itself friendly. The error
of the Machiavelian system, in this as in every other
application of the principle, lies in looking exclusively
on the wrong side of human nature, and concluding from
the known fact of the existence of a principle of evil,
that there is no such thing as a principle of good. This
mistake is precisely the same with that of the selfish system of morals maintained by La Rochefoucault, and is
not a whit less obvious than the opposite error of deny-
ing the existence of evil, and calculating on a permanent
and universal prevalence of good principles, as was done
by the partisans of perfectibility in France, and in our

day by Mr. Owen and his disciples.* The reality of both of these elements is certain, and it is equally certain, that one or the other will prevail in the relations between countries, as in those between individuals, according to the circumstances in which they are placed. The direct result of neighbourhood is to increase the

---

* I expressed on a former occasion, a somewhat favourable opinion of the system of Mr. Owen. I then knew nothing of it, excepting from an article in one of the English journals, in which it was attacked with so much flippancy and apparent injustice, as to give me a strong impression to its advantage. I have since had opportunity to converse with Mr. Owen, and to learn from his own mouth the details of his theory. He has certainly some good ideas, particularly that of employing scientific improvements to increase the comforts and abridge the labours of the working classes. His plan of a community of goods, is as old as the time of Plato, probably a great deal older; but the practicability and expediency of it have not yet been established by any decisive example. If practicable and useful any where, it would be in a society of which the population was extremely dense ; and is of course less likely to succeed at present in the United States than in almost any other country. Mr. Owen is perhaps injudicious, in attempting to connect with his economical improvements, a complete reform in religion and government. On these subjects his information seems to be less extensive than on those of a practical kind, and it may be doubted whether he will make many proselytes to this part of his theory, which he considers as by far the most important. It is but justice to this gentleman to add, that his intentions are evidently of the most benevolent character. The settlements which he is forming in the western country, considered simply as great manufacturing establishments, will prove, if they should succeed, of incalculable benefit.

intimacy of the relation between individuals or communities, but not to determine its character; and it
would be just as reasonable to say that individuals inha-
biting the same city, street, or house, are natural enemies, as to say that neighbouring nations are so. In both
cases the nature of the relation is fixed by the character
and interest of the parties; and the circumstance of
neighbourhood has no other effect than to give it in both
cases a higher degree of intimacy. Neighbours, whether nations or individuals, are not necessarily, as such,
either friends or enemies, but are only more intimate
as friends and more bitter as enemies, than they would
be if remote from each other. The principle, that neighbouring nations are natural enemies, is founded on the
fact, that as such they have a greater facility of injuring
each other, viewed in connexion with the supposition,
that nations and individuals always do each other all the
harm they can. This, as I have said, is the system of
Machiavel, and the one received in Europe, but is
alike repugnant to common sense and common humanity.
The very word *humanity*, which runs through all languages as the appropriate term for benevolence, proves
that good feelings constitute, in the opinion of the world,
the most honourable and distinctive feature, in the moral character of man ; and as neighbourhood has a necessary tendency to develope the social feelings to which
we give the name of goodness, it may be said with justice, that the direct result of this cause, when not counteracted by others, is to produce a friendly and not a
hostile relation, whether between nations or individuals.
The counteracting causes in both cases are conflicts of

interest; and as the real interests of individuals and societies never interfere with each other, such conflicts can only arise from a vicious political or individual organization or position, which leads to a false judgment respecting the interest of the party and a corresponding mistaken line of conduct. The character of individuals no doubt has its weight, even in the relations between communities; but the cause which operates with more immediate force, is the character of their political institutions. In proportion as these are conformable to reason and to nature, they will tend to produce natural and correct judgments in the persons entrusted with the government, upon all questions of administration, and of course upon those of foreign policy; and as it is the real interest of neighbouring nations to make the relation between them as friendly as it necessarily is intimate, the general effect of such institutions will be to give it this character. On the other hand, we need not look beyond the vices, which in a greater or less degree deform the political institutions of the several European nations, to find the reason why they regularly regard and treat each other as natural enemies in proportion to their proximity.

This, therefore, is the great cause upon which we have a right to depend, as a principle of permanent friendship with our neighbours in Spanish America; and which we can oppose with confidence to the sinister conclusions which the statesmen of Europe are in the habit of drawing upon this question, from their favourite and habitual theories. We believe that the political institutions prevailing through all parts of the continent, are more conformable to reason and nature than those which are established elsewhere; and that as such, their natural tendency will be to produce a relation of amity between the different communities in which they subsist; and although these institutions are not perhaps at present perfect, either in North or South America, more especially, as I have intimated before, in the latter, nevertheless, as there is a tendency in each to favour rather than discourage all reform that may appear advantageous, we have reason to anticipate that, in their future progress, they may approach more nearly to the type of perfection, rather than recede from it, and that the relations resulting from them will have a constant tendency to become more and more amicable. It is always, however, a fortunate thing, when the favourable operation of general principles is aided by the concurrence of accidental causes, and such has been the case as respects the relations between the United States and Spanish America. Under the operation of circumstances, in a great measure independent of the general cause just alluded to, these relations were established in the first instance, on a footing of entire amity and mutual good understanding; and the same circumstances have continued hitherto, and will probably continue for a long time to come, to exercise a very strong influence in preserving and maintaining them on the same basis. It was our good fortune to have the opportunity of manifesting a friendly disposition towards these new nations, at the very opening of their political existence, when they were still diffident of their resources, and were looking round anxiously for foreign succour. We

may venture perhaps to say, without fearing to be charged with an indelicate assumption of merit, that the policy pursued by the government of the United States, in
regard to the Spanish American question, is one of the
circumstances that have contributed very powerfully to
aid the colonies in establishing their independence.
Nor has this policy been less advantageous, because it
has been distinguished throughout by discretion and
good sense, as well as an enlightened regard for the
rights of humanity. We neither embarrassed our young
neighbours with officious and premature aid, before we
knew in what way we could best serve them, nor did we
wait to be the last in bidding them welcome into the
family of Christian communities. Subsequently to the
acknowledgment of their independence, it was publicly
declared by the United States, at a time when it was
known that the great continental powers had thoughts
of taking an active part on the side of Spain, that such
an interference would be considered by us as unfriendly. This declaration created between us and the new
American governments a virtual alliance against a common enemy, which, as I have already said, determines
at present, and will continue to do so for a long time to
come, the character of our foreign relations in general.
Our position in regard to the other American governments, which was naturally friendly, has assumed, therefore, in consequence of accidental circumstances, the
form of a close connexion from its commencement, and
will wear this shape for a long time to come. In this
way habit, after all one of the strongest principles of
human conduct, will confirm what nature and accident

have combined to establish ; and if ever the relation of
the two sections of the American continent, in regard
to each other, becomes unfriendly, it can only be when
the whole existing political system shall have been swept
into nothing, by some of the great changes, whether
sudden or gradual, that occur from time to time in human affairs, and are in their nature beyond the reach of
anticipation. It would be easy to confirm the above
remarks, by a reference in detail to all the transactions
that have taken place in the intercourse between the
parties; but the subject is too familiar to the American
public to require any great development. It may in
fact be considered as exhausted, (if any subject ever
was,) by the lucid expositions of this branch of our foreign relations, given in the successive messages of the
president to both houses of congress upon the Panama
mission, and in the various reports and speeches, for
which these messages furnished the occasion or pretext.
My object, therefore, in touching very succinctly upon
some of the leading points in the history of our proceedings in regard to this question, will merely be to complete in form, the brief review of the foreign policy of
the country required by this essay.

The immense importance of the emancipation of Spanish America to the world in general, and especially to
the United States, was early perceived, as might have
been expected, by the leading politicians of the country, and was justly appreciated by the body of the people. Our controversies with England on the subject of
neutral rights, formed the most interesting point in our
foreign relations, for many years preceding the close of

the late war, and, from their exceeding delicacy and difficulty, in some degree diverted the attention of the nation from all others ; but even at this time the government habitually watched with interest the progress of events in the southern regions of our continent, and took the necessary measures for obtaining early and correct information respecting them. After the conclusion of peace with England, and the probability which soon became apparent from the subsequent course of events, that our relations with Europe would be hereafter in a great measure unembarrassed by conflicts of interest or opinion, the eyes of the people were turned, with a still more intense curiosity and interest, upon the struggle for independence in the Spanish colonies. A variety of causes united in producing this effect. It was impossible not to feel a strong sympathy with communities situated precisely as we were fifty years ago, at the most critical moment of our national existence. It was impossible for a nation so warmly attached as we are to the humane and liberal principles which form the basis of our government, not to view with satisfaction a revolution, which would, in all probability, lead to the adoption of similar principles throughout the whole western continent. Independently of these considerations, it was soon perceived and felt, that our immediate interest was deeply involved in the course and issue of this contest; that the emancipation of Spanish America would form, in fact, a new era in our political existence, would elevate us from the rank of a secondary, to that of a first rate power, and would place us at the head of one of the great divisions, into which the Christian world would be

thrown by the effect of this immense revolution. Not
to have been aware of these truths would have argued
in our statesmen a want of ability and sagacity, with
which they have rarely been chargeable; but the delicacy of the crisis was equal to its importance, and to fix
the precise line of conduct which the government ought
to follow, was undoubtedly the most difficult problem
that has presented itself since the first establishment of
our independence. It was seen, however, at once, that
neither policy nor duty would permit us to shrink from
the high and responsible position in which the course
of events, or in other words the will of Providence, had
placed us. Had we been pusillanimous enough to wish
to abandon the splendid pre-eminence to which we were
called, and to neglect our duty as the first born and natural head of the flourishing family of young American
nations, we could not, in this way, have escaped from
supporting our share in the result of the commotions
going on in our neighbourhood. We must have been
either active or passive spectators of a most important
and interesting series of events, which had a deep and
necessary connexion with our own interest. In the former case it was in our power to give them to a certain
extent such a character and direction as suited our policy; in the other we made ourselves the slaves of accident, or rather laid ourselves open to certain injury, for
accident rarely helps those who are too unwise or too
indolent to help themselves. Under these circumstances,
it was hardly possible that the government or the people should have entertained a doubt as respects the
choice. All were satisfied from the first, that this was

a crisis in which the nation was called upon *to act ;* but then it was necessary to act with prudence and discretion as well as firmness. We had duties to Spain, duties to Europe, duties to ourselves, as well as duties to our southern neighbours, which were all to be taken into view, so that the moment was singularly critical as well as important. It is highly honourable to the government, that while they met the exigency with manly firmness, and pursued throughout a bold and vigorous, rather than a cautious line of conduct, they nevertheless tempered their courage so judiciously with a mixture of discretion and a just observation of the forms of civility, that no positive offence has been taken, in any quarter, at their proceedings; that these have met with general approbation at home, have already been imitated in the most important points by some of the most enlightened and powerful nations of Europe, and have been stamped, on the whole, with the favourable opinion of the civilized world. On this subject the policy of the government has never wavered for a moment, but has pursued a steady and uniform march, from the first friendly reception of the flag of the new American governments in our ports, and of their private agents at Washington, down to the nomination of ministers to assist at the congress of Panama. The several measures that have been adopted during this period, are all parts of one system, and follow each other naturally, like consecutive members in a regular series. It was, therefore, under a very indistinct and erroneous impression as to the general character of our foreign relations, that the last of the measures above alluded to, was regarded by some persons as involving the establishment of new principles, and as a departure from the settled policy of the country. Instead of this, it was only one, and that by no means the most important, of a course of measures which had, for ten years preceding, constituted the only interesting branch of our foreign relations, and was likely to do so for centuries to come. Without intending to treat this particular point in detail, (since it has already received a great deal more of the public attention than it was fairly entitled to,) I shall briefly touch upon it again at the close of this chapter.

The situation of the government, when it was first called upon to take in hand the great question of Spanish America, was the more delicate, inasmuch as the usual lights of experience and acknowledged authority were in a great measure wanting. The title of public law that shall treat of the recognition of new nations, is yet to be written ; and in the absence of written rules, there are also very few examples. The country was bound by its position, its interest, and its duty, to take the lead. It could not with propriety wait to see what others would do, and be guided or warned by their proceedings, but was compelled of necessity to act for itself; and in determining upon the time and form in which it would act, little or no aid could be derived from any foreign quarter. Under these circumstances, the first rule of policy adopted by the government, seems to have been to place itself on a perfectly solid basis at home, before it began to exercise any influence abroad ; and the executive department held itself for some time sedulously and studiously, in regard to this subject, a little in the rear of public opinion. It was in fact of the highest importance, both as respected foreign powers and ourselves, that the voice of the people should be freely and loudly uttered, by all its usual and most authoritative organs, before the government commenced a series of measures, which was to open a new era in the history of the country. The interchange of private agents, for the purpose of obtaining information, that took place before the close of the war with England, was a merely informal thing, which in no way committed the government, and is not to be reckoned in the list of public proceedings. Of these latter, the first, and a much more important one than it has sometimes been considered, was the recognition of the flag of the new states by our custom-house officers and courts of justice, for the purposes of commerce and of war upon the ocean. Whenever the public law upon this subject shall be fully settled, it is probable that this admission, and not the interchange of diplomatic agents, which is a merely formal thing, will be looked upon as the real and substantial acknowledgment of the independence of a new government. Such, however, is not the case at present, and the executive and judicial departments of the government felt themselves at liberty to go this length, at a time when prudence would not have authorised a formal exchange of ministers. In the meantime the public opinion was gradually maturing, and statesmen of ardent and energetic characters began to declare themselves with freedom, in favour of still more decisive measures ; and were naturally seconded in this by the eager, and sometimes indiscreet zeal of the pri-

vate agents of the interested powers. Anxious to avoid
even the appearance of precipitation in regard to this
momentous subject, and desirous at the same time to exhibit a proper sympathy with the declared feeling of the
country, the government, as a preliminary step, despatched a most respectable commission, appointed and
fitted out in a formal way, for the purpose of procuring
information upon the actual position of the new states.
What the general nature of their report would be, was
of course known pretty well beforehand; but it was
decorous and proper, that the information which was to
be officially acted on, should come before the world in
an official shape. While the commissioners were absent,
the policy of taking decisive measures was pressed upon
the government, by constant declarations of public opinion and feeling, in the most imposing forms; and it was
easy to see that the moment for action was ripening very
fast. Finally, when the commissioners returned with
favourable reports, after the subject had been repeatedly
taken up in congress, where nothing but the great and
well deserved confidence which was felt in the wisdom
of the executive, prevented an anticipation of the decision of the latter, then every thing was at last mature;
the president recommended the adoption of the measures necessary for an exchange of diplomatic agents,
and the recommendation was acted upon in both houses
by all but unanimous votes. Such were the fortunate
auspices, under which the government opened this new
and interesting chapter in our history; and thus it came
about, that, by a wise and prudent manner of proceeding, they were able to carry into effect resolutions of a

bold and decided cast, not only without shocking the public opinion at home in any of its divisions, but without even offending the foreign nations most immediately interested, and in point of form even injured by them. Spain, who might according to formal rules have justly declared war against us, contented herself with entering a protest, and has never interrupted her former friendly intercourse. The other continental powers had become prepared for the measure, and learned it without surprise or open demonstration of offence ; and England, observing the facility with which we had accomplished our purpose, and desirous not to be too far outstripped by us in the rendering of good offices to these thriving young candidates for national existence, made haste on her side to acknowledge their claim, and thus sealed and settled for ever the question of their emancipation and political independence. In this way only could our recognition have produced the favourable effect which it did, upon the position of the new states. Had it been made in a precipitate and careless way, before the public mind was prepared for it at home and abroad, it would have endangered, probably sacrificed our tranquillity; deprived us of the power we have since had of sustaining the cause of our neighbours, by the weight of an imposing and friendly neutrality ; deterred instead of inducing Great Britain to follow our example, and very probably provoked the continental powers of Europe to take an active part on the side of Spain. It is therefore, then, no more than an act of common justice to the government of the United States and to President Monroe, under whose administration these important proceedings took place, to say, that this distinguished statesman, and the cabinet over which he presided, consisting of Messrs. Adams, Crawford, Calhoun, and Thompson, entrusted as they were with the management of our public affairs at a most important and delicate crisis, proved themselves to be equal to their position, and discharged a very arduous duty with a singular union of firmness and discretion, and in a manner which merited as it had received the general approbation of the world. In this way too, the leading citizens of the country, who were afterwards to come forward at the head of the administration, being either members of the cabinet or of congress when this course was adopted, and having all supported it with vigour in their appropriate sphere of action, were all committed on the question, and there was no reason to fear that any one of them, whatever might be their subsequent situation, would dispute the propriety of proceedings in which he had himself been concerned, or of others dictated by the same policy which would naturally follow them.

In this way did the people of the United States, through the medium of their appropriate organs invested with the executive, legislative, and judicial powers, as well as in every other form in which their sentiments are usually declared, express their will on this important subject. The policy which was recommended before by the strongest motives of interest and duty, was now identified with the national honour, and it would have been impossible for the country to retire, without exposing itself to just reproach, from the high and responsible stand which it had assumed. No disposition of this kind, as may well be supposed, has yet been manifested; and the next proceeding of the government, in regard to this question, was marked perhaps by a still more decided spirit than that which dictated the act of recognition; I allude to the declaration made by President Monroe, in his next succeeding message to congress, that the interference of any European power, for the purpose of aiding Spain in reconquering her colonies, would be looked upon by the United States as an unfriendly act. This intimation, couched in the cool and measured language which suited the nature of the document in which it was inserted, and indeed of all state papers, may not appear at first view of a very alarming or important character; but when we consider the circumstances under which it was made, and its results, it will be found to have been a measure hardly inferior in magnitude to the act of recognition, and even bearing a stamp, as I have said, of a still more determined policy.

In regard to the recognition, it was the wish of the executive department, as I have remarked above, to hold itself a little in the rear of public opinion. Such a system was required by the nature of our government and the general rules of a sound and judicious policy. The president's declaration was a measure of a different character, and in this the executive department, with equal propriety, took the lead of all the other branches of the government, or organs of the people, and assumed the responsibility of expressing, in the first instance, the national wish. It is a part of the duty of this department to procure information of the proceedings of foreign powers, and, as far as may be practicable, of their intentions and projects, to the end that, if they are found in any way to affect our interests, we may have warning in season, and shape our course accordingly. To aid in furnishing this information, is one of the most important offices of our diplomatic agents abroad. Much of it never gives occasion to any public proceedings, and is not communicated to the people. In some cases, as in the one now in question, it leads to measures of an important character, and the advantage of possessing it is deeply felt. In the exercise of this branch of its duty, it appears that the executive department had ascertained that the continental powers of Europe were strongly disposed to assist Spain in reconquering her emancipated colonies; that negotiations were going on among them for this purpose; and that, if such a resolution were not finally adopted, it would not be for want of inclination in these powers, but because they did not think it safe. It was known that England, though involved to a certain extent in these negotiations, was not a party to the project; but it was not certain how far she would consider it prudent to declare against it, or what her precise course would be. The United States had already recognised the new governments. What under these circumstances was to be their conduct? After risking a war with Spain, because they thought it due to their position and their policy to take the lead on this great question, were they now to look on passively, and see the governments they had recognised beaten down by a world in arms, as rebellious colonies? If it was just and politic to acknowledge them, was it not, on the contrary, still more just and politic to give them countenance and encouragement afterwards? England was disposed to take a favourable part, but was still wavering. A timely demonstration of decision and vigour on our side, might perhaps induce her to exhibit corresponding sentiments on hers; and the weight of both together might avert the danger. On the other hand, however, the crisis was certainly delicate. Should we stand forward in an ostensible position, should England think it prudent to adopt a cautious system, and the continental powers proceed with vigour, we should find ourselves in some degree committed to the new states, and might yet be called upon to engage in the war. But, however critical the case, it was impossible for the executive department to enjoy the benefit of any previous display of the public opinion, because the public were not informed of the facts, and because there was not time to make them known. Negotiations were actively in progress, and a short delay in the march of our proceedings might be followed by serious results. It was a case in which the executive was bound to assume the responsibility of leading the opinion of the nation; and the administration did not long hesitate. Emulating the bold and manly virtues, so often displayed by our ancestors at every period in the history of the country; *taking counsel,* to use the noble language of the President, then secretary of state, and entrusted under the direction of President Monroe with the immediate management of our foreign affairs, *taking counsel of their duties rather than their fears,* the government determined to inform the world at once, that the nation could not see with indifference an interference of the continental powers of Europe, in the affairs of our hemisphere, for the purpose of destroying its new born independence and liberty. The declaration was made in plain and intelligible, but at the same time decorous language, without equivocation and without *fanfaronade;* and it would be difficult perhaps to cite an example of an equal effect, produced by an equally short and simple phrase. Never was the force of true eloquence, by which we mean the just and simple expression of powerful thoughts, more strikingly displayed than on this signal occasion. The burst of enthusiasm with which this declaration was received in the United States and in England ; the sort of shivering sensation with which it shook like an ague fit the old continent of Europe, proved satisfactorily enough how completely the executive had anticipated the feeling of the country, and how correct a judgment they had formed of their own position and of the line of conduct it required of them. The manner in which the declaration was received at home and abroad, was also a most favourable omen of its practical success. I happened at the time to be residing on the continent of Europe, and in a situation which naturally led me to survey with some attention the course of passing events. I well recollect, and remember to have stated explicitly in writing at the time, the very strong impression produced in all parts of the old world, by the message now alluded to. It was the first time that the government of the United States had ever been called upon, to express an opinion intended to affect immediately the general politics of the Christian system, and the novelty of the proceeding excited every where a kind of surprise. It seemed as if a new and powerful member was assuming his place, in the great Amphictyonic council of nations. The promptitude with which the decision of the government had been taken, and the firm language in which it was expressed, contributed to give it its full natural effect; and this, as I have stated before, was every where immense. In England it conquered for a moment the settled hostility of the tories, and the sullen scornful jealousy of the whigs; and we saw the singular spectacle of a general acclamation of all parties in the mother country, in favour of the political course of the United States. On the continent, the surprise occasioned by it was followed by a mingled feeling of disgust and terror. It may look perhaps like exaggeration, to represent the great alliance of powers here indicated by the word *continent,* as capable of being alarmed by any possible proceeding on the part of a government so much inferior to them as the United States now are in actual physical force. But the fact is not the less certain, and I doubt not will be fully confirmed by the concurrent testimony of competent judges. It is also by no means very difficult to be accounted for. These antiquated governments cling with a sort of agonizing grasp to the abuses, with which they are all infected; but are still to a certain extent conscious of the weakness and embarrassment, which these abuses entail upon them. They know by experience the vigour of liberal institutions, and although they have succeeded, by an immense superiority of physical force, in crushing these at home, they are still tremblingly alive upon the

subject, and watch with painful anxiety the progress
and development of such institutions in the new world.
It was quite amusing to observe the various tones that
marked the language of the different continental journals, which serve as organs to the different opinions.
The liberal writers shared the enthusiasm which was
felt in England and America, and were agreeably sur-
prised by an appearance of vigour in our proceedings,
upon which they had hardly ventured to calculate. The
ministerial politicians thought it rather beneath them to
display much anger, and spoke with affected contempt
of the temporary chief magistrate of a little republic on
the east coast of North America, pretending to give
laws to the continent of Europe.   Others, who were or
wanted to be thought ignorant of any hostile projects on
the part of the continental powers, undertook to amuse
their readers by turning into ridicule the warlike humour of the cabinet of Washington, which, as they chose
to intimate, was ready enough to fight when there was
no enemy in prospect. In the mean time, this well-timed
and vigorous declaration produced the most favourable
practical results. It contributed to strengthen, in the
British cabinet, the disposition to counteract the projects of the continent, and proved sufficient in connexion with the declarations made by England to defeat
them.   The intention of interfering in the affairs of
Spanish America was shortly after abandoned ; and in
this way the crisis passed off without any actual inconvenience.

The question has lately been moved, how far the
United States pledged themselves to their southern

neighbours, by this important declaration, that they would adopt under certain circumstances a certain line of policy. But on this point there does not seem, in fact, to be any great room for doubt. If by a pledge be understood merely the strict obligation resulting from a formal contract or treaty, it is perfectly evident, that the United States are under no such obligation to any foreign power, because they have made no contract or treaty on the subject. If by a pledge be understood the indirect obligation resulting from the expectations which may have justly been excited in the minds of interested parties by our proceedings, there can be as little doubt, that thus far we are fully pledged. Such a pledge does not deprive us of the right of reconsidering our policy at any time, and if we think we have been in the wrong, of adopting another; but it would naturally lead us not to change our system without great consideration and a just and sufficient motive. The interest of many foreign powers, indeed of the whole Christian world, is in a greater or less degree involved in the decisions, that may be taken on important points in our foreign relations by the government of the United States. Under such circumstances, a judicious and consistent course is enjoined upon us by our duty to others as well as to ourselves; and if we were to proceed in a precipitate or vacillating way, we might properly be charged not only with neglecting our own reputation and interests, but with sporting wantonly and even dishonourably, with the vast influence that Providence has entrusted to us. Such, and such only, as it seems to me, is the pledge which we may be supposed to have given to any foreign power.*

Thus far, however, no disposition has been shown by the government to deviate from the track which was entered upon with so much consideration and has been pursued under auspices so favourable; nor is there any reason to fear, that the policy of the nation will be marked in future with vacillation or uncertainty, in regard to this subject. The great success which has attended all our proceedings, is a sufficient guarantee

---

* As respects this supposed pledge, the President of the United States of Mexico remarks, in his address to the congress of those states, at the close of their last session, (May 1826,) that *the memorable promise of President Monroe is not sustained by the present government of the United States of the North, and that the compact made on this subject has been broken.* Every one who knows any thing about the matter, knows that no compact was ever made upon this subject with Mexico, or any other government; and that the policy professed by President Monroe has been constantly pursued ever since, and never more actively than since the commencement of the present administration. The want of precision, (to say nothing of gratitude and good policy,) exhibited by Mr. Vittoria in this part of the speech, is truly remarkable. The same defect is observable in the style employed in mentioning our country, which the president calls " the United States of the North," instead of the United States of America. The chief magistrate of a great republic ought to know that it is usual, in official papers, to designate friendly powers under the names which they assume, unless it is contended to contest them, which I hope is not the case here. After borrowing one half of our name, it would be hardly fair in the Mexicans to rob us of the other.

that the views which dictated them will continue to prevail among the people. Success, though an uncertain test of merit, is a pretty certain one of popularity and favour. Had the leading part we have taken, in regard to Spanish America, involved us in war with Spain, disturbed our pacific relations with any other foreign power, and failed of producing any important advantages to our southern neighbours, the expediency of it would have doubtless been called in question. But when a course of measures which has placed us for the time being in the commanding position of *the leading Christian power*, and aided very considerably in securing the independence of Spanish America, has, at the same time, not only not committed the tranquillity of the country, but has actually ameliorated the state of our foreign relations with Europe, and been applauded, approved, and finally imitated, by those powers with whom it is most important for us to be on good terms; when these splendid results have been obtained, without other loss and expense to the nation than the outfit and salary of a few foreign ministers, there is little reason to doubt that a policy, which has been so eminently successful, will continue to be, as it has been hitherto, uncommonly popular. Since the adoption of the two decisive measures upon which I have dwelt in detail, no others of equal moment have been resorted to, because no occasion of equal interest has presented itself; but the government has pursued with activity and steadiness the line of conduct which these leading acts prescribed. Immediately after the recognition of the new American governments. negotiations were opened with them for the purpose of establishing our commercial intercourse on a proper footing, and have been in general attended with success. In the mean time, the influence of the United States has been actively employed at the court of Madrid, in endeavouring to bring about a general pacification in America; and with the leading powers of Europe, in urging them to concur in these endeavours. With a view of contributing to the accomplishment of the same great object, and of better securing our own domestic interests, the government have also counselled the Spanish American states not to disturb for the present the existing position of the islands of Cuba and Porto Rico. For instituting and prosecuting these negotiations, the administration has been, I believe, represented, in the course of some debate in congress, as playing the part of a *busy body* in the cabinets of Europe. It strikes me, however, that to employ the influence naturally belonging to the nation, in promoting its honour and highest domestic interests, in aiding the progress of other communities towards the attainment of independence and liberty, in labouring to effect the restoration of peace, and to stop the effusion of human blood, is a *business* of which no government need to be ashamed. It strikes me too, that to succeed in a greater or less extent in many of these objects, without committing the public tranquillity, and without expending a dollar or a drop of blood, is pretty good proof that the government has been busy to some purpose. But it would be hardly fair to criticise too formally these little bursts of petulance that occur at times in the progress of debate, and which the authors themselves would, perhaps, in a cooler moment, be the first to disavow.

The last measure in the order of time, connected with this subject, is the appointment of ministers plenipotentiary to assist at the congress of Panama. Of the whole series of proceedings, this is the only one which has met with opposition from any party in congress or the nation; and with all the respect due to the station and character of some of the persons, who appear to disapprove it, we may perhaps with safety affirm, that it was of all these measures the one least open to any plausible objection. After the full justification of it afforded by the president's message, and by the proceedings in congress, especially the report of the committee of foreign affairs of the house of representatives, and the eloquent and judicious speech of Mr. Webster, it would be entirely superfluous to enlarge upon the subject here. The substance of the argument may be resumed in a very few words. The degree of importance that may belong to this and to the congress of Panama, and of course to the question whether the United States ought or ought not to be represented there, was and still is uncertain, and will depend upon the progress of events in Europe and America. But however this may be, our position in regard to the Spanish American powers has long been settled; and whatever may finally be the results of the congress, it was not so much a matter of propriety or expediency, as a matter of course, that we should be invited to assist at it, and that we should accept the invitation, provided that our known and standing policy upon this subject be the true one. If the system of

friendly relations which we have adopted towards our
southern neighbours be right, then this measure was
right. If the system be ill-judged and inexpedient,
then this measure was of course inexpedient; or rather,
the proposition of any new measure adopted in pursu-
ance of the existing system, would furnish a proper opportunity for attacking the system itself. In order to
prove that the appointment of ministers to assist at the
congress of Panama was wrong, it would be necessary
to prove, in the first place, that the recognition of the
independence of Spanish America was wrong, the declaration of President Monroe wrong, and all our subsequent negotiations on the same subject wrong. It
would be necessary even to go further, and show that
the conduct of Great Britain, France, Holland, and
other European powers, who to a greater or less extent
have copied our measures, has been wrong; that all the
enlightened men at home and abroad, who have warmly
approved them, were wrong; that the people of the
United States, who urgently pressed their adoption on
the government, and have stamped them in like manner
with unequivocal marks of approbation, were wrong.
If all this can be made out, why then of course the mission to Panama, which was a natural consequence and
accompaniment of these previous and most decisive and
important proceedings, was also wrong.

Is this nothing?
Why then the world and all that's in 't is nothing,
The covering sky is nothing, Bohemia nothing,
My wife is nothing, nor nothing have these nothings,
If this be nothing.

Our policy, whatever it is, must be all of a piece; and there is neither honour nor advantage in blowing hot and cold in the same breath. A general reprobation of the standing system of the country in regard to South America, was therefore the only tenable ground from which the measure could be attacked; but this ground was not taken by the persons who appeared to disapprove it; so that their opposition, whatever may have been its real motive, rested on a false basis, and proved, as might have been anticipated, ineffectual.

There is little danger in fact, that the opposition of this or any future day will seriously undertake to question the correctness of our general policy in regard to Spanish America. It was adopted under the urgent recommendation and with the hearty approval of the whole people of the United States. It has been consecrated by the favour of the wise and good throughout the world, and by the imitation of some of the greatest powers of Christendom. It has finally been crowned with complete success; has given us a higher and more dignified place among the nations, materially improved the state of our foreign connexions, essentially aided the cause of liberty and humanity, and the interest of our southern neighbours, and all this without subjecting us to any expense or inconvenience, or involving us in the least political embarrassment. If any person or party were at any time ill-advised enough (as respects their own interests) to attack a system adopted under such auspices and attended with such results, it is evident that the recoil of the weapon would be more dangerous than the blow. The proceedings of the opposition last winter had perhaps an indirect bearing of this kind, and thus far must have had an immediate tendency to strengthen the administration. But such a course is too unpopular to be directly and systematically pursued ; and we may safely calculate, that, under all changes of persons and parties, the existing policy in regard to Spanish America will be steadily upheld, and will long constitute the leading principle of our foreign relations, to the great advantage of the country and the signal glory of its principal authors and advisers.

CHAPTER IX.

Fiftieth Anniversary of the Declaration of Indepen-
dence.—Death of Messrs. Adams and Jefferson.

DURING the time that I have been employed in preparing these pages, the fiftieth anniversary of the declaration
of independence has passed over.   The general reflections naturally suggested by this most interesting occasion, are precisely those which also belong to the scope
and subject of the present work.   To survey with gratitude the goodly heritage which has been allotted us,
the honourable position we have been called to occupy
among the nations, and the glorious future destinies that
seem to be opening upon us; to remember with filial affection and reverence the ancestors to whose wisdom and
virtue we are indebted, under Providence, for these
blessings, and to realize the solemn duties which their
possession imposes upon us, are the feelings and employments suggested by the day.   They are also those
to which I have successively adverted in greater or less
detail; and I should therefore not have thought it necessary to devote a particular section to the commemoration of this anniversary, had not the extraordinary
events by which it has been signalized, made it, independently of its original intrinsic interest, one of the
most remarkable seasons in the whole period of the his-

tory of man.   If any one of the few remaining veteran patriots who signed the declaration of independence, had been called to a better world on one of the anniversaries of that day, the coincidence would have been regarded with justice as singularly beautiful.   Had this anniversary also happened to be the one, which by the common consent of the world is always marked out in reference to any series of public events as worthy of especial notice, and has received the auspicious and consecrated title of a *jubilee*, we should have thought the accident still more worthy of attention. Again, had the two most distinguished surviving civil fathers of the country, closed their long career of honour and service on the same day, whatever might have been its date, the melancholy interest excited by the circumstance would have been mingled with a sort of pleasing wonder. But that the day marked by such a coincidence, should be also at once the anniversary and jubilee of our national birthday, is a thing which approaches the miraculous, and which we should not have believed possible, if we had not seen it happen.   Such a close was indeed suitable to such lives.   We might almost imagine that Providence had expressly prolonged the old age of these two patriarchs beyond the ordinary length, and disposed the termination of it, in order to distinguish, in this appropriate and unexpected manner, the occasion and the authors of it.   To think of mourning over such deaths would be almost a mockery.   They can be only viewed as the height and consummation of mortal glory. The tears we shed are the sweet and natural flow of the deep feelings of gratitude, admiration, respect, and

love, which we have always cherished for these illustrious men, and which now revives with new force, at
the moment when we lose them.

Whatever may have been the merits of others, it is
generally admitted that Adams and Jefferson were the
civil fathers of our independence. Hancock and Henry,
Samuel Adams, Dickinson, and their associates, executed
the labours that prepared the way for this resolution;
Washington and his military coadjutors sustained it in
the field. Hamilton and Madison, with their fellow
labourers, completed the work, by procuring the adoption of the federal constitution. In all these, and in
every other action of our long revolutionary struggle,
and our subsequent political history, John Adams and
Jefferson bore a leading part; but to them belongs more
peculiarly the honour of having been the immediate
authors and advisers of the declaration of independence.
This was the decisive act, which required, no doubt, in
order to produce its effects, to be properly supported,
but without which all the labours, losses, and achievments of our fathers would have proved entirely fruit-
less. It was therefore in a manner an epitome of the
whole revolution, and the patriots whose influence was
more particularly exercised at the critical moment when
this determination was adopted, may be called in a more
literal sense than any others, the political fathers of our
country. These no doubt were John Adams and Jefferson. They had both concurred in advising the measure, and were both of a committee that prepared the
declaration. Jefferson as chairman drafted the paper;
but in these cases the mere writing a formal instrument

is a matter of inferior consequence, and his agency on
the whole was probably not more effective upon this occasion than that of his coadjutor. He affirmed himself,
at a later period of his life, that in the congress of that
day John Adams was *the pillar of independence.* When,
in a former chapter, I attempted a feeble sketch of the
merits and services of some of our revolutionary worthies, I found myself with regret restrained by the delicacy due to living characters, from alluding otherwise
than in a cursory and general way, to the two (in civil
life) most distinguished among them. This objection is
now removed, and I venture to hope that a more de-
tailed notice of their characters will not be thought out
of place in this essay. Ill-timed it can hardly of course
appear at such a moment as this.

The great length to which the life of both these patriots was extended, though diversified throughout with
labours, cares, and hardships, that are generally supposed to impair the vital powers, proves the native vigour
of their constitutions both physical and mental. The
hardy Saxon stock has in fact rarely found a more con-
genial soil, than the mountains of New England and
Virginia. President Adams seems to have combined all
the higher qualities that distinguish the best specimens
of this noble race; the keen sensibility that indicates
genius; the strong instinctive feeling of moral obligation, which we understand by *virtue;* and the high
manly spirit which commonly accompanies the union of
the two. One who means well and knows that he has
talent to sustain his meaning, is rarely prone to the
lower arts of simulation and dissimulation, which to him,

as Lord Bacon has it, are *a hindrance and a poorness,* and which were at all times singularly foreign from the character of President Adams. To these essential qualities he added indefatigable industry, the pure and amiable graces of private life, and a free and cheerful humour that always threw a sunny light over his own prospects and the feelings of all around him. This was a character which would have ensured its possessor, under any circumstances (not wholly accidental), a happy, useful, and honourable life; and which, if occasion favoured, must necessarily have conducted him as it did to the highest eminence of public trust and glory. When he entered the world, the professional career was, as in fact it is now, the one most attractive to generous minds. He commenced it with the zeal and industry belonging to his nature, and was rapidly rising to distinction at the bar, when the crisis in our relations with the mother country, which terminated in the revolution, was first perceived to be rapidly approaching. He describes himself, in one of those charming private letters which he addressed to his friends in his later years, and which, if published, would form the most interesting portion of his writings, as a full faced fresh coloured youth, seated as a listener among the junior members of the bar, at that memorable session of court, when James Otis argued the question of the writs of assistance. With the fairest prospects of professional advancement and its consequents, wealth and honour, opening before him, he had every thing to lose, and apparently little or nothing to gain, by meddling with the business of revolution. But we find him nevertheless, with all the higher and better spirits of the time, enlisting heart and hand in this great cause; and contributing most powerfully, as an orator, writer, and active citizen, to its success. He was probably the most learned politician in the eastern section of the country. His newspaper essays, and his treatise on the canon and feudal laws, evince the extent of his researches and the depth of his reflections, and did much to fix and ascertain the basis of positive right, upon which the friends of liberty rested their pretensions. Such were the preliminary studies and labours by which he prepared the way for his entry into congress, where he was destined to perform the most memorable act of his life, by concurring, as a leading member, in the declaration that gave a national existence to the country. Independence with him was no new or sudden thought. His letters written soon after he left college, and recently published, prove that he anticipated even then, when there was no appearance of any serious contention with Great Britain, an ultimate and not very distant separation. Such, it is understood, was the tenor of his conversation while a practising lawyer, when the idea was entertained by very few, and when the open avowal of it would have probably been dangerous. To this great point his whole efforts seem to have been directed after he took his seat in congress, and he was, as I remarked above, probably the person who did more than any other in the country, to determine the momentous resolution of the 4th of July 1776. The part which he took on this occasion, was consonant with the natural boldness and vigour of his character, but had, nevertheless, not been determined on without the fullest deliberation, and a perfect sense of the importance of the measure, and the perils which surrounded it. In his letter written on the evening that the resolution for independence was adopted, and which has since been repeatedly published, he predicts with prophetic sagacity, the splendid results of that memorable day, which are now so rapidly realizing, but which would then have appeared like idle dreams to one who had had a less fearless confidence in the truth of his principles and the justice of his cause. He pronounced the day to be a great and glorious one, pregnant with rich blessings for his country and the human race, and foretold that its future anniversaries would be seasons of public rejoicings. Fifty years afterwards, this venerable patriot, reviving for a moment on his death bed, at the noise of the celebration he had thus predicted, pronounced it again to be a great and glorious day. His dying lips declared with these last accents the accomplishment of the prophecies, with which his faith in God and love for his country had inspired him half a century before. There is nothing more sublime and beautiful than this, I will not say in poetic fiction, which always falls below the majesty of truth, but in the finest passages of ancient or modern history.

To give existence to a mighty nation, is a thing which does not happen twice in the course of his life to the same individual; and the part which was taken by President Adams in determining the resolution of independence, must therefore, as I have said above, be regarded as the most important act he ever performed.

But in those critical days it was not the custom for any one to rest upon his laurels; and the performance of one important act was only a prelude to the undertaking of another. Soon after the declaration of the 4th of July, President Adams was intrusted, in conjunction with Dr. Franklin, Mr. Jefferson, Mr. Jay, and occasionally others, with the conduct of our negotiations abroad, and took the lead in this important branch of the public affairs, from this time forward till the close of the war. The success of these negotiations in all parts of Europe, viewed in connexion with their extreme delicacy and difficulty, is the best commentary on the ability of the agents. The parsimonious and wary Dutch were persuaded to lend us money, and to commit themselves to a war with Great Britain. The arbitrary government of France was prevailed upon to contract a close alliance with a cluster of infant democracies. Finally, an honourable peace was concluded with the mother country, after a short war of seven years, on a footing of reciprocal equality and independence, and without the least sacrifice by us of pride or principle. In regard to some parts of the last negotiations, it is understood that there was a difference of opinion between President Adams and his illustrious colleague Dr. Franklin, which was decided in favour of the former by the adhesion of Mr. Jay. Both no doubt were right; that is, both acted with the purest intentions, according to the best of their belief and ability. The views of Adams exhibited the spirit and decision which always marked his character. He took counsel of his duties rather than his fears. Franklin at eighty years of age, was cautious and wary:

but the end has justified the boldness of his colleague. Among the remarkable passages of these negotiations, may be mentioned the memorable first treaty with Prussia, to which I have alluded in a former chapter, and which will hereafter be regarded as forming an epoch in the history of public law. In these quiet and easy times, we can hardly realize the unremitted labours of the revolutionary patriots. It was only an episode in this course of continual exertion, for President Adams abroad to cross the Atlantic, and, during a short visit to his native state, to found, in conjunction with his namesake and kinsman, Samuel Adams, the constitution of Massachusetts, which has served as a model for most of the others throughout the union. After the close of the war he resided as minister in England, until his election to the vice-presidency under the new government.

Accustomed to a constant exercise of his highest intellectual faculties, President Adams took advantage of this comparatively less busy period, to engage in a course of literary labours, which, with the studies necessary to the execution of them, would now be thought sufficient to occupy the whole life of an industrious man. While he remained in England, he wrote his defence of the constitutions, and during his vice-presidency, his discourses on Davila; both works distinguished by extensive and solid learning, an independent mode of thinking, and the most correct and elevated moral principles and feelings. The theory of government developed in the former, which supposes that the only security of personal rights, lies in the maintenance of a balance between two or three distinct representations of

the community, though ingeniously and learnedly supported, may perhaps be regarded as somewhat questionable. The objection to it is, that it seems to attach
too much importance to the mere external forms of legislation and administration, and too little to the condition of the people. In the modern and more generally
received doctrine of representative government, the
condition of the people is considered as controlling the
forms of legislation, and they become of course comparatively unimportant. There are, however, some high
speculative authorities, in favour of the views of President Adams, particularly that of Montesquieu, the master of political science. He appears to have been led
to adopt them, in part, by a natural disgust at the wild
exaggerations of some of the modern political writers of
the continent of Europe, and the defence was, in fact,
intended in the first instance, as an answer to a tract by
the Abbé de Mably, in which some of the crude notions
then current were as crudely applied to our institutions.
The discourses on Davila are written in the manner of
Machiavel's celebrated discourses of the first decade of
Livy; and the subject is not less important and interesting. Davila was the historian of the religious civil
wars, that occurred in France in the sixteenth and seventeenth centuries; and perhaps no series of events in
the modern history of Europe, offers an equally fruitful
field for philosophical remarks on the general principles
of political science. These works of President Adams
are not among the number of those, which by the nature
of their subjects pass immediately into a very extensive
circulation; but they have been generally read and

justly appreciated by competent judges. In the estimate of their value, the partial incorrectness or correctness of particular theories is of little consequence. They
will always be recurred to as the honest speculations of
a powerful, practised, and well-stored mind, upon the
most important subjects, and will gradually acquire a
classical character. Their style is well adapted to the
matter, being perfectly plain and unpretending, and at
the same time pure, perspicuous, and for the most part
correct. It would perhaps admit of some improvement
on the score of point and polish. In these last respects,
President Adams's mode of writing improved with age,
and we find in his later private letters, a natural and
easy flow of language, and often a poetical beauty, which
is not observable to the same extent in his earlier productions. It is much to be wished, that a selection from
his voluminous correspondence, may hereafter be presented in print to the public. These honourable literary recreations, which would have been the monopolizing
labours of a less active mind, were brought to a close by
a new declaration of the love and confidence of his
countrymen, which called him to the head of the government, as the successor of Washington in the presidency.

The period of his administration that followed, is
perhaps the least agreeable one to contemplate, in the
whole course of his long and busy career; not because
his measures were in any way unworthy of his character, but because the country was at that time distracted
with party dissensions, and did not always do justice to
the purity of his intentions and the manly uprightness

of his policy. As president of the United States, it was his lot to fall on evil days, when, without much fault or even error on any side, the wisest, best, and greatest men of the nation, who had stood by each other like friends and brothers through the whole revolution, were converted for the moment into personal enemies and chiefs of opposite parties. I say there was but little fault or even error on any side, because the struggle was in fact in a great measure about foreign interests and foreign affairs, and was an indirect result of a sort of violent crisis which then agitated the whole civilized world. The mistake of those persons, in the United States, who warmly sympathised in the earlier movements of the French revolution, was natural and excusable. The opinion of others, who viewed them with more distrust, and of whom President Adams was one, does not require to be defended, because it has been justified by the event and is now universal; yet this difference between opinions sincere, natural, and laudable on both sides, was the principle of the bitter exacerbation of parties that raged at the precise period of Mr. Adams's administration. He was individually as little implicated in the merely controversial feelings excited by these disputes, as perhaps any person in the country. The madness of the French authorities made it necessary to protect our commerce by an armed force; but so far was the president from entering into this *quasi* war with any sort of political feeling, that he gave offence to some of his more zealous counsellors, by the readiness with which he availed himself of an opening for the adjustment of the difficulty, afforded by some

changes in the government of France. By the effect
of the party dissensions and prejudices which then prevailed, he was, however, not re-elected to the presidency; but he left the office with unsullied reputation.
The idle clamour which was raised against one or two
of his measures, is now forgotten, and it is generally
admitted, that he displayed throughout the fearless and
manly vigour which had always belonged to his character, and well understood the true policy of the country. We owe to him the creation of the navy, at one
time obnoxious to a part of the public, but now universally and justly a favourite with all. This single measure would alone be sufficient, independent of all his
other services, to entitle him to the lasting gratitude of
his country. The indiscretion of some of those who
were or should have been his political friends and supporters, probably did more than any errors of his own,
to give to his administration a temporary aspect of ill-
success. It will not be regarded hereafter as one of the
least remarkable in the annals of our government. The
judicious biographer of Washington has done much to
rectify the errors that were formerly entertained by
some on this subject. Time and the progress of events
have done still more; and the future historian will complete the work. The friends of President Adams may
leave it to him with undoubting confidence.

The long interval of twenty-five years, which elapsed
between the close of President Adams's administration
and his death, was passed in a dignified and studious
retirement, and was probably one of the happiest periods of his life. He had reached the age when the

busiest spirits are willing to rest from active labour;
his literary taste afforded him ample occupation of the
most interesting kind ; and he employed much of every
day in reading and epistolary correspondence. He was
uncommonly happy in his family connexions. He saw
the prejudices which had at one moment been excited
against him giving way from year to year, and found
himself surrounded by a new generation, who looked up
to him with reverence and love, as a political father.
In this generation he had the proud satisfaction to find
his own family taking an honourable lead, and to see his
son rise, through a long course of public services, to
succeed him in the presidency. These interesting events
filled up his last years with new and most agreeable
emotions, and contributed probably to preserve unimpaired, to a very extraordinary degree, his intellectual
and moral sensibility. He exhibited an example of dignified and cheerful old age, such as I have never witnessed in any other person. His health was perfectly
good, and his countenance retained, up to the age of
ninety-one, the serene and fresh appearance that generally indicates youth. His manner remained as it had
always been, noble and commanding, but at the same
time uncommonly easy and courteous. His conversation
was of the most rich and various character, and though
dwelling in preference on high and serious matters, was
always in a cheerful and animated tone. He was well
versed in polite literature, ancient and modern, had
studied profoundly the great subjects of religion and
government, and knew how to impart the rich fruits of
his experience and researches. without assumption or

dogmatism, and in a perfectly natural way. I have met with no person of any age, whose conversation was of a more intellectual cast; and with none whose conversation of this description was adorned in an equal degree, with a real and unaffected urbanity of manner. So venerable and interesting was, at this time, the appearance of President Adams, that I have sometimes found my eyes suffused with tears, by the mere emotion of being in his company. The political events of later years came so nearly home to his own family, that it may well be supposed they were as familiar to him in all their details, as those of any other period of his life. But his attention was not absorbed by these most interesting occurrences. I remember to have conversed with him at considerable length, a few weeks after the last presidential election, upon a delicate topic connected with religion, and found him, at a time of life when powerful minds are not always exempt from superstition, uniting the piety of a believer with the cheerful firmness of a true philosopher. He was still alive on the theory of government, and amused himself freely at the expense of the English radical Major Cartwright, who had just before published a heavy work on the British constitution, better meant on the whole than executed; and he sportively challenged me to an argument with him, upon the merits of his own system of checks and balances, to which I had on a previous occasion taken the liberty of proposing some objections. Although his sight and hearing were partially impaired, I left him with a full conviction that his mental faculties were still in full perfection. It is needless, however, to multiply proofs of this, since the public letters which he continued to write till within a few weeks of his death, and even the last words that moved his lips, evinced the possession of entire intellectual and moral vigour. Such was the serene and happy old age of this great and good man. It was the fit reward of a life distinguished throughout by industry, temperance, and every other public and private virtue, and may serve as an answer to the querulous moans of some discontented souls on the wretchedness of old age, and of human life in general. The last fortunate event that happened to him, was, to be permitted to close his labours as he did. We may well apply to him, with the proper variations of details, the remarks of an elegant Latin historian concerning one of the patriots of ancient Rome. You will hardly find in any person of any nation, age, or rank, an example of equal good fortune; for besides the signal success and high honours that marked his public life, besides attaining the first posts in the government, distinguishing himself by an active and patriotic opposition to the enemies of his country, and living to a very extraordinary old age, he left behind him a flourishing family at the height of reputation and success. An end like this should hardly be called death, but rather a joyful termination of life. *Hoc est nimirum magis feliciter de vita migrare quam mori.*

Of Mr. Jefferson, whom I had not the honour of personally knowing, I must speak of course with less fulness and detail. He too seems to have been endowed by nature with all the higher mental qualities, and his early distinction proves the exemplary industry with

which he turned his talents to account. He must have
been one of the youngest members of congress, his age
being about thirty-two, at the time when he was placed
at the head of the committee for preparing the declaration of independence. The spirit which animates this
celebrated paper, and the vigorous resolution with which
its author had directed his efforts towards the promo-
tion of the great object of it, from the time of his appearance in congress, evince the natural energy and
firmness of his character. At the same time, these qualities were probably tempered in him with a larger in-
fusion of policy, than they were in some of his distinguished contemporaries, and this circumstance contributed much to his success in the world. He combined
with his active disposition and talents, a strong taste for
contemplative pursuits, and was early smitten with the
charms of " divine philosophy." Although he nowhere
makes in his published writings, an ostentatious or im-
proper display of learning, it is easy to see that they are
the productions of a disciplined and studious mind. His
notes on Virginia, which are among the earliest of them,
prove that he had already explored with a curious eye,
the various departments of intellectual, moral, and physical science; and had speculated with a free and independent spirit, upon the facts that fell within his observation. It is known that he continued through life, to
devote his leisure hours to these delightful recreations.
His range of study included not only the great subjects
just mentioned, which form the theoretical basis of all
knowledge, but also the subsidiary branches that teach
the application of the former to the uses of life, such as

the ancient and modern languages, and mathematics
pure and mixed.   He descended even from his habitually elevated region of inquiry, to the common walks of
practical labour; was much engaged in agricultural pursuits, and proposed himself an improvement of the
plough.   He was curious in short with regard to every
part of useful or elegant learning, and nothing that
seemed likely to contribute to the general good escaped his attention.   He also possessed a strong taste for
the fine arts, and is said to have lived much, while
abroad, in the society of the eminent artists of Europe.
His style of writing, though not a perfect model, is more
correct and elegant than that of any contemporary
statesman, and has more of the point and precision that
mark the manner of a close thinker.   The stores of various knowledge, with which he had stocked his memory, gave a rich fulness to his thoughts, even of mere
matters of business ; and we see through the lucid current of his language, the beds of gold over which it
flows.   As one star differeth from another in glory, we
may admit without injustice to their fame, that the different revolutionary worthies possessed, each in a higher degree than the rest, some peculiar excellence ; and
it will probably be noted hereafter, as the distinctive
merit of Jefferson, that, next to Franklin, he was the
most philosophical statesman of this illustrious group.
This quality has in fact been assigned him, by the general consent of his enemies as well as friends ; the former having commonly reproached him with a too strong
inclination to act upon abstract theories, which is only
an unfavourable form of stating the same trait of character.   It will probably be found, if (to use a common

phrase) we come to the rights of the matter, that philosophy (as Voltaire said of wit) does no harm even in business. Plato, we know, affirmed, that men would never be properly governed, until kings became philosophers, or philosophers kings.

The most important act in the life of Mr. Jefferson, as in that of President Adams, was the part he took in determining the declaration of independence; and if Adams, on account of his more advanced age, and the remarkable energy of his character, had probably more substantial influence than any other person in bringing about this event, it was the fortune of Jefferson to connect his name with it in a very particular way, by being called upon to write the document which published it to the world. It is no doubt true, that the substance of such a paper is given by the occasion, and that the mere merit of clothing it, however fitly, in words, is one of a comparatively inferior order; but it is one of those merits of inferior order, which contribute materially towards bringing into public notice other and loftier ones. The patriotism, energy, and substantial talent of Mr. Jefferson, were much higher qualities than his skill in composition; but this latter talent, (the one that probably marked him out as the chairman of the committee,) gave him, on this great occasion, a place apart, and in some degree more conspicuous than that of any other member of congress, which will constitute for ever a singular title of honour. The propriety with which the instrument is drawn, fully justified the choice of the writer. It is wholly free from the noisy flourish or *fanfaronade*, which a vulgar pen would have run into at once. It commences with a simple statement of a few

incontestable general principles, proceeds to recapitulate in plain language the wrongs of the country, and
ends with a firm declaration of the great fact which it
was mainly intended to announce. The form of the
paper is, therefore, as it was highly important that it
should be, perfectly suited to the substance; but it is
not in the choice of words or contexture of phrases, that
we are to look for the real essence of this *unique* document. Its true value lies in that it is the written contemporary record of the event which it published, and
which, according to a high European authority, quoted
in a preceding chapter, opened a new era in the history
of the world. As this era advances, and as the importance of it is more and more distinctly perceived, the
circumstances that marked its commencement will become constantly more and more interesting. If our
hopes are realized, the declaration of independence will
be acknowledged hereafter throughout the world, as
the *great charter* of human liberty and happiness. To
have been called to write such a paper, was a piece of
good fortune, which could only have happened to a
truly great man, and it is one which a truly good man
need not be ashamed to envy.

While the war lasted, Mr. Jefferson was constantly
employed in the most important duties. He appears to
have preferred such as required his presence in the
country, and is understood to have refused a foreign
mission; but when Dr. Franklin returned from France,
after the peace, Mr. Jefferson consented to take his
place. The occupation of our diplomatic agents were
now less urgent and complicated than they had been,
and left them more at leisure for the observation of pas-

sing events, and for miscellaneous pursuits and studies. The philosophical habits of Mr. Jefferson enabled him to employ, with great profit, the time which he passed at Paris, in extending his knowledge and cultivating his taste. It has been thought by some, that his views on speculative subjects were unfavourably modified, by the effect of his association with the literary men of the continent of Europe; but I am not aware that there is any foundation for this suspicion. The liberal notions on almost all important subjects, which appear in his notes on Virginia, a work published before he went to Europe, as they could not well be improved, do not appear to have been changed for the worse. He has been charged with irreligion; but this wanton calumny was a mere repetition of the base and cowardly attacks that have been resorted to so often in all ages, in order to shake the reputation of the best and often the most religious men. It was known that Mr. Jefferson sympathised warmly in the early movements of the French revolution; and as some of the philosophers and statesmen who were engaged in them, professed a loose doctrine on religious and moral subjects, Mr. Jefferson's enemies made no scruple, though without the least shadow of evidence, of imputing to him all their errors. This artifice is too gross and easy to deceive any person of discernment, and is not very creditable to the generosity of those who resorted to it. Mr. Jefferson, instead of being justly obnoxious to the charge of impiety, was probably one of the most sincerely religious men in the community. Many of his published letters, particularly one addressed to a Quaker, that has often been reprinted, breathe, on this subject, a most amiable and at the same time perfectly orthodox spirit, which cannot have been affected, because there are certain tones that can only come from the heart, and which no dissembler, however cunning, can imitate. The anticipations which he was led to form of the results of the French revolution, were somewhat more favourable than the event has justified; and his residence in France may have contributed to the formation of these opinions. But this error was a practical and not a speculative one. The principles of the French reformers can hardly be called in question with propriety, by us, because they were substantially the same with those of our revolution, and had been learned in fact in the school of the patriots and sages of '76. As respects theory, therefore, Mr. Jefferson instead of being a pupil was one of the teachers. He was the author of the code which the national assembly were attempting to introduce in France. For him to approve his own principles, and take a warm interest in the proceedings of a powerful nation labouring to reduce them to practice, was a matter of course; and to believe in the practicability of what he had so much reason to wish and to hope, was, to say the least, a very natural error. It was indeed an error so universal, at the time, among the generous and enlightened friends of liberty, that we have more reason to admire the extraordinary sagacity of the few persons who foresaw from the very first, the fatal termination of such brilliant prospects, than to wonder at the contrary opinion of those who anticipated nothing but good. The enthusiasm which was felt by Mr. Jefferson, was almost universal throughout the United States. It was, indeed, no trifling motive of self satisfaction for a people just springing into life, to see their example imitated by the greatest and most celebrated nation in Europe. Clouds began to gather very soon over this fair morning, and innocent blood to flow in torrents down the streets of Paris; but it was still by no means certain that all was lost. Many good and wise men indulged the hope, that these were passing troubles incident to all violent political changes, and that after a while a better system would gain the ascendancy. Others were now convinced of that which they had before feared. In this way there grew up a difference of opinion upon the subject, which became soon after the leading point of controversy, between the two political parties. Mr. Jefferson's feelings still inclined to the favourable side, and were the same, in this respect, with those of a great majority of the people of the United States ; so that his error, as it may now without hesitation be admitted to have been, was of the number of those *indiscretions*, which, as Shakspeare says, *often serve us well, when deep laid plots do fail*. The nature of his sentiments, in regard to the French revolution, contributed very much to give him the immense popularity, which first raised and then re-elected him to the presidency, sustained him in so remarkable a way through the course of his administration, and continued to attend him up to the very close of his life; while the sounder views of Mr. Adams (as they are now considered by all), were the immediate cause of his temporary unpopularity with a part of his countrymen. The presidency of Mr. Jefferson fell on times as easy and tranquil, as those immediately preceding had been stormy and difficult. Our foreign relations had assumed a favourable aspect, in consequence of the turn of affairs in Europe. The bitterness of party feeling gradually subsided, under the influence of the great and growing popularity of the government. Industry and commerce flourished beyond all former precedent, and these eight years will always be regarded as one of the most brilliant periods in the history of the country, as they also were one of the most agreeable and prosperous in the life of Mr. Jefferson. At the end of his second term, he finally closed his public career, by declining to be considered a candidate for re-election, and thus crowned his long course of service to his country, by an act which gave another beautiful proof of the truly philosophic temper of his mind. Whether this act was as advantageous to the country, as it was creditable to himself, may well be questioned. He was still in the vigour of his faculties, and, as the event has proved, might have served the people with constantly increasing usefulness, for two or three more terms. The repeated re-election of tried public servants, under such circumstances as those in which he was then placed, would be favourable rather than dangerous to liberty.

The life of Mr. Jefferson after he retired from office, was, like that of President Adams, not less happy and hardly less useful to the nation, although more quiet than the preceding portion. He returned with new ardour to his favourite studies, which occupied in the most agreeable way a considerable part of his leisure. His house was habitually frequented by guests of the highest respectability and intelligence. No foreigner of note visited the country without paying his respects at Monticello, and it became to his countrymen a sort of political oracle, which was resorted to on all doubtful and important occasions. The prejudices that had been felt against him in times of party dissension, gradually subsided. They were wholly unknown to the rising generation, and were nearly or quite forgotten by those who had once cherished them with violence. For years before their death, he was in habitual and friendly correspondence with President Adams; and the letters they exchanged, many of which have been published, exhibit an amiable philosophy, and a generous forgetfulness on either side, of their temporary misunderstanding, in the highest degree honourable to both. On several occasions, Mr. Jefferson, even in retirement, exercised a beneficial influence on the progress of the public affairs. When the British commander in chief, with a wanton and insolent contempt of common humanity and public law, burned the national buildings at Washington, and with them the library, Mr. Jefferson came forward in the midst of the momentary consternation excited by this shameless proceeding, and revived the spirits of his countrymen, by reminding them that it was only a century and a half since the Hollanders had burned the British fleet at Chatham. He also placed at their disposal his own collection of books, a much larger and better one than the other, and thus laid the foundation of a new public institution, which, if properly sustained, will one day be an ornament to the country. During his last years he was much occupied, in conjunction with his friend and political associate, Mr. Madison, in establish-

ing the university of Virginia. The service rendered
to his native state and country, by his labours in promoting this single object, would entitle him, independently of all his other merits, to the lasting veneration
and gratitude of the people. His conversation is said
to have been in the highest degree rich, various, and
instructive, and his mode of entertaining his friends at
once cordial and unceremonious. Every one was charm-
ed with his unaffected affability, and left him with new
respect for his character and talents. His manner
through life was plain and easy, rather than elegant,
being the natural unstudied impression of good feelings
and powerful thoughts. His correspondence, which often
found its way into the newspapers, presented a beautiful image of a mind, at peace with itself and all the
world; full of charity for others, and actively bent in
promoting the general good; looking backward with
honest satisfaction on a well spent life, and forward with
cheerful resignation to its close. I have often thought
and remarked, that the history of man does not offer, in
any of its proudest passages, a spectacle more honourable to our nature, than the old age of these our revolutionary fathers. This charming picture, which appeared before too complete to admit of improvement,
has finally received a new and as it were supernatural
finish, in the almost miraculous coincidence, which we
have lately witnessed, and will hardly in future be surpassed or equalled.

Compare now the splendid talents, the sublime and
simple virtues, the ardent and unwearied devotion to
the public, the noble disinterestedness, the blameless

youth and divine old age of these men, with what we know of the politicians and generals of modern Europe, at their best estate; and say whether there be not something in popular institutions, that seems to favour specifically the growth of public virtue. I know that great and good minds are formed, from time to time, under all governments and in every part of the world, and that the continent, from which our fathers proceeded, was never barren of these celestial fruits. But in arbitrary governments they appear like exotics; and we look in vain through the history of absolute monarchies, even at their brilliant moments, for the traces of a principle that favours the formation of such characters. The heroes of the great Corneille were the only specimens of Greek and Roman virtue, to be found at the court of Louis XIV. The ante-chambers of Bonaparte were not overrun with Dewitts and Scipios. It has been in fact established by Montesquieu, as an axiom in political science, that public virtue is the natural product and essential principle of popular government. The hasty observations which I have hazarded in a preceding chapter, on the subject of our institutions, tend, as far as they have any weight, to support this theory. It seems in fact to be confirmed by the experience of all ages, and no period has ever exhibited a more striking illustration of its truth, than is seen in the glorious company of our revolutionary patriots. The examples they have left us will surely not be lost to their posterity, and if the theory be true, the institutions which they founded and bequeathed to us, will remain a fruitful and perpetual source of virtues like their own.

The death of these two fathers of the country, especially considering the extraordinary circumstances under
which it occurred, naturally revives with new force,
our interest in the events and characters of the revolution, and has reminded me of a wish that I have often
felt and expressed, that there were somewhere in the
country some one spot, consecrated more immediately
to their memory. The place that I should choose for
this purpose, would be Mount Vernon, a territory well
adapted to it by its central situation in the union, its
vicinity to the capital, its natural picturesque beauties,
and its noble position on the banks of one of the finest
rivers in the world, but especially fitted for this object
above all other grounds, from having been the residence
of Washington. It has sometimes struck me as a sort of
profanation, that the dwelling which was made holy to
the American people, by having been the scene of his
earthly pilgrimage, should be afterwards devoted to the
ordinary uses of life; and without intending the most
distant reflection on the conduct of its present occupant,
(whose leisure and privacy are as sacred as those of any
other individual,) it has seemed to me a painful thing,
that the people should not be permitted, at all times and
seasons, to come and pay their vows in perfect freedom,
at the tomb of their political father. I could wish that
every one might have the privilege of going there, and
visiting at his discretion, every nook and corner of the
house and garden, and meditating for hours together, if
he pleased, in the most retired and secret places. The
public good would be promoted by it, because no citizen could return from such an expedition without find

ing his patriotism heightened, and his best and purest feelings encouraged and confirmed. It is evident, however, that the people can never enjoy this advantage in its full extent, while the property belongs to any single individual. Some restrictions must be imposed upon the freedom of access, and the disagreeable scenes which from time to time will necessarily grow out of them, without being proper occasions of blame upon any one, should, if possible, be avoided, in regard to all matters connected with the memory of the great genius of this spot. Independently of this, the very civility, the mere presence of a gentleman on whom you cannot but feel that you are in some degree intruding, and who is probably a stranger to you, is a check upon the sentiments which the scene would naturally excite. You are conscious that you ought not to stay too long, take a hasty survey of the house, walk rapidly through the grounds, drop a tear perhaps at the hero's tomb, bring away some little relic from the woods, and, with a still hungry longing to pass several hours or days in this divine retreat, you hasten to relieve the family from a situation, which by constant repetition must be to them fastidious and irksome. Such were my feelings when I made this pilgrimage, although I had every reason to be gratified with the attention and kindness with which I was received. I should therefore wish, on every account, that Mount Vernon might be purchased by the people, and held as a national property. This arrangement would not only be advantageous to the country, but is, in fact, required by common justice to the family of General Washington. The people do in reality, by

continually resorting to this place, appropriate it to their
own use; and although they cannot have the full enjoyment of it, while it is occupied as a private residence,
they also, on their side, prevent the owner from making
that undisturbed and tranquil use of his property which
every citizen has a right to claim. The sacrifice that
would be necessary, in order to acquire this estate, is
too trifling to be mentioned; and although the heirs of
Washington must of course set a high value on his patri-
monial domain, they would naturally be proud and happy to cede it to the country, for the honourable purpose
of being consecrated, as a perpetual monumental ground,
to the memory of our revolutionary patriots and heroes.
I repeat, therefore, that I should desire on every account, that Mount Vernon might be purchased by the
people, and devoted at once to this noble object. The
house and grounds should be kept in perfect order, and
as nearly as possible in the same state in which they
were left by Washington; and a superintendant, with
the necessary assistants, should be placed on the spot to
attend to these cares, and to give to visitors such information as they might wish. When the house, which is
of wood, should exhibit any appearances of a tendency
to decay, it might be built over (like that of Peter the
Great at St. Petersburgh) by a stone edifice, imitating
it as nearly as possible in its exterior, which would preserve it from the weather and prevent it from going to
ruin. Within the house should be placed portraits of
the heroes and patriots of the revolution, and on some
elevated spot, on the grounds, should be erected an
equestrian statue of Washington, that might catch from

a distance the view of citizens coming up the river to visit the place, and serve as a suitable indication to them, that they had reached the end of their journey. This might be regarded as the monument which the faith of the nation has for years been pledged to execute, for which the remains of Washington were obtained from his widow, and which the people are bound, not merely in justice and patriotism, but in common decency, to erect immediately. This imposing figure towering majestically above the clumps of trees that adorn the ground, would form a noble object as seen from the river. Every ship that passed would strike her topsails in honour of it, as the mariners of Athens, when they entered the Piræus, on their return voyages, were accustomed to salute the tomb of Themistocles, that stood at the head of that harbour. Within the house, as I observed above, might be placed the portraits of the civil and military associates of its great proprietor. In the principal hall should stand his own, by Stuart, with that of his aid-de-camp and confidential friend General Hamilton on one side, and on the other the fine likeness by Scheffer, of the nation's guest, which now hangs in the hall of the house of representatives. Under the latter might be placed the key of the Bastile, which Lafayette himself presented to Washington, and which is now exhibited in the outer hall. After these would naturally follow the portraits of Knox, Lincoln, Greene, Lee, Gates, Morgan, Sumpter, and the rest. Warren, the young martyr of Bunker Hill, should obtain a conspicuous place among them, and the hero of Bennington should not be omitted. Another principal room should be devoted to the commemoration of those who served the country in civil life. At the head of them I would station Franklin, John Adams, and Jefferson, with the members of the continental congress grouped around them, as they are in Trumbull's picture. On their right hand should appear the others, whose services were most conspicuous in the earlier scenes that preceded the decisive action. Among them would be seen the open face and manly person of Samuel Adams, as represented by Copley, in the fine portrait now in possession of the grandson of the noble proscript, Mr. Samuel Adams Wells, of Boston, who would readily cede it for this patriotic purpose. By the side of this our more than Cato, might stand Patrick Henry our untaught Demosthenes, John Dickinson the lettered farmer, and James Otis. In another of the rooms should be collected the younger generation who were associated with Washington in completing the work of the revolution, by reforming the government and introducing the present federal union. I would have here another portrait of Washington, in a civil dress, as President, and another of Hamilton on account of his signal services on this occasion. Madison and Jay would of course accompany the latter, on either side, and after them would come the active friends and supporters of the constitution throughout the country; the cloudy, careworn countenance of Parsons, then, however, a blooming young man, the radiant visage of Ames, and the fine manly features of Rufus King, with the others their fellow labourers in the various states. With this group the list should close; for I would not make Mount Vernon a Westminster Hall or a general mausoleum for all the illustrious dead; but would devote it specifically to the honour of the revolutionary worthies and the founders of the government. The merit of these, as respects the country, will always remain of a singular kind, whatever titles of honour may hereafter be won by others. In the military hall I should place apart, with some distinct note of infamy fastened upon it, the portrait of Benedict Arnold, the only apostate that England ever gained from our glorious cause, as a sort of perpetual monition to future generations to beware of treason; and in the civil one, in like manner, that of Thomas Paine, who, after rendering some real service to the cause of liberty, disgraced it, or rather himself, by a scandalous abuse of sacred things. In some more private apartment should be united the portraits of the family of Washington. This interesting gallery would at once furnish the house in a manner suitable to its high destination, and concur in promoting the great objects of the scheme. The national flag should be always displayed above the building, to mark it as public property, and the estate might, for purposes of jurisdiction, be considered as an appendage to the District of Columbia.

The access to Mount Vernon under this arrangement, should be perfectly free to every one, at all times and seasons, effectual measures having been first taken to prevent disorder and injury to the property. Steamboats should rather be encouraged to land passengers on the ground than dissuaded from it; and the place should be open alike on Sundays and working days, for no more pious act can be performed by a citizen of the United States, than that of signifying his respect and gratitude for the person, who was raised up by Providence, to accomplish the deliverance of the country. Under these circumstances, the resort to the spot would probably be much greater than it has ever been before; and it would gradually come to be regarded as a sort of sacred ground, like the plains of Elis in ancient Greece, where the Olympic games were celebrated at the end of every four years. Mount Vernon too would perhaps be made the theatre of public rejoicings, upon our great national festival. The citizens of the neighbourhood would naturally meet there upon that occasion; and as the importance of the day was more and more felt, and the reverence for our political fathers went on increasing, as it will, from year to year, it would not be singular if many of the most respectable persons from all parts of the country should avail themselves of that opportunity, (the season being favourable for travelling,) to visit the place. The festivities would probably be continued for several days, and accompanied by devotional and literary exercises, poems, plays, orations, and other entertainments of all descriptions. The drama of the Greeks grew out of an annual religious festival, which lasted four or five days in succession, and during which tragedies and comedies, founded in the history and manners of the country, were acted without intermission from morning till night, this being the only time when they were performed. If we ever have a national theatre in the United States, it will be by the effect of some such institution as I have now hinted at, and not by attempting to naturalize in our cities the modern European drama, the forms of which are as foreign to our habits and morals as they are to our soil, and which will never be any thing in our hemisphere, but a paltry and contemptible abortion. Here too some new Herodotus might perhaps read to his assembled countrymen, the (yet unwritten) history of the achievments of their fathers, and of the almost fabulous adventures of the first settlers; some modern Pindar restore the reputation of lyric poetry, by devoting it to the praise of heroism and virtue, instead of making it (as it has generally been made of late) a pander to vice. Such a festival as this, held perhaps once in three or four years, would produce no trifling effect, in maintaining among the people a high national spirit, and cherishing that principle of *public virtue*, which we are taught to consider as the essence of our government. On the birth day of General Washington, which falls about the middle of the annual session of congress, it would be natural for the members of that body, and of the executive and judicial departments, to suspend their official duties, and commemorate the joyful occasion by visiting Mount Vernon, and by performing there such solemn public exercises as might appear to be suitable. It is precisely at this period of a session, that the members of congress, warmed by discussion, fretted by contradiction, and probably fatigued by the inconveniences of a rather uncomfortable residence, begin to lose the good temper, which generally marks their proceedings for some time after the opening. I am apt to think that a public celebration of the 22d of February at Mount Vernon, intervening in this way at a critical moment, would tend very strongly to keep up the cordiality and cheerfulness of our legislators till the close even of a long session ; and this would be no slight advantage. It would serve to check many little bursts of petulance, which their authors must afterwards regret, and which do no honour to the country.

Such, however, is the plan which I have sometimes contemplated as a suitable method of doing honour to our revolutionary fathers and of diffusing a national spirit through the country, and which has now been recalled to my mind by the decease of two of the last survivors of the number. It will doubtless be pronounced visionary, by those who consider every thing as such, that does not come within the routine of daily usage. I confess that I see nothing in it, either impracticable or irrational ; and as respects several points in the arrangement, it is required, as I have observed above, not merely by considerations of a higher order, but I think of justice, convenience, and even common propriety. The expense would be trifling, the advantages, direct and indirect, of importance. It belongs to the riper and more practised wisdom of our enlightened lawgivers, to decide whether the suggestions I have made are worthy to be acted upon.

CHAPTER X.

Conclusion.—Prospects of the Future Situation of America, and its Influence on the Fortunes of the World.

It was a favourite and much disputed question, for a considerable time after the discovery of our continent by Columbus, whether this event had been or would be on the whole advantageous to Europe. The first consequences resulting from it were, in fact, of a nature to render the point for a moment at least extremely doubtful. There was nothing very consonant to the feelings of a humane and generous heart, in the conquest of the flourishing empires of Peru and Mexico, by a horde of invaders, much below their inhabitants in real civilization, and superior to them in the same way in which a vigorous, well armed, and remorseless highwayman, is superior to the peaceable citizen whom he attacks in his house or in the street. The only compensation for these horrors was the supply of a few additional articles of luxury to the sensualists of Europe, and even this poor benefit was more than neutralized, by the importation of new diseases that accompanied the cargo. Had it been necessary to close the account for ever, while it remained in this state, it must be owned that our species would not have been very deeply in debt to the enterprising Genoese pilot, who had given a new world to Castile and Leon. But even then it was not difficult for such as looked a little below the surface of events, to perceive, in the discovery of America, the germ of a great and most auspicious change in the condition of the Christian nations, and ultimately of the human race. The old soil of Europe was occupied, and occupied on principles not the most favourable to the progress and prosperity of the inhabitants. The communities among which it was distributed, had established themselves in a barbarous age, and every thing about them was more or less tinctured with the vices inherent in such an origin. The division of property, and the laws that regulate its transmission, the great social institutions that fix the rights and duties of citizens, the forms of government and religion, the *constitution,* in a word, of all these countries, was the work of unenlightened heads and rude hands. Organized in this way, and crowded together upon a comparatively limited territory, the European nations were engaged in constant wars which wasted their numbers and their substance, vitiated their character, and withdrew their attention from objects of real importance. To reform this state of things from within, was an almost hopeless task. The vices I have specified were so deeply engrained in the system, so many personal interests were involved in the maintenance of them, that the least attempt at social improvement was little else than a signal for new scenes of horror, which sacrificed the happiness of one or two generations without effecting any considerable good. The most remarkable effort of this kind was that of Luther, to correct some existing abuses in the forms of religion; and this, after desolating the greater part of Europe with an almost uninterrupted war of a hundred and fifty years, left things in the main very nearly as it found them. It would seem, therefore, that had it not been for the discovery of America, the Christian nations would not probably have made any great advances in civilization, beyond the point at which they stood about the middle of the seventeenth century, and at the close of the long war of the reformation. They would proba- bly have continued, by the effect of a sort of epidemic and incurable political madness resulting from the vices of their institutions, to ravage one another as before, with constant wars, until some one military state should have arisen sufficiently active and successful to subju- gate the rest; and which, being organized on the same vicious principles, would have soon settled for them the question of the possible extent of human perfectibility, by bringing on with great rapidity a return of their for- mer barbarism. This we know to have been the history and termination of the European civilization of a former epoch, which commenced in the obscure period of the fabulous ages, produced in its first stage the simple arts and manners of the early Italians, then displayed the ripe and perfect glory of Grecian taste and Roman vir- tue, and beginning soon after to decline, under the in- fluence of vicious institutions, finally sunk for ever with the ascendancy of the Cæsars. The repetition of a similar course of events in modern Europe, was proba- ble, as I have stated before, on general grounds; and an observer who confined his view to Europe, might

perceive even now strong symptoms of a not very distant and rapidly approaching catastrophe, of a precisely
similar or still more formidable kind. We see, in fact,
an immense military empire formed and forming in the
north-eastern quarter of Europe, resting its rear on the
boundless regions of Asia, its right flank on the north
pole, and its left on the deserts of Tartary and Turkey,
and from this inaccessible and impregnable position advancing with giant steps to the conquest of the west. In
such a power it is impossible not to recognise the future
master of Europe; and if the ascendancy of Russia does
not bring with it a return of barbarism, it will evidently
not be because the institutions of that empire are modelled, at present, on a wise and liberal plan, (although
they are perhaps as good as the state of the people would
admit,) but because the principle of civilization and
improvement will be powerfully sustained by aid from
abroad, that is, from America. We also know that the
progress which has actually been made in civilization
by the Christian nations, since the period when, as I
have intimated above, it would have come to a stand,
without the discovery of America, may be traced in fact
more or less directly to that event. The immediate
cause has been the great development of commerce and
industry, and this in turn has been principally owing to
the spring supplied by the colonization of our continent.
The discovery of America furnished, in fact, to the
friends of improvement, the *point d'appui* which Archi-
medes required, in order to move the world, and which
seems to be as necessary in morals as in physics. With
this basis to rest upon, they have exercised and are con-

tinuing to exercise a most favourable influence upon the
state of society in Europe and the condition of our race.
Having dwelt at large in the preceding chapters, upon
the interesting crisis in the political relations of the two
continents, which forms the principal subject of the present work, it only remains, in order to complete the
plan, to describe the nature and extent of the moral influence to which I have just alluded. For this purpose
it is necessary to take into view the probable future, as
well as the present condition of our western world. The
value of our institutions and the weight of our example
will not be distinctly felt, as long as the whole population of our continent forms a comparatively small mass,
and while we remain inferior to the nations of Europe
in numbers, wealth, disposable political power, and the
elegant and useful arts of life. It is by observing the
rapid development of our resources, and the point to
which this must shortly bring us, that we realize fully
the immense importance of the discovery and colonization of America to the fortunes of mankind.

One of the most remarkable features in the probable
future as well as the past progress of our country, is the
rapid and before unprecedented increase of population
that has taken place among us, and, without some unfavourable change in our political condition, must continue for centuries to come. This circumstance is at
once a proof and a principal co-operating cause of our
extraordinary prosperity. That the source of the
wealth of nations lies in the bone and muscle of their
citizens, their true defence, not in batteries and fortifi-
cations, but in *high minded men,* are doctrines handed

down to us from remote antiquity and generally approved in all ages. It remained for a writer of the present day to start the strange paradox, (which, by a singular caprice of public opinion, was for a time pretty universally admitted as true,) that an increase in the numbers of the people (excepting in some peculiar cases) is a public misfortune, and that it is the business of a wise legislator to check population and not to encourage it. It is generally known, however, and Mr. Malthus is the first to admit, that labour is the only source of wealth. What then creates more wealth or capital? why of course more labour. And what furnishes an addition of labour? clearly the increase of population, which increases the number of labourers. Again, we all know and freely admit, that next to a sufficient supply of actual labour, the most important thing to the public welfare is the division of it, which leads to its proper and scientific application, and greatly augments its products. Now what cause produces the division of labour? not, as some fantastically suppose, an instinctive disposition in the human mind *to truck, barter, and exchange,* the reality of which it would be difficult to establish, but the increase of population, which, by increasing the number of labourers in proportion to the work actually in hand, enables each to devote himself to a particular department; and thus augments at once the quantity and quality of the products of the labour of all. It is evident, therefore, that the increase of population, instead of being, according to the singular theory alluded to above, a principle of evil, is, in fact, the great natural spring of the welfare of states. It is the immediate result of our strongest instincts, and takes place every where, where the benevolent efforts of nature are not counteracted by the effect of physical and moral evil, in some of their various forms. In proportion to the rapidity with which it occurs in any community, it proves the absence of all counteracting causes of this description; and the unprecedented augmentation of numbers that has been observed in the United States ever since the formation of its first settlements, furnishes a splendid commentary on the advantages of our position, even under the colonial system. These advantages, however, did not lie, as the abovementioned theory supposes, in the facility afforded by the great extent of the territory, taken in connexion with the original scantiness of the population, for obtaining by labour an abundant supply of the means of subsistence. Labour will furnish this any where, and is in general more productive in proportion to the density of population, because more skilfully applied. There is no difficulty in finding countries where labour will produce abundant fruits. *The difficulty is to find a place where men are permitted to enjoy the fruits of their labour,* and this was the signal distinction of the United States, even as colonies. This blessing of Providence (for it is one and nothing else) will turn a sand-bank or an ice-berg into a paradise of plenty, as it has been seen to do in Holland and Switzerland; and will make the wilderness blossom like a rose, as it has done with us; while without it, the most fertile and delightful spots upon the globe, the environs of Rome, the plains of Castile, the garden of Eden itself, are first depopulated and then become uninhabita-

ble.   This was the great advantage which we enjoyed
over the Spanish and Portuguese colonies, whose territory was more extensive, more fertile, and in other respects better situated than ours, but whose population
was probably not greater at the moment of their emancipation from the yoke of Europe than at the time of
the conquest.   It is still composed, as it was then, in
great part of the original natives.   Ours on the contrary has gone on doubling, about once in twenty or five
and twenty years, ever since the settlement of the country ; and since the declaration of independence has continued to advance in the same or a greater ratio, having
probably quadrupled in the forty-three years which
have intervened since the peace of '83.   It is important
to trace this rapid increase of population to its true
cause, and not to be misled by the vain imagination of
mere theorists ; because it is in this way only that we
can fully appreciate the value of our political institutions.   If this increase (which has been the main and
immediate cause of our progress in wealth and power)
had been owing merely to the extent and fertility of our
territory, taken in connexion with the original scantiness of our numbers, then our form of government, whatever it might have been, would have had nothing to do
with our success.   Such is the theory of Malthus, in its
application to us and other nations ; and the same doctrine has at times been advanced by writers among ourselves.   The truth is that our form of government, or in
other words our liberty, is the only distinction, which we
have enjoyed over various communities in every other
respect as well or better situated than ourselves, and is.

therefore, the real cause of all our prosperity. To suppose, with many European statesmen, that these institutions will not be permanent, precisely because they are
not vicious, or, as they express it, that they are too
beautiful to be practicable, would be to suppose that vice
is the law of nature, or in other words, that evil is good
and good evil, a heresy expressly condemned by Scripture as well as common sense. I have considered this
point in a preceding chapter, where I have attempted
to explain the nature of the real security of our liberty;
and have, I trust, succeeded in showing that it is a perfectly satisfactory one. Having every reason to depend
upon the permanence of our forms of government for
an indefinite length of time to come, we may also calculate with confidence upon a continuation for a corresponding period, of the same progress in population,
civilization, and wealth, which has hitherto resulted
from it.*

The same cause which has produced these magnificent effects in our country, but which has not yet been

---

* The principles stated in the text, on the subject of the
economical effect of an increase of population, are proposed
rather more at large in the work entitled, *New Ideas on Population, with remarks on the theories of Godwin and Malthus, by
A. H. Everett*. New theories, as such, are rather suspicious;
and it may therefore be proper to add, that those ideas are only
new, inasmuch as they differ from those which have been pretty
generally received in England and in this country for some
years past, as the authority of the popular journals. The work
of Mr. Everett is, in fact, a defence of the old and common opinion against a modern paradox.

in operation on any other portion of the continent, will
gradually begin to display its efficacy in Spanish and
Portuguese America, and may, after a while, lead to a
progress in wealth and population, similar if not equal
to that which has taken place with us. I have hazarded
some doubts, in a preceding chapter, whether the institutions which have lately been established in these vast
regions, are strictly conformable to the state of society
and the character and condition of the people. If they
be not, they cannot be permanent, not because they are
too beautiful to be practicable, but because no form can
ever long subsist without a corresponding substance. I
have even ventured to raise the question, whether the
legislators of these new nations acted prudently in seek-
ing to imitate so closely as they have done, the forms in
use here; whether they had not, in fact, wholly mistaken the proper basis of their system, and whether, considering the state of property, opinion, and feeling in
the communities which they were called upon to organize, religion ought not to have been, for them, what
liberty was and is for us. Events that have occurred
since I wrote those remarks, in the republic of Colombia, which was previously, to all appearance, the most
secure and stable of all these governments, seem to lend
some show of probability to these ideas. I am far from
wishing, however, as I trust I have sufficiently shown in
the course of the work, to indulge in sinister conjectures
respecting the future prospects of these states, still less
to give an unfavourable view of their present condition.
Their independence appears to me to be established;
and I ardently desire that their institutions may be found

sufficiently well adapted to their situation to go quietly into practice. In that case, they need not wish, nor we for them, for better; as our own experience amply proves. If, on the contrary, as there is some reason to fear, these institutions which have been to us the sources of so much happiness, should be found with them to be impracticable, they will have to pass through another period of revolution and anarchy before they attain a settled condition. The result of every such period is in a greater or less degree accidental, and always uncertain. It might end in the establishment of vicious institutions, and thus nip for ever, in the bud, the brilliant promise of these young nations. To anticipate this would, however, be to look unnecessarily on the dark side of the possible future. It may rather be hoped that the intestine troubles which now exist, or may hereafter break out in these countries, will finally terminate in the introduction of the best forms of government which circumstances render possible. These, if not at first in theory perfect, would nevertheless be active principles of improvement, and by gradually ameliorating the condition of society, would prepare the way for an ultimate modification of their own provisions according to some superior plan. In the mean time, any government founded with good intentions on the best practicable principles, would secure to a considerable extent the personal rights of individuals, and would thus lead to a more or less rapid progress in national wealth and greatness. The South may therefore be expected to follow us, perhaps at a considerable distance, *proximus sed longo intervallo,* in the brilliant career which we have long been pursuing; may also advance with rapidity in population, wealth, and civilization; and establish, as we have done, a cluster of powerful, prosperous, tranquil, and well governed republics, which may add their resources and influence to ours, in giving political importance to the common continent. All this is yet wholly *in futuro*, or very partially and imperfectly accomplished. That it will finally be effected, I for one most sincerely hope, and, in part at least, believe.

Although the remarkable increase of population that has taken place in the United States, and the rapid progress in wealth and civilization consequent upon it, have not been owing, as is thought by some, to the extent of our territory, taken in connexion with the original scantiness of the number of the first settlers, but to the nature of our political institutions, nevertheless this immense geographical expansion is one of the most important elements to be taken into view, in making an estimate of our future condition. Population and wealth may increase with as much rapidity upon a small territory, as upon a large one; and it has in fact so happened, that most previous examples of any very striking results of this description are to be found in communities of moderate dimensions, such as Holland, Switzerland, the Italian republics, Ireland, and England. In these cases, the misfortune is that the prosperity of the society is not founded on a sufficiently firm basis to be secure, and that at all events the political importance it confers can never rise above a certain point. A wealthy and populous community of small geographical extent, though stronger in proportion to its territory than other countries, and able to cope with a somewhat larger but less prosperous state, loses its advantage when the disproportion becomes too great, and must fall if attacked by a very powerful neighbour. In this way Holland was repeatedly overrun by the French armies, before and after the revolution; and in this way England, had it not been for the extraordinary resources growing out of her colonial and naval establishments, must have sunk under the overwhelming masses of material power, at the disposal of Napoleon. It seems to be the natural lot of small and wealthy nations to sustain repeated assaults of this description, and, after parrying them a while, to be crushed at last by some one more terrible than the rest. Thus the Greeks, after beating off the Persian army, were conquered in succession without much difficulty by the Macedonians and the Romans. The Hollanders defended themselves triumphantly for more than half a century against the whole strength of the Spanish empire, then the dominant European power, only to see their territory, almost without resistance on their part, occupied, as I have said before, by any neighbour, France, Prussia, or England, that chooses to enter it. England herself had hardly time to breathe from her long and desperate struggle with Napoleon, before she found herself threatened by a still more dangerous political Colossus, which must finally trample down her independence and liberty. An extensive geographical basis, with the material resources which accompany it, is therefore a necessary condition of national security and greatness. The territorial extent of

every country is, in fact, the natural measure of its
wealth, population, and political importance, and furnishes in connexion with the form of its government the
actual one. A bad government will reduce an empire,
however extensive, to comparative imbecility, and even
finally break it up into fragments and ruin it for ever;
while, on the other hand, a good government will elevate a small state above its natural position, and may
even, by enlarging its territory, endow it with a lasting
and solid accession of power. This was the process
alluded to by Themistocles, when he said, that although
he could not play upon the flute, he knew how to make
a great state out of a little one. The concurrence of
an extensive territorial basis and a good government is,
therefore, the principle of great and lasting political
importance. If the view which I have taken of our institutions be at all correct, this combination never existed, in any other country, to any thing like the extent
in which it is realized with us. With a territory equal
to that of the greatest empires of ancient or modern
times, with a government far superior, as we think, to
any one that was ever tried before, unless the auspices
under which we have entered on our march of national
existence, should, contrary to every reasonable anticipation, prove fallacious, we must become, and that at no
very distant period, a more populous, wealthy, and powerful community than any the world has ever seen.
Supposing the number of our citizens to increase as it
has done, from the first settlement of the country up to
the present day, (and as it must continue to do, unless
arrested by disastrous political events,) it will amount

at the close of the present century, to about eighty millions, a population twice as large as that of Russia at present. By the middle of the next century, it will reach three hundred millions, and will then be equal to the most exaggerated estimates of the population of China, and much exceed those of later date and more authentic character. Continuing to advance on the same principles, it will arrive, in less than two centuries, at the sum of twelve hundred millions, and will then considerably exceed the present estimated population of the globe. But if, to avoid the appearance of exaggeration, we close our prospects at the second of these periods, we shall then (in less than eighty years from this time) possess a population greater than that of any single nation ever known, and nearly twice as great as that of all Europe at the present day. As the state of population is the surest index of the whole economical situation of countries, our advances in this respect will be, as they constantly have been, attended with a proportional progress in wealth and prosperity. The immediate results of this cause are a proportional increase in the number of labourers, a more perfect division of labour, and increased skill in the application of it. The general result of the combined action of these elements is a great augmentation in the quantity, and improvement in the quality of all products, or, in other words, of wealth. The same cause therefore, to wit, the goodness of the government, which creates the increase of population, creates a corresponding increase in wealth, and will make the nation not only the greatest, but in proportion to the number of its inhabitants the richest and most flourishing on the globe. If, eighty years hence, the population of the United States should be twice as large as that of all Europe put together, their wealth, taken collectively, will be five or six times as great, and that of any ten or twenty millions of their inhabitants, taken indistinctly from the mass, will be greater in the same ratio than that of any corresponding number of the inhabitants of Europe. I make this statement rather to illustrate my ideas, than to give an exact account of the probable fact, as the disproportion in favour of the United States, in respect of wealth, must according to any reasonable estimate be far greater than the one here supposed. The high degree of political importance, which our country will possess under these circumstances, may well be imagined; since the political importance of a nation is only another expression of its wealth, population, geographical extent, and form of government. Superior in each and all of these particulars, to the whole European commonwealth taken together, the United States, at the close of this century, will outweigh very much in political importance, the combined power of its members; and instead of having any thing to apprehend from their injustice or violence, will be naturally courted by them all as a useful friend and ally, and will have it in their power to exercise a most beneficial influence upon their institutions and policy.

Such, at no very distant period, (since it is one which will be reached by numbers now living,) will probably be the economical and political situation of our country. But in considering the future prospects of our continent, it is necessary to keep in view the Spanish and Portuguese American states which occupy so large a part of the surface. These also are all possessed of the extensive geographical basis, which forms one of the two essential elements of national greatness; and if, as we may venture to hope, their political institutions either are already, or will become hereafter, sufficiently solid, and at the same time liberal, to admit of a rapid progress in wealth and population among their respective communities, they too will attain very shortly the importance of the greatest nations of ancient and modern times. It can hardly be anticipated, from present appearances, that they will enter immediately on a career as brilliant as that which the United States have long been pursuing; but, without doing all that we have done and are likely to do, they may still do much. If Mexico, for instance, which is now supposed to contain about six millions of inhabitants, should double its population only once in forty or fifty years, it would still be equal in this respect, at the close of this century, to the average of the first rate European powers of the present day, and by the middle of the next would rise to the level of Russia. Colombia, hitherto a leading Spanish American state, is much inferior to Mexico in population, and, just at this moment, is somewhat unfortunately situated in regard to its government. It is, however, not worse off in either particular, than our own country was at the close of the revolutionary war, and has only to exercise the necessary wisdom and energy to ensure success. The same remarks apply in substance to the others. There is, therefore, reason to suppose, that in the course of this and the following century, the American continent will be able to boast of possessing several nations, not inferior to the mightiest power of the old world, besides others of less consequence, and one at least, far exceeding in wealth, population, and importance, any other body politic of ancient or modern times. Such, on a very cursory survey, are the probable future prospects of America. It remains to notice the influence of this state of things at home and abroad, or in other words, its effect on the character and happiness, first of the inhabitants of our own continent, and then of the world at large. We shall then be able to realize, with more precision, how far the success of Columbus has been injurious or beneficial to the fortunes of the human race.

One of the first and most certain immediate results of the rapid progress of our continent, in wealth and population, will be a great improvement of the present state of the sciences, physical and moral, and the modes of applying them to the practical uses of life. This is not a loose conjecture, founded merely on some supposed connexion between political prosperity and the progress of knowledge; but a strict deduction from acknowledged principles applied to existing facts. The immediate effects of the increase of population are, as I have stated above, an increase of the number of labourers, a more perfect division of labour, and an increase of skill in the application of it. Now the increase of skill, in the application of labour to the practical uses of life, is in other words an improvement in the theory and practice of the physical sciences. This improvement is one of the two principal means by which the increase of population produces the favourable effect which regularly follows it, in the condition of a community, the division of labour being important only as it leads to an increase of skill. Hence, when we see, as with us, an increase of population working out its natural consequences in a great augmentation of wealth and power, we know that the means by which it produces these effects are in active operation, and that rapid improvements are steadily going on in the theory and application of physical science. This, therefore, is not an accidental but a certain consequence of the present condition of our country. The assurance which we have a right to feel upon this head, on theoretical grounds, is also fully confirmed by experience. The singular success of our countrymen, in mechanical invention, as well by discovering new principles as by making new applications of such as were known before, has become notorious, especially within the last fifty or sixty years. The world is in fact indebted to us for a very large portion of the important theoretical and practical advances that have been made within that time in physical science. A description, in detail, of what our countrymen have done in this way, would fill volumes. In order to be aware of the value of these discoveries, we need only recollect, as among the most important, the creation of the science of electricity, the invention of the quadrant, the improvements in naval architecture, the beautiful compound blow-pipe of Dr. Hare, (claimed, I believe, like the quadrant, by some poor-spirited European plagiarist,) the cotton-gin of Whitney, the *century of inventions*, each, in the French phrase, more happy than the rest, of that miracle of genius, Jacob Perkins, from his machine for cutting nails to his late improvement in the steam-engine, which, should it ultimately prove to be practicable, will put a new face upon the whole business of mechanics; and finally the steam-boat, that splendid achievement of the genius of Fulton, which has already put a new face upon the internal commerce of the United States. These great discoveries and improvements, among others, serve to show the singular progress of skill in the application of labour that has taken place among us, and has in fact given a sort of reputation for mechanical talent to the country. It has been concluded by many, that the citizens of the United States possessed as such some peculiar aptitude for this department of intellectual activity, a position which it would be exceedingly difficult not merely to prove but to make intelligible. The truth is, as I have stated above, that this development of skill and progress in physical science is a consequence not accidental, but natural and necessary, of the rapid advances of population. While the cause continues to operate, (which will be, unless the government be changed, for an indefinite length of time to come,) it is a matter of certainty, rather than conjecture, that it will continue to produce the same effects. To say in detail what these effects will be, or in other words what discoveries will be made, would be to anticipate them. The importance of those that are making every year sufficiently proves that the field is by no means exhausted, and furnishes a standard by which to estimate the amount of the contributions that may be added to the present stock in a course of centuries.

As respects the progress of moral science, of which the principal branch is politics, (because the nature of the government determines in a great degree the morality of the individual,) less probably remains to be done. If at least there be any correctness in the views which I have taken of the subject, in a preceding chapter, our institutions, founded originally under the most favourable circumstances, and gradually improved by the effect of a succession of fortunate events, may now be considered as conformable in all their essential and important points to reason and natural justice, or in other words, as perfect. In the main, therefore, they would admit of no alteration for the better. In some comparatively minor matters of practice and detail, it is possible that useful changes may be indicated by longer experience, and whenever they shall be, they will be adopted without difficulty or danger. Whether the branch of sovereign power, which regulates the modes in which the laws shall be clothed with the sanction of religion, will always be exercised precisely in the same way in which it is now, is, perhaps, as I have hinted before, a matter of doubt. The general question respecting the effect which will be produced by the progress of knowledge in our country, upon the public opinion on the subject of the forms of religion, is in fact extremely curious, and far from admitting of a very prompt solution. As our faith is founded substantially, on the steadfast and immoveable rock of truth, the veneration which is now so universally entertained for it, will probably increase rather than diminish; but as all the forms under which it is professed, are in a greater or less degree mixed up with error, they may be expected to undergo various alterations; and it is a matter of interesting conjecture, whether all these forms will continue to exist and flourish, side by side, as they now do; whether any one or more of them will obtain a complete ascendancy over the others, or whether all will finally give way to some new construction of the sacred record, which all the sects receive alike as the common rule of belief and practice, although they differ so in regard to its meaning. Will the Roman Catholics, who are now very active in many parts of the country, who have lately made proselytes even in the heart of orthodox New England, who have their College of Jesuits at Washington, and at times their deputies in congress, continue to advance, as they fondly expect, until they have reclaimed us all from our wanderings and gathered us into the fold of holy mother Church? Will the Unitarian doctrine, which has lately diffused itself so widely among the better educated classes, gradually penetrate into the mass of the people, as it has already done in some of our cities, and finally become the prevailing belief of any considerable portion of the union? or will the Church of England successfully counteract this opinion, even among the wealthy and enlightened, by the effect of a solemn and imposing exterior, and, though hardly at home on any foreign soil, retain its ascendancy over the minds and affections of many of our most respected citizens? Will the uneducated teachers of various names persevere with as much acceptance as heretofore, in attempting to explain to the public a subject, which it is much to be feared they scarcely understand themselves, however truly pious they may often be in feeling and in spirit? Finally, is it possible that from the midst of this chaos of conflicting sects, some new form of the common faith may ultimately spring up, more consonant to the real sense of Scripture, and better accommodated to practical uses, than any now existing? These, as I have said, are interesting questions; but it hardly comes within the scope of the present essay to discuss them in detail: I leave the inquiry with pleasure in the abler hands of our learned and exemplary clergy of all opinions. Among the branches of morals, political economy is one that will probably make advances among us; and it will, at any rate, be employed for the first time as a rule of public conduct. In ethics, or the theory of private conduct, which is written by nature in all our hearts, there is little improvement to be made. The great point here is to prevail upon the people to do what they know well enough to be their duty, and the strong inducement to private virtue held out by our institutions and position is, as I shall presently state, their greatest practical excellence.

Having thus stated or suggested in the form of inquiry some improvements that may probably or possibly be made among us in moral and physical science, it may be well to mention some other changes occasionally proposed as improvements, that will probably not be realized. It is an easy artifice with the interested enemies of the progress of civilization, to accuse its friends of enthusiasm and extravagance; and it must be owned that the language of the latter, however well meant and honest, has at times given countenance to the charge.

I will therefore add, to avoid misconstruction, that I do
not anticipate with Condorcet, that men will ever become immortal on the face of the earth; with Godwin,
that we shall learn to do without religion, government,
property, or marriage ; or with Mrs. Godwin, that w.e
shall ever introduce a complete political equality of the
sexes. I do not expect that Mr. Owen will *Owenise*
the United States in five years, or that these states will
ever consent to be *codified* by Jeremy Bentham ; nor
do I believe that Captain Symmes will turn out a second
Newton. I apprehend, on the contrary, that the term
of human life will remain as heretofore, at the ancient
date of threescore years and ten ; that we shall keep up
the old relation of governor and citizen, master and ser-
vant, man and wife, parent and child, with I trust a
better understanding and more diligent practice of the
duties belonging to them ; that instead of throwing our
property and women into common stock, we shall, as we
advance in civilization, employ additional skill and care
in administering the one and watching over the other ;
and that with all the improvements we are able to make
in our condition here, we shall never be so well satisfied
with it, as to lose the desire and hope of exchanging it
for a better one hereafter. If this avowal of belief and
not belief, shall be considered by any of the abovementioned persons as classing me among the adherents of
antiquated prejudices, I shall with all due humility undergo the charge ; and cheerfully relinquishing all pretensions to any share, as a citizen of the United States,
in the terrestrial paradises that may be discovered above
or below the surface of the country, and within or with-

out the polar verge, shall proceed to state very briefly the effect upon the character and happiness of the people, of the less magnificent, but still not wholly contemptible changes for the better, which I have indicated above as being likely to happen.

The practical effect of the improvements in political science that have been already introduced among us, is, as I have stated, that every one enjoys the fruits of his own labour, the deductions which are made from them for account of government being too trifling to be taken into calculation. This is a first and indispensable preliminary to any favourable change in the condition of a community. This being premised, the operation of the improvements that have been or may be made in physical science, is to increase the comforts and abridge the necessary labour of all. It is thought by some, and particularly Mr. Say, that the effect of such improvements is merely to increase the total amount of products, and to change the direction of labour without abridging it; but this observation, though true in certain cases, is not universally so. The demand for all articles of real utility or convenience, is limited by the extent of population for the time being. If the labour necessary for obtaining these articles be abridged by improvements in physical science, one result will be the application of a part of the labour thus economised to the making of new articles, less essential perhaps, but still useful, convenient, and agreeable. In this way, as I observed before, the comforts of life will be augmented for all. But here too a limit is set to the productions of new articles, by this very consideration of increased comfort. Whenever the enjoyment that can be derived from an additional ornament or luxury, is more than counterbalanced to the community by the additional labour required for obtaining it, it will cease to be produced. If a rational community can supply themselves with necessaries and comforts, by labouring on an average three or four hours every day, they will probably be induced to labour three or four more, in order to obtain other comforts or luxuries; but will never condemn themselves to twelve or fifteen hours of daily toil, in order to add to these a few trifles of conventional or imaginary value. Where the real wants of life can be supplied by moderate labour, it will never, in general, be excessive; and the effect of the improvements in physical science will therefore be, as I have stated above, to abridge the labour and increase the comforts of all. The surplus time of the community will be devoted to social intercourse and intellectual improvement. The favourable operation of such a state of things upon character and morals, hardly need to be described. Man, under these circumstances, ceases to be a mechanical tool or a beast of burden, and takes his proper rank in the world as a moral and rational being. His faculties are exercised, his heart is enlarged, and his spirit gladdened and refreshed. The good principle of his nature is developed, and the evil are kept in check. He is in short, according to the measure of his capacity as an imperfect creature, virtuous and happy. I am no believer, as I have declared above, in earthly Utopias or in the entire extirpation of misery and vice. I know, we all know by fatal experience, the frailty of our constitution; and there seems to be no more reason to hope that we shall ever be absolutely good and perfectly happy in this world, than there is to fear that we shall ever be completely vicious and miserable. But I see no ground for assuming the present state of civilization in Europe or America, as the *nec plus ultra* of our possible attainments, rather than that of China or New Holland. We find the different branches of the human family, according to the circumstances in which they are placed, exhibiting the most various and opposite characters; and if the situation of the United States be as much more favourable than that of most other communities of ancient and modern times, as I have been led to believe and represent it, I can imagine no cause why they may not attain a height of civilization, or in other words, a degree of wealth, knowledge, virtue, and happiness, as much above that of the present population of Europe and America, as the latter is above that of the degenerate tribes of Africa, or the Kanzas and Omawhaws of our own continent.

The future state of the elegant and ornamental arts in this country, is another question more curious perhaps than important, but which I should also be disposed to decide in favour of their progress. It seems to be thought by some, that these are a kind of exotic plants, which can only flourish in an unnatural, that is a vicious atmosphere; and that a really good government affords them as such no encouragement or protection. Where the solid fruits of labour are abundant and within the reach of all, it is argued that nobody will waste his time in acquiring and exercising talents that are of little real value to the public, and are rarely profitable to their possessors. Others hold, on the contrary, that a free and prosperous country is the natural home of all the fine as well as useful arts. They maintain, for example, that poetry and eloquence, the highest of them all, are the forms in which superior minds communicate the delicate impressions made upon them by the beauties of nature and their own lofty imaginations, to other minds less favoured by education and original constitution; and it is said (with some show of reason) that these forms will arrive most surely at perfection, wherever the occasions of such communication are most favourable and frequent, which is doubtless the case in free governments. The same is true, with proper qualifications, of painting, music, architecture, and the rest. Art, in fact, is the mirror of nature; and can it be affirmed with probability, that the image it presents will be least beautiful where the original exists in the greatest perfection? Is the pecuniary advantage afforded to the artist by a large and flourishing community less likely to be steady and ample, than that which results from the capricious bounty of a few rich individuals, or less fitted to give to art its true and natural direction? Is there not something more awakening to a generous mind, in the prospect of deserving and obtaining the applause of an intelligent and sympathizing nation, than in all the pensions that kings can bestow? Would Herodotus have exchanged the rapturous shouts with which the reading of his history was received by the Greeks, at the Olympic games, for the patronage of any Persian satrap? Or if all these notions be vain and idle, does not recent experience show that the bookseller is, after all, the best Mæcenas? Instead of apprehending a degeneracy of the arts among us, I am prone to believe, on the contrary, that they will flourish here much more than they have done in Europe, where some of them have never thriven, and hardly one has equalled the standard of antiquity.

But however this point may be settled, which is after all one of little practical moment, and considering the example which we shall hold out to Europe as merely that of a nation more populous, wealthy, powerful, virtuous, and happy than any one which has ever been known before, we may still inquire, whether this example will produce no effect, in recommending to other nations the adoption of the institutions which create this superiority? When they see our improved system of social machinery in full, easy, and steady operation, producing results so much more favourable than those which are in use elsewhere, is it in human nature that they should not borrow or imitate so great an invention? I think not, and cannot but anticipate, that the success of our institutions will exercise a very auspicious influence of a quiet and pacific kind, upon those of the old world. Much, however, will depend on the progress of events in Europe itself, and the nature of the political movements that may successively modify its position and foreign relations. We can therefore only calculate, with some degree of certainty, on the continued progress and full success of the cause of civilization and humanity in our own vast continent; but even this is a prospect sufficiently glorious to excite the enthusiasm and gratitude of every elevated mind, and to rank the discoverer of America among the greatest benefactors of the human race.

It is time, however, to conclude these reflections. Notwithstanding the disclaims I have made of Utopian dreams and baseless theories of all kinds, I am aware that some persons (who would perhaps regret to see them realized,) will charge even the most moderate anticipations, in which I have ventured to indulge, with exaggeration. I can only say that I have advanced no conjectures, without giving what I think good reasons for them; and that if the latter can be refuted, I am quite prepared to abandon the former. Other persons perhaps may doubt the expediency of holding up these favourable pictures of our own institutions, and future prospects. Why nourish in this way, they may say, a national vanity already perhaps sufficiently exalted? If we are really a favoured and a prosperous nation, let us rather thank God for it, and enjoy our blessings in silence, than excite the envy and malignity of other less fortunate communities, by empty boasting. If we occupy a high and commanding stand in the political system, let us not, by indiscreetly vaunting our strength and advantages, induce other governments to attempt to deprive us of them. In these remarks, there is some degree of force; and I should regret to be considered, by competent judges, as having passed the line of discretion, in speaking of the political importance and future greatness of our union. But in order to appreciate fully the value of our liberty, it is absolutely necessary that we should, in the first place, correctly estimate the advantages, for which we are indebted to it; and in order to discharge our duties as a nation, we must know our precise position as such, in the system of which we form a part. On both these subjects there are various opinions. Some deny that our liberty has contributed at all to our progress in wealth and greatness. Others contend that we have nothing to do as a people with foreign relations. Both these doctrines are, in my opinion, of dangerous tendency, and I have endeavoured, in the course of the preceding work, to prove their incorrectness. If I have represented the government as occupying a lofty station among the leading powers of the world, it has been with a view of impressing upon the minds of our rulers and of the nation, the deep responsibility under which they act, in consequence of the immense influence, which is necessarily attached to their position, and which they must exercise even in refusing to exercise it. If I have presented a flattering image of our present situation and future prospects, it has been for the purpose of showing more distinctly the inestimable worth of the political institutions which have made us what we are. Should one or both of these great objects be in any way effected, I shall think myself, I will not say rewarded for the trouble of writing this work, which has been to me a pleasure, *labor ipse voluptas,* but fully satisfied with its success.

THE END.